THE
GREAT AMERICAN FAIR

**THE WORLD'S
COLUMBIAN EXPOSITION & AMERICAN CULTURE**

The Ferris Wheel on the Midway *(Courtesy Chicago Historical Society)*

THE
GREAT AMERICAN FAIR

THE WORLD'S
COLUMBIAN EXPOSITION & AMERICAN CULTURE

Reid Badger

Nelson Hall nh **Chicago**

Badger, Reid.
    The great American fair.

    Bibliography: p.
    Includes index.
    1.   Chicago.   World's Columbian Exposition, 1893.
I.   Title.
T500.B1B3   909.81'074'017311   79-11774
ISBN 0-88229-448-2 (Cloth)
ISBN 0-88229-692-2 (Paper)

Manufactured in the United States of America

10   9   8   7   6   5   4   3   2   1

FOR LEE

CONTENTS

We, too, entertain, we ordinary puritanical Americans, some shadowy notions of a time, when, at more frequent intervals than now, men shall draw in a delighted breath and cry, "Oh, that this moment might endure forever!" We believe in this far-off time, because, at least once or twice in a lifetime, each of us experiences such a moment, or, feeling the wind of its retreating wing, knows that it has just gone by. It may have been in the spell-bound glow of some magical sunset, or at the sound of a solemn music, or in the sudden apprehension of a long-sought truth, or at the thrill and tightening of resolution in some crisis, or in the presence of some fair marble image of a thought that keeps its beauty and serenity while we fret and fade. It may even have been at some vision, seen in the multitude of business, of a new republic revealed to the traveling imagination, like a shining city set on a hill in the flash of a midnight storm. Till life itself yields such moments less charily, it is incumbent upon the artist to send them as often as he can.

Stuart P. Sherman
"The National Genius" in
Atlantic Monthly, January 1921

PREFACE

Cultural history in the broadest sense of the term is the study of shared experience—be it of a family, a tribe, or a nation. Its practical function is nothing less than the preservation of the collective memory which is as vital to the ongoing life of the group as is private memory to the psychological continuity of the individual self. Cultural history is our public memory, and just as it is important to the individual that his memory be clear and complete, so also is it important that a society's cultural history be accurate and fully integrated. The difficulty lies in the fact that while there are reliable records of particular individual experiences and hard evidence to permit accuracy in assessing the political, economic, social, or intellectual aspects of the collective experience, knowledge of shared experience as a whole (which may be something else than merely the sum of the various components) has been more elusive.

My interest in Chicago's world's fair of 1893 developed over the course of several years of studying various aspects of late nineteenth century American civilization. Time and again I encountered serious and often thoughtful references—on both the popular and the highest cultural levels—to the world's fairs of this period as indicators of one or another important cultural trend. It became increasingly clear that whatever the modern estimate of the significance of recent fairs, the nineteenth century tended to take theirs seriously indeed. And in no case was this more evident than in the World's Columbian Exposition held in Chicago in 1893. Eventually, I became convinced that these unique events might provide the cultural historian with a focal point, a microcosm perhaps, for investigating the general experience of the culture at a particular point in time, and I determined to use the Chicago fair as a test case for the hypothesis.

The project divided itself into two separate, though interrelated, areas of research. The first of these was simply to determine the extent to which the Columbian Exposition could be said to be a representative cultural event. This required a general consideration of the great world's fairs within the context of nineteenth century Western culture, their relationship to American culture, and finally an analysis of the particular significance of an American world's fair in the City of Chicago in the early 1890s. The second major question, following closely upon the first, was to determine what light, if any, a study of the world's fair itself (its history, operation, and symbolic meaning) might shed upon the overall psychological or emotional condition of American society in the 1890s. The book was not intended, finally, to be a full and complete analysis of every aspect of the fair, but rather to establish the place of the Chicago exposition within the broad context of American culture in the nineties and to offer an interpretation of its overall meaning in terms of that culture.

Anyone who writes a book within the broad field of cultural history incurs innumerable intellectual debts. Scholarship is, after all, a cumulative and cooperative process and I have depended heavily on the original work of many outstanding students of late nineteenth century American life. I would also like to acknowledge the contribution of various doctoral and masters degree candidates. Theses and dissertations are important resources for any scholar, but rarely do they receive the recognition or attention they deserve. Syracuse University generously provided me with support for a year's uninterrupted research and Ralph Ketcham, also of Syracuse University, encouraged my initial interest in the project and continued to contribute his invaluable criticism and suggestions along the way. A number of friends, colleagues, and students in American Studies at the University of Alabama read or discussed with me various parts of the manuscript and helped me to clarify both my expression and my meaning. The College of Arts and Sciences of the University of Alabama helped also with the typing and manuscript preparation costs. The extent of the debt which I owe to my wife, Lee, I trust is clear from the dedication. And finally, I am indebted to the Cayuga County Historical Society and the Chicago Historical Society for their special assistance and cooperation in making their unique collections available to me, and I am most grateful to the people of Chicago for whom historical consciousness is a civic duty.

PROLOGUE: *OPENING DAY*

As the whole of Greek life was symbolized in the Acropolis, so in the drama at Jackson Park yesterday the whole life of America and of other civilized nations was portrayed.

Daily Inter Ocean
May 2, 1893

May 1, 1893, the opening day of the World's Columbian Exposition, arrived cold and misty. A threat of rain hung over the elaborate ceremonies that were to mark the beginning of the six-month celebration of Chicago, the United States of America, the achievement of Christopher Columbus, and the progress of civilization. At the Union League Club two lineal descendants of the great explorer breakfasted on oysters, roast woodchucks, veal chops with Castilian sauce, strawberry shortcake with kirsch, cognac, and other delicacies, while outside in the sprawling city thousands of parents and children packed lunch baskets, collected umbrellas, and assembled themselves for the trip to Jackson Park to witness the event Chicago, and indeed the entire country, had been anticipating for over three years.[1] A few minutes past nine o'clock President Grover Cleveland emerged from the Lexington Hotel on Michigan Avenue and, accompanied by Presidents Thomas Palmer of the National Commission and Harlow Higinbotham of the Exposition Company, entered the awaiting presidential carriage. Immediately a bugle sounded the command to march and a mounted full dress escort of Chicago Hussars, Park Police, Illinois National Guardsmen, and United States Cavalry swung into line and started south, to be followed by a procession of twenty-two carriages drawn by highstepping horses.

In addition to the presidents of the United States, the world's fair National Commission, and the local Exposition Company, the parading dignitaries included Vice President Adlai Stevenson, the secretaries of State, Treasury, Navy, Interior, and Agriculture, various world's fair directors and officers, Governor Altgeld of Illinois, the Duke and Duchess of Veragua and other Spanish notables, and in the last carriage the exuberant and popular world's fair mayor of Chicago, Carter Harrison.

As the pageant moved smartly down Michigan Avenue "aflame with flags and bunting and alive with cheering thousands" and turned in to the fairgrounds at the Midway Plaisance, a roar "like that of distant thunder" was heard from the groups of Egyptians, Algerians, Javanese, Irish, and other foreign nationals who had assembled outside their decorated Midway concession areas.[2] And as the presidential carriage passed, four trained lions from Hagenbeck's Zoological Circus bellowed ferociously, the circus band blared "America," the Algerians gave their famous yell, and the dancing girls lowered their veils—the highest tribute, it was said, that they could pay.[3]

In the Court of Honor, an enormous crowd of some three hundred fifty to five hundred thousand men, women, and children gathered in the mud at the base of the platform which had been erected at the eastern front of Richard Morris Hunt's domed Administration Building. The sea of expectant faces stretched down both sides of the Grand Basin to the Peristyle at the opposite end. At 11:15 A.M. President Cleveland, followed by his cabinet, the world's fair officials, the Spaniards and other dignitaries, appeared at the landing of the stairway and as they took their seats on the platform amid deafening cheers the push toward the grandstand nearly caused a serious panic. Choristers sang a "Columbian Hymn" while down below the shouting, crushing, and fainting among men, women, children, Columbian Guards, police, and reporters was "like a scene from Doré."[4] A man leaped up on one of the press tables and yelled at the mob: "For God's sake stand back; you are killing these women in front"; while high up on the portico of the Administration Building several Oglala Sioux braves in full ceremonial dress watched with detached curiousity the chaos below.[5] Theodore Thomas' orchestra quickly struck up the "Columbian March" by John K. Paine and, amazingly enough, a certain amount of order was restored, sufficient at least for Director-General Davis to introduce the Reverend W. H. Milburn, the United States Senate's blind chaplain, to offer the invocation. Following the reverend's proclamation of a "sabbatic year for the whole human race," for which he was cheered by those who thought he was giving a speech, Miss Jessie Couthoui read the requisite epic poem praising Columbus' vision "full of light" and his mission "to show the world the way."[6] The orchestra offered a Wagnerian overture, Director-General Davis congratulated the individuals and groups responsible for producing the fair, and without formal introduction President Cleveland rose to speak.

The sun, as if to give nature's blessing to the proceedings, finally burst forth from behind the clouds, bringing the fairylike marble palaces and shimmering lagoons to life as the nation's leader faced the resounding cheers and sea of waving handkerchiefs. "Never before in any land," said the *Daily Inter Ocean,* "did any crowned monarch receive such homage of so many nations as was thus bestowed on this plain blackcoated American who acted as the representative of the American people."[7] This great exposition, said the president, was a tribute to the nation, and he praised the "stupendous results of American enterprise" which demonstrate "the unparalleled advancement and wonderful accomplishments of a young nation, and present the triumphs of a vigorous, self-reliant and independent people." In conclusion, he offered his own "vision of light"; "As by a touch the machinery that gives light to this vast Exposition is set in motion, so at the same instant let our hopes and aspirations awaken forces which in all time to come shall influence the welfare, the dignity, and the freedom of mankind."[8]

Shortly after noon, his half-heard speech concluded, President Cleveland pressed the golden button (actually a gilded telegraph key) setting the fair in motion. Instantaneously, as the electric circuit was closed, came a low rumble of machinery; water gushed from MacMonnies' Columbian Fountain; the flags of the United States, Castile, and Columbus' sovereigns Isabella and Ferdinand were unfurled on the main flag-staffs; banners and streamers of all colors fluttered from the buildings, while whistles from the steam launches in the Grand Canal joined the chimes from the domed palaces and the heavier boom of the USS *Michigan*'s cannons in the harbor. Two hundred white doves were released from the Peristyle, the shroud fell from the giant gilded statue of the Republic in the Grand Basin, and the orchestra began "America."[9] As the multitude gazed enchanted at the spectacle, amid cries of "Ah-h-h," one among them felt her purse snatched from her. It was Jane Addams, the mistress of Hull House.[10]

The curtain was up on the great American world's fair, "the beginning of an Olympian Era." But that same day the papers also reported from Wall Street that "repeated raids were made on leading shares."[11] The celebration of American progress and prosperity and the achievement of all mankind would be conducted during a crippling world-wide depression. In six months the dream city would be a memory and Mayor Harrison would be dead from a deranged spoilsman's bullet. In slightly more than a year the two figures, President Cleveland and Governor Altgeld, who now sat together on the grandstand, would be facing each other in a bitter constitutional battle arising from the Pullman strike. And within five years the two nations who were being especially honored by the exposition, the United States and Spain, would be at war. The World's Columbian Exposition, the greatest international fair of its time, which was to express the continuity of progressive American civilization, and open a new epoch in man's comprehension and control of nature, expressed far more clearly the confusions and contradictions that existed at the core of the society, between what was believed, desired, and desperately hoped for, and what was becoming inescapably more real and actual.

INTRODUCTION:
THE GREAT WORLD'S FAIR AND VICTORIAN CULTURE

Change is inevitable. In a progressive country change is constant.

Disraeli

The day of the great world's fairs has long since passed. Large scale displays and spectacles, calling themselves "World's Fairs" and attracting record millions, may continue to be produced from time to time, and will undoubtedly continue to find their admirers, but they will be viewed increasingly as remnants of an earlier age, costly curiosities whose ultimate value is as questionable as is their relevance to modern life. Conditioned by recent experience to accept, if not embrace, complexity, novelty, and uncertainty, the modern mind finds it difficult to understand the singular optimism and simplistic world vision that is reflected in the great world's fairs. Industrialism, nationalism, urbanization, and the rise of science—the forces and factors which produced and made possible the great fairs—have come to be seen as ambiguous benefactors of mankind, and therefore an institution that expresses such uncritical faith in the swift and universal progress of civilization is hard to treat seriously. Nevertheless, while there are good reasons for denying major cultural significance to the world's fairs of the recent past, the tendency to dismiss the fairs of an earlier period as well has hindered an accurate assessment of their potential value as prime sources for understanding an age in which their significance was to most people beyond question.

The great world's fairs of the second half of the nineteenth and early part of the twentieth centuries were an expression of a particular period of Western cultural development and were the result of a special combination of historical forces, conditions, and beliefs, and they continued to appear as long as these factors existed—and even for some years after they had been supplanted by newer forces, conditions, and ideas. Between 1851 and 1925, it was unusual for a year to pass without at least one major international exhibition, and in several years more than one great fair vied for the world's attention. During this period the basic form and operational pattern of the world's fair was established and it began to take on an almost institutional character. Indeed, the world's fair seems to have been one of the few truly international institutions of Western culture of the period. The major reason for this is not difficult to discover. In a period of rapid industrial and technological change, affecting all aspects of Western culture, the great world's fairs provided an objective focus for cultural self-examination and self-expression. Beginning as large international industrial displays and showcases for the new inventions and discoveries of science and technology, they quickly became committed to the much more ambitious and comprehensive aim of revealing culture in all its dimensions.[1]

Immediate practical benefits became less and less important as the symbolic character of the institution was established. In static and isolated societies there is no great impulse toward cultural reexamination. The fundamental relations and definitions that are embedded within the patterns of life are understood because they are assumed and unchallenged.

Cultural identity does not exist as a problem or a question. In a dynamic society undergoing basic transformations, on the other hand, as in Western culture of the mid-nineteenth century, the idea of cultural definition becomes problematic and pervasive. The industrial and technological revolutions were changing the basic relations and patterns of Western life, while increasing knowledge about other cultures challenged cultural isolationism and complacency. Both of these factors fostered a self-conscious cultural reexamination that became increasingly more complicated and difficult.

The emergence of the world's fair as a symbolic cultural expression during this period is but one of several developments that testify to the self-consciousness of the age. Like the tortured intellectual and literary experiments, the political, theological, and economic debates, and the social and educational movements of the late nineteenth century, the great world's fairs in the broadest sense represented the Victorian era's attempt to both acknowledge the reality of rapid change and to understand and control its direction. Unlike some of these others, the world's fairs operated on a broader and more simplistic level and illustrated more clearly, perhaps, the age's faith that man could have his revolution and control it too. The two elements could not forever be held in balance, however, and when they began to crack the great world's fairs which were their physical manifestation from the first lost their original cultural significance. While it lasted, the Victorian faith made the great world's fairs important focal points and sensitive indicators of Western culture.

Part One:
THE BACKGROUND

A World's Fair (I prefer the popular descriptive title) is the clearing-house of civilization.

> Thomas W. Palmer
> President, National Commission
> World's Columbian Exposition

1

The Crystal Palace and the Origins of the Institution

Queen Victoria opened the first true world's fair in Hyde Park, London, on May 1, 1851. Although important multinational trade fairs had been known since the ancient Greeks, and national or local exhibitions of arts and industrial products had become familiar to many European countries in more recent times, the London World's Fair of 1851 presented in its totality something entirely new. It was the first conscious attempt to give comprehensive expression, in a concrete and popularly accessible form, to the major forces and concerns which underlay nineteenth century Western culture in general and mid-century British culture in particular. The fair was both a product of and a response to the great changes marked by the French Revolution and the Industrial Revolution. While eighteenth-century thinkers debated the question of whether

real change could take place in less than a millenium, whether man could actually bring about change in a single lifetime, the men and women of the nineteenth century found accelerating change all around them a fact of their daily lives. "The eighteenth century speculated about whether change was possible. The nineteenth knew deliriously that it was."[1]

Prince Albert, royal consort to Queen Victoria, had been impressed by the vigorous expansion of British industry and commerce and (by the late 1840s) had taken an active interest in various small exhibitions of British manufactures. He was also aware that since the mid-eighteenth century almost every country in Europe had held exhibitions of national products, and especially that the French had successfully introduced a system of competitive prizes to stimulate industrial development in their officially sanctioned exhibitions.[2] In 1849 Prince Albert became the most influential promoter of a plan for a British exhibition which would be grander in scale, size, and cost, and of a wider range of international participation than any similar undertaking hitherto attempted. Its appeal would not be limited as before merely to traders, manufacturers of special products, or the curious, but would be directed toward a much broader national and international audience. The fair would be a great celebration of British acceptance of change, growth, and expansion, and it would encourage through comparisons and competition further manmade change and development. As an international event it would also demonstrate the benefits of free trade among nations and point the way toward world peace and brotherhood which, as Winston Churchill later remarked, "it was then supposed must inevitably result from the unhampered traffic in goods."[3]

Diversity, change, growth, universality, and an optimism toward the ever-evolving future were the large ideas to be given objective form in the great British world's fair. Just the fact of its being conceivable bore witness to the increase of new materials, inventions, and products, of improved transportation and communications, of new techniques in temporary architectural engineering, of the popular vogue for travel, exploration, and secular knowledge, and of novel methods and attitudes toward managing popular enterprises that were expected to attract millions of people.

From the very first, however, the celebration of change was to be only a part of the fair's purpose and plan. The nineteenth century had discovered that real change was possible but it sought also to understand it, and this meant determining its direction and goal. Even in England, purposeless change—real novelty—was inconceivable to all but a handful of thinkers. Uncontrolled change was destructive, chaotic, anarchic, and sacrilegious. To men of Prince Albert's background, the French Revolution and the recent upheavals of 1848 pointed out the dangers of uncontrolled popular belief in swift change. From his viewpoint, there was an obvious

need for a second message at the fair, one which would channel the general energy and optimism of the country toward safer and more constructive paths. The thematic solution, just as obvious, lay exposed all across the surface of a British society which at mid-century was rapidly expanding its economy, extending its commercial and political power, and standing at the summit of world industrial leadership.

Thomas B. Macaulay published the first volume of his *History of England* in 1848 and in the opening chapter he wrote that the "history of our own country in the last hundred and sixty years is eminently the history of physical, moral, and intellectual improvement."[4] This wedding of two of the most important and pervasive concepts of the nineteenth century, progress and nationalism, provided an acceptable and popularly understandable answer to the questions raised by the recognition of rapid change. The idea of progress was acceptable because it accounted for the operation of change without the violent disruptions of revolution and chaos; it implied a gradualness and inevitability that gave hope without encouraging or fostering radicalism. It was understandable because it made sense out of the visible fact of change while requiring few conscious sacrifices in the older habits and patterns of thought.

Nationalism, the sense of national destiny and glory, provided an appropriate goal or purpose for progressive change. It was of practical value to monarchs and national leaders who had reason to be worried about their popular support and their hold on positions of power; it was equally appealing to the general public who could identify themselves with their country and could take some degree of self-pride from national achievement, but who found it difficult to personally understand themselves in relation to a wider world of which the only direct knowledge they had was of hostility. Nationalism countered the inherent divisiveness and confusion of rapid change by offering a unifying principle which was not so abstract as to be beyond the popular understanding. The first great world's fair, as planned, would be both a massive demonstration and celebration of change and at the same time an object lesson in how to understand that demonstration. In one voice, in its details, it would praise innovation and diversity, while in another, in its orchestration and conduct, it would sing of patriotic unity and restraint.

The Royal Society of Arts, with Prince Albert's urging, became the chief sponsor of the parliamentary approval its international nature required. Desiring to further a closer relationship between manufacturing and technological development and the fine arts, the society saw the fair as an opportunity for British artisans to learn valuable lessons that would encourage improvement in both areas.[5] The proposal for such a comprehensive international and popular event, however, still faced conservative opposition from those in England, and on the Continent, who were at first unable to recognize its advantages. In the British Parliament and in the public press it was argued that England would be overrun by bands of criminals, revolutionaries, and disease carriers; that English morality and loyalty to the crown would be weakened; that the English economy would be disrupted; and that it would end as a financial disaster.[6] Even after the proposal passed the House of Commons and a royal commission headed by Prince Albert began to publicize the details of the plan, sour predictions of failure and disaster continued.

Just a month before the great fair opened, Prince Albert wrote of the persistence of its opponents: "The strangers [the foreigners who would be attracted to London], they give out, are to commence a thorough revolution here, to murder Victoria and myself, and to proclaim the Red Republic in England. The plague is certain to come from the confluence of such vast multitudes and to swallow-up those whom the increased price of everything has not already swept away. For all this I am to be responsible and against all this I am to make efficient provision."[7]

On the Continent, especially following the upheavals of 1848, national isolationism and mutual suspicion led many governments to be fearful of contacts between their citizens and British institutions and ideas. The Prussian king was initially so alarmed by the prospect that he refused to allow the Prince and Princess (later the Emperor William and Empress Augusta) to accept Queen Victoria's official invitation. More doubts were expressed when Joseph Paxton's plans for the enormous exhibition hall were made known. The Crystal Palace, that most extraordinary and memorable symbol of the 1851 world's fair, was at first thought to be incapable of withstanding the elements, and many nervous individuals stayed away from the opening ceremonies out of fear that the guns fired to salute the Queen's arrival would bring the glass shattering down upon them.[8]

In spite of the prophecies of failure, however, by the time the fair closed its doors on October 11, it was judged on all sides and by all standards a triumphant success and the opposition, "which may be reckoned the last major outbreak of English parochialism," was silenced by the results.[9] Nearly fourteen thousand exhibitors, half of them British, had sent displays which were then carefully ordered and shown under the four classifications of raw materials, machinery and mechanical inventions, manufactures, and sculpture and the plastic arts, to demonstrate the progress achieved in each field. In all, six million people visited the fair, a daily average of forty-three thousand, and the Royal Commission, which had financed the project largely from private donations, was left with enough surplus capital to endow a national museum in South Kensington.[10]

Paxton's 108-foot-high Crystal Palace, covering nineteen of the fair's twenty-six acres, became in Churchill's words "the marvel of the decade," a revelation of what could be done architecturally with steel and glass.[11] It established a precedent for the future important role that large, quickly assembled, temporary architecture would play in the great world's fairs. Prince Albert was personally vindicated and the queen delighted by the success of the fair. "God bless my dearest Albert! God bless my dearest country, which has shown itself so great today!" she wrote in her diary following opening day.[12] The exhibits of British machinery captured most of the prizes and awards and the English exhibits in other areas, except textiles and fine arts, were nearly as impressive.

The great British world's fair probably encouraged the further development of British industry, and it certainly pointed out areas in which England had much to learn from the accomplishments of other nations. Not only did England learn, but the Continent, and especially Germany, learned of the superiority of British industry and manufacturing and the public display quite possibly served to foster a greater demand for British exports. The significant increase in British trade in the years following the fair seemed to many people to be proof positive of the fair's contribution, and undoubtedly the objective of stimulating British national spirit, confidence, and unity was achieved.[13] The queen's several visits to the fair seemed to arouse in her subjects a sense of personal loyalty and national pride. "Never had the throne," Churchill wrote, "been so firmly grounded in the affections of the people."[14] Assembling the nation's most progressive achievements in one place and under one roof, and identifying the government officially with the display, provided not only a sense of British security as to its position in the world, but also seemed to commit the government to maintain and extend it.

Furthermore, however fortunate or unfortunate it may be judged, the surge of nationalism in the late nineteenth century also led to national aggressiveness and territorial expansion. Searching for satisfactory answers to questions raised by the whirl of physical and intellectual change, the nineteenth century settled upon a dynamic nationalism that became im-perialism. It is not surprising, then, that an aristocrat of 1912 could nostalgically view the Crystal Palace, which at that time still stood, "as a memorial of the initial stage of England's Imperial Era; for though many may only date this from the day when Lord Beaconsfield's genius evolved the idea of crowning Queen Victoria Empress of India, he no doubt read, with subtle intuition, the thought in the public mind, and we may assume that the great Exhibition of 1851 was a powerful factor in its birth."[15] Regardless of how honestly Prince Albert believed that the fair would contribute to the breakdown of provincialism and signal the beginning of an era of world peace and understanding, it was also an object lesson in competitive nationalism. Few men foresaw that the Crimean War would follow close upon it.

The consequences of the ideas embodied and encouraged by the great British world's fair were not, perhaps, so clear then as they may seem to be today, and yet there is something to be said for the Englishman who found only his own sense of national identification and self-confidence awakened by his country's novel experiment in mass showmanship. He had seen England's best achievements matched against those of the rest of the world, in what he wished to believe was fair competition, and he had seen his country emerge victorious, a demonstrated leader in the Victorian era's contest with the disturbing forces of modern civilization.

2

The Growth and Character of the Institution

Whatever the actual results of the first great world's fair for England, the idea quickly caught the imagination of the rest of the world. In the next seventy-five years well over one hundred major exhibitions were staged that claimed world's fair stature. So widespread was the attempt to imitate London's success that it would not be an exaggeration to say that the world's fair, between 1851 and 1925, became a significant institution of Western culture. Understandably, the largest and most numerous fairs were held in Western Europe, England, and the United States, where industrialization was further advanced, but important efforts were also made in Australia, India, South America, and Eastern Europe, where it was hoped that industrialization might be encouraged. The popularity of the world's fair was due not only to the fact that

it expressed and accounted for several of the larger questions of the period, but also to the comprehensiveness of its aim, the goal as one writer put it "to try to take in the world and every occupation and interest of mankind,"[1] which thus provided a wide latitude for national, local, and individual expression. By presenting the opportunity for a nation to show its most progressive and representative achievements, it required that culture to define itself and thus forced upon it a certain kind of self-consciousness. In addition, the transitory nature of the fairs tended to encourage the view that a world's fair offered only a snapshot of civilization at one stage in its development. It gave no final word on any subject, but simply the latest, most progressive word. A world's fair challenged a nation to reveal itself at a particular moment in time, while reassuring it that within the overall progressive scheme no one would expect it to be the same next year.

The rapid developments in the applied sciences, transportation, and communications in the second half of the century made it possible for each successive world's fair to proclaim a new stage in the evolution of man's control of nature and to place the host country's bid to a position in the vanguard of the race before an ever larger audience.

As in the first great world's fair, succeeding fairs showcased industrial and mechanical inventions and developments. At London in 1851, British machinery, agricultural implements, and firearms received the most attention; again at London, in 1862, the Bessemer steel process and the potential of rubber products were demonstrated; at Paris in 1867, it was German gasoline motors and aluminum; at Philadelphia in 1876, the telephone and the typewriter; at Paris in 1878 motor cars, refrigeration, and electricity; at Chicago in 1893, the electric light bulb and alternating current; at Buffalo in 1901, the storage battery and the wireless; at St. Louis in 1904, the radio tube. The list of such innovations that received initial world-wide exposure at the world's fairs is nearly inexhaustible, and it is one of the most often mentioned features of the great world's fairs that has carried over into the more recent twentieth century spectacles. The New York World's Fair of 1939, for example, boasted the television, air conditioning, and plastics, while the Brussels World's Fair of 1958 revealed the nuclear reactor and the atomic clock.[2]

Important as was this aspect of the great world's fairs, the display of mechanical and scientific novelties was never their exclusive or primary purpose. It was appropriate that England should highlight industrial achievement in 1851, because the most significant developments and most obvious changes in the culture were occurring in applied science. To identify with the forces of change meant to identify largely with materialism. Following the London World's Fair, however, the great world's fairs increasingly gave space to displays of natural history, science, agriculture and livestock, educational methods, and the fine arts. Indeed, the connection between

the fine arts and industry was apparent from the earlier association of the Society of Arts with the sponsoring of the first world's fair. A leading nation in nineteenth-century civilization could never, it was thought, be a mechanical sophisticate and an esthetic primitive. A nation's art needed also to demonstrate progressive achievement, and yet within that overall demonstration art at the world's fairs came to have a particularly functional character. If the great world's fairs celebrated change by showcasing the innovations of applied science, they sought in art a means of controlling and understanding that change. From the start, as Lewis Mumford has remarked of the American "Brown Decades," the dominant theme of nineteenth century materialism required a compensating alternative.[3] This explains why architecture, that peculiar combination of esthetics, engineering, and social utility, became such a notable feature of the great world's fairs.

Large international fairs became a possibility in the mid-nineneenth century only because of the development of modern engineering methods that permitted the erection of expansive and relatively cheap buildings in a very short time.[4] Great world's fair architecture, however, rarely revealed any startlingly original principles, but restricted itself instead to the adaptation of older techniques and designs to the new practical problems presented by the requirements of the world's fairs themselves. The Crystal Palace of London in 1851, for example, was thought to be a uniquely innovative structure, whereas it was in fact an exaggerated greenhouse *in design* and an extension of previous advances made in the iron and steel industry as a result of railway bridge building *in construction*. This does not, of course, detract from Paxton's achievement in demonstrating new and influential uses for older ideas and techniques, but it does suggest the limits of architectural creativity especially in artistic design that were permitted within the framework of the great world's fairs. The true modernists in architecture, as in art generally, were never allowed much freedom at the fairs, because art in the Victorian world was the expression of idealized beauty, harmony, control, and grandeur, and functioned as a stylized human counterpoint to the materialistic trends. The world's fairs required illustrations of progress in art, that is, refinements of the Victorian idea of art, but radical innovations in art (just as in politics) would be out of place at the fair. In the Victorian balance, art was set over and against industry and mechanics and thus was expected to express its opposite spirit.

As the nonmanufacturing exhibits gained greater prominence in the fairs following London in 1851, the idea that a world's fair should also concentrate and express the progress of mankind in his intellectual, moral, and spiritual existence began receiving increasing support. In part, this was simply an extension of the argument that a world's fair has as one of its major objectives the exchange of knowledge and encouragement of mutual understanding among all nations and peoples. It is also related to the goal of illustrating progress in an ever wider and more comprehensive sphere. More directly, however, the demand for more attention to the nonmaterial aspects of civilization was an obvious reaction to the growing fears engendered by the increasing number and diversity of novel mechanical and industrial exhibits.

The French gave the nonmaterial a special emphasis in their world's fairs and it was they who first instituted, in 1889, a series of intellectual and religious congresses to be held concurrently with the operation of the fair. As in the industrial, mechanical, and fine arts exhibits, the congresses, to which leading figures in various fields of knowledge and activity were invited, were intended to share information, stimulate new thought and effort, and above all indicate progressive development. Much has been claimed for such congresses as agents of change or as forecasters of social and intellectual trends, but on balance such claims are seldom justified.[5] As in the material exhibits, the architecture and artistic displays, and the physical organization, world's fair congresses were more directly revealing of the current state of thought than prophetic or catalytic.

Nevertheless, since the world's fairs were such popular events and received such wide coverage in the public press, travel guides, and periodicals, they were seen by many reformers and educators as a medium of mass communication which might be used to change attitudes and spread such ideas as universal brotherhood, world peace, human dignity, and social improvement. As developments in transportation made it possible for more people from farther and farther away to attend the great fairs, there was a real opportunity for acquainting different nationalities and cultures with each other and encouraging mutual respect and understanding. Actually, although there were some noble efforts made, the potential was never fully exploited. Where it was realized, it existed as a relatively minor theme beneath the period's pervasive national rivalries and quest for national prestige.

Beginning with the Crystal Palace, the great world's fairs intentionally served some narrower national purpose either directly or indirectly. Usually some date of patriotic significance or important national achievement was symbolized or commemorated. The Vienna World's Fair of 1873 was a demonstration of Austria's full recovery from the War of 1866; the Philadelphia World's Fair of 1876 celebrated the centennial anniversary of American independence; and the Paris World's Fair of 1878 was proof that the Third Republic was established and could accomplish as much as the emperor had done. Napoleon III's desire to present a French spectacle more magnificent than England's, and to strengthen his hold upon the growing French capitalist class, are said to have been the primary motives for the Paris world's fairs of 1855 and 1867.[6]

The first world's fair was organized and financed through private subscription and received governmental support only in the form of the granting of a royal charter. Members of the crown family and the government did, however, publicly associate themselves with the affair by serving in the management, and by their personal praise and frequent attendance. Thereafter, direct governmental involvement administratively and financially grew significantly. The Paris World's Fair of 1855 returned only about $1.25 for every $10.00 expended in operation and construction costs, largely because Napoleon III wanted all the people of France to see his great production and so ordered the admission price to be kept to an absolute minimum (on some days only four cents). The French government made up the deficit. Not only to support their own world's fairs did governments begin to grant direct subsidies, but also to support the private displays of their manufacturers and artisans in foreign fairs.

Making an impressive showing abroad became almost as much a question of national pride as the holding of a successful fair at home. The idea of international comparison and competition was based upon the presupposition that the world would be reasonably well represented, so that one of the reasons put forth for supporting the world's fairs of other countries was that it would insure reciprocation. The most common arguments offered in favor of participation in foreign world's fairs, however, were that it would increase trade by increasing foreign demand for home products, stimulate industrial and artistic development, and raise the country in the world's estimation. Taken in a negative sense, and revealing the insecurity that lay behind the Victorian optimism, it was said that failure to make a good showing would not only contribute to the loss of world trade, but would also be interpreted as marking the beginning of the degeneracy of the national culture.[7]

The connection in the Victorian scheme between private exhibits and their public or national significance helps explain the growth in public support for private industrial and manufacturing displays in foreign fairs. The British Government, for example, began making grants to English exhibitors for the Paris World's Fair of 1867, and it soon thereafter became customary for foreign nations to appoint their own official commissioners to be responsible for insuring a creditable performance. It was also at Paris in 1867 that the French Government inaugurated another standard feature of the great world fairs. By inviting foreign nations to erect their own national buildings, the French gave recognition to the growth of official international commitment to the institution.

The great world's fairs were an institutional expression of the late nineteenth century as a period of industrial and commercial expansion, of national rivalry and prestige, and of the desire to find more customers and markets for local products. With a growing emphasis on productivity, came also a growing concern with consumption which the fairs were expected to stimulate through their function as mass advertizers. The economic motives, however, were always indirect, predicated on anticipated results that could never be completely proven. Few actual sales or contracts were effected at the fairs themselves. Similarly, the success of a world's fair in general was never thought to be an exclusively economic matter. Since the first London World's Fair, there has usually been a real if not apparent deficit in actual receipts over costs, so that commissioners-in-charge and supporters of the institution have had to emphasize the indirect gains to trade, to industry, or to tourism.

In addition to national rivalry and economic ambition, the great world's fairs of the late nineteenth and early twentieth centuries reflected the rise of the city as an important economic and social factor and as a center of national and individual identity and pride. Great fairs could only occur in great cities where the necessary facilities, accommodations, talents, and funds were concentrated, and it was recognized from the very first that the millions who came to see the fair would also see the city. Indeed, it may well be true, as it was often held to be, that the greatest exhibit of a great world's fair was the city in which it was held. Thus, the great fairs easily became mirrors for metropolitan as well as national ambition and pride. One of the major reasons for Napoleon III's promotion of the Parisian fairs of 1855 and 1867, and one might reasonably suggest a prime motive for all the Paris fairs, was to silence London's claim, put forward in 1851, to be the capital city of Europe. City rivalry was apparent not only in the London and Paris world's fairs of the period but also in the fairs held at Vienna, Brussels, Amsterdam, Antwerp, Sydney, and Melbourne, and it was a particularly notable feature of the American fairs. "In the life of a city," wrote one observer, "the moment arrives when it must give a world's fair. A fair, according to economists, results from an accumulation of goods. A world's fair might be said to result from an accumulation of pride—not the competitive feeling whipped up by chambers of commerce, but the pride of cities, a splendid emotion."[8] Nevertheless, the indirect economic gains to cities resulting from world's fairs were considered important. Money spent by visitors on hotels and food, new business attracted to the area, new values added to real estate and factories—however impossible to calculate—were real values and were used as arguments by fair promoters to encourage heavy financial support and cooperation by city governments and city leaders.

3

America and the Great World's Fairs

Although the basic form and character of the institution evolved mainly in Western Europe, the country which produced the greatest number of world's fairs was the United States. American interest and participation during the last half of the nineteenth and early twentieth centuries, like the British and French, reflected the expansion of national spirit, enterprise, and world consciousness. From the beginning, however, American representation at foreign world's fairs was more hesitating and private. Participation was not taken for granted until the late 1880s, and public support for U.S. exhibitors faced strong and persistent opposition at home.[1] As to the advisability of participating in the London World's Fair of 1851, proponents had to answer the widely held charge that it was to be a "mammoth speculation" sponsored by John Bull for his own selfish ends and that Americans could not expect decent treatment in Europe.[2] When efforts to obtain a congressional appropriation failed, many American agriculturists and industrialists were unwilling to send their exhibits. The American effort toward the first great world's fair was essentially private and disorganized, compared to most other foreign displays, and the results of this first venture showed the limits of that approach.

Congress had granted the use of the USS *Lawrence* to transport the United States' exhibits to London, but when it arrived, much to the delight of the British press, there were no funds for unloading and transportation. In addition, in their early moments of enthusiasm, the Americans had reserved much more space than they now could fill. In the midst of the crisis, a private American banker in London, George Peabody, realized the implications of this embarrassment and came to the rescue with $15,000 of his own money. In spite of Peabody's noble efforts in transporting, arranging, and decorating the American display, the British press continued to criticize the U.S. performance, especially in the weakness of the arts shown. A few individual exhibits of agricultural technology and mechanical invention received reluctant notice, but the general preliminary conclusion seemed to be that the American display proved the United States was what the English had all along thought it was, a typical adolescent republic—long in ambition, but short in accomplishment. "The Americans say," chuckled *Punch,* "that the reason they have sent nothing to the Exhibition is, that the productions of their industry are . . . too gigantic to be brought over; and . . . the reality is so impossible to be understood or described, that the only way to give us any idea of it was to leave it all to our imagination."[3]

Following tests by an international jury, and especially after the prizes were awarded, the American exhibits were given a much more thorough and favorable appraisal. Although the United States had contributed only 534 of the nearly fourteen thousand exhibits shown at the Crystal Palace, America had captured proportionately a greater share of prizes than any other country, including Great Britain.[4] McCormick, Goodyear, the Borden "meat biscuit," Dick engine tools and presses, and the Bond device for astronomical observation all received Council Medals for original design. Afterwards, while a general inferiority in splendor and glamor was still mentioned, the utility, comfort, efficiency, and mass appeal of American products began to receive notice.[5] And when the New York clipper *America* won the first race for the International Silver Trophy (later known as the America's Cup) on August 28, even *Punch* made amends:

> YANKEE DOODLE sent to town
> His goods for exhibition;
> Everybody ran him down,

> And laughed at his position:
> They thought him all the world behind;
> A goney, muff, or noodle;
> Laugh on, good people—never mind—
> Says quiet YANKEE DOODLE. . . .

> Your gunsmiths of their skill may crack,
> But that again don't mention;
> I guess that COLT's revolvers whack
> Their very first invention.
> By YANKEE DOODLE, too, you're beat
> Downright in Agriculture,
> With his machine for reaping wheat
> Chaw'd up as by a vulture. . . .

> You also fancied, in your pride,
> Which truly is tarnation,
> Them British locks of yourn defied
> The rogues of all creation;

> But CHUBBS' and BRAMAH's HOBBS has picked,
> And you must now be viewed all
> As having been completely licked
> By glorious YANKEE DOODLE. . . .[6]

By the close of the fair the British press, pleased with the great event and confident of their country's overall supremacy, could afford to grant the American achievement, and as Merle Curti has written, "the final British reactions indicated that American participation, despite the shortcomings of the exhibit, greatly exalted the country in the eyes of other lands."[7] Nevertheless, American sensitivity to the initial British criticism was made clear in a defiant verse published in Boston the following year:

> John Bull, you laugh in proud emotion
> At our small wares sent o'er the ocean
>
> . . . .
>
> But to my own plain Yankee notion
> We're in the right.

You laughed aloud, in high disdain
At our machine that cuts the grain;
And swallowed down your words again.
                    Conceited John.

We beat you, John, at all that *pays;*
'Tis idle in these stirring days,
To fool your time, and only raise
                    What's old tomorrow![8]

The American section at the next great world's fair at Paris in 1855 did not sustain the final optimistic predictions of London. There were several excellent manufactured articles, and Goodyear won another award, but the meager 54 American exhibitions (after space had been reserved for 1,200) was a severe disappointment to the French. During the Civil War period United States participation continued to be largely unofficial and undistinguished and, with the exception of American machines and engines, was afforded little favorable attention. After the war, however, at Paris in 1867 and Vienna in 1873, the United States provided the first really impressive material proof of her expansion and progress, and indicated through the first substantial congressional appropriations a change, however slight, in the official attitude toward the value of the institution.[9] At Paris, American natural resources and especially American agricultural potential was acknowledged. The United States might eventually feed the world as she had already "captured the imagination and the future of the political world."[10] In technology and consumer goods, the American displays impressed many Europeans with their "originality, inventiveness, peculiarity, and novelty"; in social relations, a new department at Paris, the American model farms received general praise as did the American rural schools at Vienna.

In other areas, however, the U.S. displays were less distinguished. In literature and the fine and decorative arts the American exhibits were generally weak and unoriginal, and European criticism overall emphasized that American products, though useful, lacked grace, design, color, elegance, and elaboration. Poor organization and mismanagement also plagued the United States' representation at both fairs. At Paris, the Americans failed to provide several promised displays, did not have proper inventories, sent managers unfamiliar with French customs or language, and were slow in receiving Congressional appropriations and in preparing their section. At Vienna, Massachusetts State Commissioner Charles Francis Adams blamed mismanagement for a poor showing, which he likened to a "Worcester County Fair," and for an embarrassing scandal that arose over the selling of New York liquor, previously admitted duty-free for exhibit, at the American bar.[11]

In spite of these problems, the mounting world reputation of American technology and acknowledged standing in the agricultural and fishing industries by the late 1870s encouraged further American participation in the international fairs of the eighties and nineties. In this period, American representation not only at the great world's fairs at Paris in 1878 and 1889 and London in 1886, but at the smaller more specialized events like the fisheries exhibits in Berlin in 1880 and London in 1883, or the Columbian Historical Exhibition in Madrid in 1892, became predictable and even expected. American machinery continued to receive most of the awards and medals at the large fairs, but it was also becoming clear that Americans were sensitive to the persistent criticism of American lack of design, refinement, and craftsmanship, and that there was a growing desire to correct the impression of American inferiority in these areas. By the end of the Paris World's Fair of 1889, in which the United States received 53 grand prizes, 198 gold medals, 266 silvers, 233 bronzes, and 233 honorable mentions, it could be reasonably asserted, on the basis of American participation in the world's fairs since 1851, that the country had demonstrated a potential for international leadership and an official acceptance of such a role for herself.

The growth of American participation in foreign world's fairs reflected the adoption of many of the standard European arguments for supporting the institution. In addition to increasing American prestige in the world, the United States could learn valuable lessons from the artistic and industrial displays. This would improve the quality of American production and contribute to the spread of useful knowledge. American trade would be enhanced by making full use of the great fairs as a cheap method of mass international advertising and would help secure new markets for the expanding economy. Such reasoning eventually prevailed over concerns that Europeans would steal American secrets, grab American markets, and that the United States would never be given an honest opportunity in Europe. It was even suggested that a creditable showing would help convince the most skilled and intelligent "portion of the productive classes" to emigrate, and that it would increase the attractiveness of American bonds to European investors.[12]

Other arguments advanced during the period reflected a growth in American patriotism, sense of world mission, and a desire to surpass the Old World. In the congressional debates over participation at Paris in 1867, it was suggested that America was duty-bound to inform Europe about America and to show what could be done under the American political system. World's fairs were "a contest between the products of labor under democratic liberty, and those under monarchical despotism," declared Henry Raymond of New York.[13] The independence, strength, and unity of the country would be manifested; the nation would show itself as the model for other republics; and American support for sister republics would be demonstrated by participation in any fairs they might hold. For the French world's fairs of 1878 and 1889, it was said that the United States should contribute extensive displays as a token of appreciation for French aid in the Revolutionary War. Additional reasons put forward illustrated the affect upon American pride of European criticism of the inadequacies of the early American displays and the patronizing attitude toward America that was prevalent in many areas of Europe. Americans wanted not just the respect of Europe, but its admiration as well.

A clearer reflection of American attitudes, perhaps, was the immediate desire following the Great London World's Fair of 1851 to produce a great American world's fair on American soil. The first American effort to sponsor a world's fair occurred in New York City in 1853. An obvious attempt to imitate London's success, it was opened two months behind schedule by President Pierce on July 12 in its own Crystal Palace.[14] Erected at Reservoir Square on Fifth Avenue and Forty-Second Street (now the New York Public Library and Bryant Park) after plans sent from England, the hastily conceived production of a group of local businessmen immediately ran into difficulties. Only a few foreign exhibitors were represented, the roof of the glass palace leaked, and attendance was slack. In spite of Horace Greeley's promotion and P. T. Barnum's management, the "Exhibition of the Industry of All Nations" could not be saved and it closed quietly the following year. In 1858, despite twenty-one million gallons of water in the adjacent reservoir, the New York Crystal Palace burned to the ground in half an hour.[15] Lacking true national support or interest, the very most that may be said for the New York World's Fair of 1853 is that it reflected to a degree "the pride of a great city, becoming suddenly conscious that its police and politicians were scandalous, and its manners less refined than those of Boston or Philadelphia; or, of course, London—which was still America's spiritual capital."[16]

New York was indeed becoming aware of itself as an established, dynamic metropolis. Already the nation's largest city, it had its Central Park, was acquiring a certain decorum, and had become one of the great world ports in the age of the clipper ship. But the transportation and industrial transformation of the country had yet to be felt deeply enough to give the necessary widespread impetus for a Great World's Fair in America, and the Civil War had yet to shock the nation into a self-conscious need for cultural stock taking.

Shortly after the end of the Civil War, Professor John L. Campbell of Wabash College began suggesting that a great international exhibition held in conjunction with the one hundredth anniversary of the Declaration of Independence would be an effective way to demonstrate the restoration of the American Union and would help to heal the wounds of war. Three years later the Franklin Institute of Philadelphia picked up the idea, adding that obviously its fair city—the home of Franklin, the Liberty Bell, and Independence Hall—would be the appropriate location. Boston, Baltimore, Washington, and New York also entered determined bids for the honor, but Philadelphia had history and an earlier start on its side and so Congress responded in 1873 by passing a bill creating a Centennial Commission and naming Philadelphia as the Centennial City.

The first world's fair on a grand scale ever held in the United States was opened on May 10, 1876, by President Grant and the Emperor Dom Pedro of Brazil.[17] The presence of a monarch, some had insisted, would be an insult to American republicanism, but the official invitation was extended anyway, indicating that acceptance of the international situation as it was seemed to be more important than encouraging changes.[18] Occupying 236 acres of Fairmount Park in Philadelphia, the fair impressively presented over one hundred and fifty structures erected by states, territories, and foreign governments. By the time the fair closed on November 10, over eight million visitors had paid to see the thirty thousand exhibits representing thirty-two countries.[19] In the midst of one of the most severe financial panics of the century, the Centennial Commission had raised nearly nine million dollars from the federal government, the State of Pennsylvania, the City of Philadelphia, and private citizens, and although the fair actually lost money, Americans could justly take pride in their country's "first adequate expression in a material way of the dignity, wealth, and resources of the nation."[20] Most foreign visitors were genuinely impressed by America's first great world's fair, and Europe's changing attitude toward the nation was symbolized by the playing of a Richard Wagner composition written especially for the Centennial.

The particular focus of America's first great fair was unquestionably the machine. American and foreign visitors marvelled at such exhibits as Bell's telephone, the Westinghouse air brake, Edison's duplex telegraph, the typewriter, the refrigerator car, the sewing machine, and other illustrations of American mechanical inventiveness. And in the very center of Machinery Hall, a symbol of the machine age itself and transmitting power to the eight thousand other machines in the building, stood the giant Corliss steam engine, a double vertical engine raised three and a half feet above the floor like a vast idol upon a fifty-six foot diameter platform. "The cylinders were forty-four inches in diameter with a ten-foot stroke, and between the two engines revolved a flywheel weighing fifty-six tons, thirty feet in diameter, with a twenty-four-inch face. This made thirty-six stately revolutions every minute to govern 1,400 horsepower of energy furnished from twenty tubular boilers outside the building."[21] The opening of the fair itself was accomplished when President Grant and Emperor Dom Pedro together turned the huge valves that started the monster.

But if America's celebration of the machine and the progressive changes it signified was a source of national pride and foreign admiration, the comparison of American exhibits with those of other nations in different areas of achievement showed, as in the recent foreign fairs, an imbalance in Victorian terms in the overall development of American civilization. Not only in the fine arts of painting and sculpture, but in handcrafts, furniture design, personal adornment and home decoration, the European and—somewhat surprisingly—the Japanese displays showed that America had much to accomplish before it could fairly claim to stand in the same rank with countries whose cultures were centuries old.[22] This situation may have actually been acknowledged at Philadelphia, since there does not seem to have been any serious intention in the architectural design or planning of the Fair's buildings to rival the recent grand architectural triumphs of Paris or Vienna, and perhaps there was a tacit agreement (undoubtedly fortunate) to grant at America'a first great fair the deficiency in the arts and decorative crafts in order to present the actual achievements in mechanics.[23] In any case, following the centennial there was a marked increase in the demand in America for engraved furniture, bric-à-brac, chandeliers, and sculptures—a wave of "tastefulness that was known at the time as the 'Artistic Craze,'" wrote Russell Lynes. Heavily imitative of European standards, it was a "tremendous straining toward artistic achievement that was doomed from the start. It was all show—show of technique, show of rich materials, show of virtuosity—with no driving conviction behind it, no intellectual substance, and no fight."[24]

However divorced from the everyday realities of American life, however inexpressive of American character, the "Artistic Craze" did imply a recognition of the importance of the arts in an overall assessment of national progress, it did help to raise in the popular mind the status of the American artist within the culture, and it did influence a movement in the last quarter of the century toward the building and endowment of art museums and art collections.[25]

The Philadelphia World's Fair of 1876, as the first great American fair, indicated a general acceptance of the basic function and meaning of the institution and an awareness of its suitability to the United States in the last half of the nineteenth century. Like other industrially developing nations, in Europe and elsewhere, America was changing swiftly. There was a need to comprehend the direction and meaning of change. Here too, and even perhaps more so than in Europe, the association between industry, commerce, and government in the common goals of progress and nationalism seemed natural and unforced. The historically ambiguous nature of American attitudes toward the European fatherland made the world's fair an unusually clear reflector of American rivalry with Europe on the one hand, and of its susceptibility and sensitivity to European standards on the other. In addition, the period was one of growing American international interest and world involvement, and the popularity of the international exhibition illustrated—as did the travel books and romances—a trend away from provincialism and toward cosmopolitanism. Nonetheless, the Philadelphia World's Fair of 1876 and its forerunner of 1853 illustrated several important differences between the European and the American approach to the institution.

Even for the fair that commemorated the birth of the nation, official United States financial and administrative support was minimal when the official governmental commitments of other nations is considered. In Europe by 1876, it was the general policy of nations hosting world's fairs to subsidize the expenses of their fairs prior to opening the doors and, often, to supply the management personnel directly from various governmental department staffs. With the solvency of the enterprise guaranteed by the government, private industrialists and artists were more easily encouraged to display their products. The organization and operation of U.S. fairs, on the other hand, has remained since 1853 largely the responsibility of private individuals who form companies (usually nonprofit membership corporations), provide the administration, construct the buildings, gather the exhibits, and pay the expenses for the most part by selling bonds to the public. Even when a significant appropriation is obtained from Congress, it is usually accompanied by restrictions that limit its value. At Philadelphia, for instance, the congressional appropriation of over two million dollars was made in the form of a loan that had to be repaid by the World's Fair Commission as the close of the fair. While such procedures have freed American fairs from the direct control of the federal or state governments, they have also forced American fair managers to be more concerned with financial operations.

Although very few American or European world's fairs were ever profitable in a direct investment sense, or were ever expected to be, in America the deficits that remained at the close of a fair had to be covered by the individual stockholders and not by the government or the people in general. Thus, while American fairs have been more responsive to local and individual direction than their European counterparts, they have also been more interested in maximizing gate receipts, concession revenues, and exhibitor fees, and with minimizing their costs. What is surprising is not that American fairs had a materialistic quality that was absent in similar European events, but that without extensive governmental support the United States produced so many of the costly spectacles. Between 1876 and 1915, the country held fourteen major fairs of international scope, five of which (Philadelphia 1876, Chicago 1893, Buffalo 1901, St. Louis 1904, and San Francisco 1915) qualify as great world's fairs. The popularity of the institution in America cannot be explained as easily as in some other countries by reference to its practical political usefulness for particular governments. In America, the absence of direct government control and supervision allowed the world's fair to be at once more disorganized and informal and a more broadly sensitive indicator of popular culture. The adaptability of the institution in America helps explain why the form, at least, has proved so serviceable to successive generations.

A second major difference between American fairs and those of other nations, as illustrated by the New York World's Fair and especially by the centennial, was their peculiarly heightened symbolic meaning for American cities. The great world's fair, as has been previously noted, was historically an institution appropriate only for great cities whose expansion in size and international importance followed the Industrial Revolution. To host a world's fair was not only a mark of national progress and leadership but also a demonstration of metropolitan influence and pride. Moreover, world's fairs contributed to the growth of urban consciousness and city rivalry by providing an objective focus.

In Europe, however, city rivalry was closely associated with national competitiveness. The rivalry between Paris and London in the late nineteenth century is reflected in the successive great world's fairs of 1851, 1855, 1862, and 1867, but it is also clear that such city competition was closely related to the national rivalry between France and England as well. It seems hardly necessary to state that Paris and London stood for France and England respectively, just as Vienna stood for Austria. In America, on the other hand, there was no clearly acknowledged urban center or capital which could represent the country in its own eyes to the world. Washington, of course, was the seat of the federal government and the administrative capital of the nation. But it was not the oldest,

nor the largest, nor the most dynamic city; neither was it the most centrally located, geographically or demographically. Thus, beginning with the centennial, any suggestion of holding a world's fair in the United States involved first the settling of the question of its urban location. This procedure was usually accomplished through public discussion in the national Congress, the merits of each hopeful city's case being the subject of often heated and acrimonious political debate.

Once a decision was reached and a world's fair city determined, the urban and regional ambitions, antagonisms, and jealousies that had been exposed and intensified by the debate often limited the degree of cooperation that Congress could then achieve toward providing adequate support and backing. In addition, once a city had been chosen to represent the nation before the world, the other cities and regions which had had their ambitions sidetracked and their claims denied found themselves watching and analyzing with skeptical completeness their sister's performance.

In America in the latter part of the nineteenth century, then, the world's fair provided a forum for city ambition and rivalry within the country itself.[26] It also forced upon the nation and the world's fair city a certain national self-consciousness and concern for national self-definition. The city's image and reputation depended upon how well it represented the United States to the rest of the world, while the nation, in order to evaluate the success or failure of that symbolic representation, had to consider the basis of its own character. This, in turn, insured that America's world's fairs would be the subject of thorough analysis and wide cultural interpretation of great significance to the entire society. In America, where there was no London or Paris, the great world's fairs raised deeper cultural questions.[27]

In addition to the relative lack of governmental control and the heightened significance of urban rivalry, the American world's fairs placed a greater emphasis, though it was not advertised as such, on popular entertainment features. In part, this was due to the need for increasing revenues to which popular concessions and sideshows would contribute and to the relatively less rigid controls placed on what should and should not be a part of a world's fair. More generally, it was in keeping with the popular, mass, consumer trend in the nation at large, a trend that Europeans often noted in the design and usefulness of American mechanical inventions and products. Managers of American fairs found early on that Americans tired and lost interest if they were fed a diet only of heavy symbolic messages. Americans wanted to be informed, but they also wanted to be entertained, and thus from the first, when P. T. Barnum took over as president of the New York World's Fair of 1853, American fairs in order to be popular successes were as much show as tell.

Popular show business in the United States, in fact, grew up with the great American world's fairs and was an important ingredient in all of them.[28] At Philadelphia, the amusement concessions permitted within the grounds were restricted to a miniature railroad for transporting visitors, various international restaurants, beer gardens, soda shops, and clam bars, and the Sawyer Observatory—a massive iron structure that lifted customers up three hundred feet for a view of the fairgrounds and the surrounding countryside.[29] There were no buildings devoted primarily to fun within the limits of Fairmount Park, but outside the gates more than a mile of saloons, amusement booths, and side shows sprang up in numerous ramshackle stalls and houses. Shantyville, as it was known, was the out-of-bounds "recreation" zone of the centennial, a collection of cheap wooden structures housing variety shows and "such marvelous attractions as the 'learned pigs' and the 'five-legged cow.'"[30] Whether it was because Shantytown was a bigger money-maker than the fair proper, or because there seemed no way to prohibit such amusement sections, the managers of subsequent American fairs decided to bring the amusement areas within the gates where they would at least be subject to some degree of control.

More welcome, perhaps, than the entertainers and sideshowmen were the professional, religious, social, and reformist groups who found in the world's fairs an opportunity to hold their meetings, contact their members, and spread their mes-sages among the throngs of visitors. Over one hundred of such groups chose to meet in Philadelphia during the summer of 1876, beginning a tradition that has lasted to some degree up to the present.

In many ways the Philadelphia World's Fair of 1876 was a resounding success. It set world records in attendance, in the expanse of the fairgrounds, in receipts, and in the size of a single exhibition building. In the number of exhibits shown, only Paris in 1867 had a greater number up to that time, and in total cost, only Vienna in 1873 exceeded it. In the logic of world's fairs of the late nineteenth century, such statistics were thought to be significant indicators of progressive development and, as each new world's fair was judged according to its establishment of new standards, statistical data was continually referenced. The qualitative achievement of civilization was more difficult to determine but it was generally sought in appraisals of the fine arts and decorative arts displayed and the overall architectural design and plan. Such evaluations were based, naturally, upon Victorian and beaux-arts standards. The centennial, although it could boast a separate art building and a fairly representative collection of European art, did not attempt in its architectural design to rival the impressive achievements of Paris or Vienna. The United States made a strong bid to be considered as a major world leader in a material and quantitative way, but as many European visitors were to remark, the nation had yet to demonstrate that it had achieved maturity in the qualitative aspects of its civilization.

In its national meaning also, the Philadelphia World's Fair was a somewhat ambiguous spectacle. On the one hand, and despite the large deficit that remained, the results of the fair were a source of satisfaction to the managers and of pride for Philadelphians. Citizens who visited the fair from other regions could gain a patriotic sense of national progressive achievement from the entry of the country into the international arena, and the nation's newspapers and magazines helped to broadcast that confident message. But, in 1876, there were actually few visitors from west of the Alleghenies, as distances, transportation facilities, and costs were restrictive.[31] As a national enterprise, a world's fair had to attract a representative part of the nation as well as represent it. In addition, Philadelphia had been granted the centennial not so much because the city was representative of the country in 1876, but because it had the best claim to have represented the nation at the time of its founding in 1776. The fair looked to the American past, not to the American present or future; the city itself was a memorial to the original unity of the eighteenth rather than the promise and diversity of the nineteenth and twentieth centuries. Philadelphia was the first great effort of the United States in international show business, but it was not the last nor the greatest.

Following the centennial, large fairs were held in Denver, Louisville, New Orleans, Cincinnati, and Detroit, but each of these was limited to local significance and failed to attain the major national symbolic importance of the great world's fairs. By the late 1880s, however, plans were being formulated and interest being aroused in a new American world's fair to be held in conjunction with the celebration of the four hundredth anniversary of Columbus' discovery of the New World. Here was a grand opportunity to proclaim America's greatness before the world, to show the enormous strides in cultural achievement since the centennial, to set to rest forever the quibbles about American cultural inferiority, and, not incidentally, to foster patriotic harmony in a period of mounting domestic conflict. It would also, of course, surpass the centennial in all particulars; it would be more representative of the country, sum up its development more completely, and point more directly and confidently toward the grand future. By overshadowing the latest spectacles at Paris in 1878 and 1889, it would conclusively demonstrate the passing of world leadership from the Old to the New World and would symbolize the fulfillment of the mission and vision of Columbus. To accomplish this, to be the greatest American world's fair, it would have to be the greatest world's fair of all.

Part Two:
THE SETTING

America, my country, is almost a continent and hardly yet
a nation, for no nation can be considered historically as such
until it has achieved within itself a city to which all roads
lead, and from which there goes out an authority.

Ezra Pound

4

Energy and Uncertainty

The centennial year of 1876, and especially the Philadelphia World's Fair which was the outstanding centennial event, provided a natural opportunity for Americans to examine their past, to reflect upon their present, and to seek an identity upon which to base their ideas about the future. And yet, even granting that "there in an effervescent microcosm of parades and encampments, of excitement, effort, and confident expectation, was the essence of the Republic," there seemed to be little serious consideration given to the consequences of the great changes that were transforming the country in that post-Civil War industrial era.[1] Perhaps it was enough on the nation's birthday, as the country recovered from the panic of 1873, to pay homage to the past and reassert the general faith in the future with naïve patriotic confidence.

Few people who wondered at the giant Corliss engine, the exhibition's favorite attraction, understood its significance for an older tradition of individual craftsmanship, small towns, and independent farms. They accepted it symbolically as a demonstration of the genius, power, and greatness of the American people, but they did not consider what living with it would actually be like.

William Dean Howells, a native Midwesterner and the editor of the *Atlantic Monthly*, found the huge engine "an athlete of steel and iron with not a superfluous ounce of metal on it." But while he acknowledged that the industrial arts were the best expression of the "national genius," he was unable to see that the functional design and simplicity of the great engine might be the harbinger of a new, more appropriate, and even necessary American artistic tradition in it-self.[2] Instead, like most people, he saw only its material power, and like most people he sensed the inadequacy of American efforts in Victorian terms to comprehend its meaning. And yet Howells did not doubt that "by and by the inspired marbles, the breathing canvases, the great literature" would come, and he was satisfied that "for the present America is voluble in the strong metals and their infinite uses."[3]

Indeed, the machine was not a new force in American life in the 1870s; it had changed the course of the national history in earlier periods in often remarkable and important ways—the long rifle, textile machinery, the cotton gin, the six-shooter—but in the last third of the nineteenth century its impact became pervasive, confusing even American ideas of normal sexual relationships. A popular vaudeville expression of this confusion, which never failed to be received with gales of laughter in the nineties, involved a man crooning, "Here I sit with my typewriter on my knee."[4] Paradoxically, it was precisely because the changes were so great that the self-conscious insecurity of the period sought comfort and command of the situation through an increasing reliance upon traditional forms of thought and expression. And yet, even defining the traditional in America was problematic—was it essentially transplanted European, New England puritan, antebellum southern, western frontiersman or adventurer, Jeffersonian yeoman, or Hamiltonian urbanite? Was there any one culturally unifying tradition which might serve as support in times of need?

At the Philadelphia centennial, American independence was celebrated as the singular event in the national past, but technology, especially in the forms of the transcontinental railroad and the trans-Atlantic cable, was making interdependence the reality to be somehow understood and accommodated. The international character of the centennial offered evidence of the trend toward cosmopolitanism while its aggregation of exhibits from the states and territories indicated a growing recognition of the diverse character and changing importance of the various sections of the country in the national life. And yet, as in the case of the Corliss engine, there seems to have been little attempt consciously to consider the implications. The country's mind was still dominated in the 1870s by the Northeast and the Southeast. The West was a faraway, undefined land of mystery, "Olympian in its distance" and so remote that the celebrators of the Fourth of July in Philadelphia had not yet learned of Custer's Last Stand, nine days after the disaster.[5]

In the 1870s writers and especially poets were still considered important citizens and public figures, and no one would have thought of commemorating any large public event without the benediction of at least one notable literary figure. At Philadelphia, the Centennial Commission's choice of three poets for the opening ceremonies was significant. Sidney Lanier, from the South, was persuaded to contribute a cantata, Bayard Taylor of Pennsylvania to offer a hymn, and Henry Wadsworth Longfellow from New England to write an ode.

When Longfellow declined the honor, William Cullen Bryant, Oliver Wendell Holmes, and James Russell Lowell—all New Englanders—were approached in turn without success. (Holmes, however, did agree later to do a hymn for the Independence Day celebration). Each of these venerable New Englanders was beyond the period of his best work, but the committee was bound to have a representative of their tradition and so finally, nearly at the last minute, prevailed upon the sixty-nine-year-old John Greenleaf Whittier to write a short hymn, Taylor agreeing to undertake the ode.[6] In their persistence the committee ignored perhaps the most capable writer of an American song of the period, Walt Whitman. He was old enough, certainly, at fifty-seven, but *Leaves of Grass* was thought obscene and had been banned in several cities.[7] Of the western writers who might have been candidates, Joaquin Miller (the "Bryon of the Sierras") was the best known poet, but he was considered too flamboyant and slightly uncouth by the East.

Bret Harte was still a controversial figure and no one could be sure how Mark Twain might respond to such a solemn occasion. Melville was completely forgotten (his long poem *Clarel* was published in 1876 but no one read it), Emily Dickinson was undiscovered, and Helen Hunt Jackson, the most famous woman poet of her day, was thought to be less than original.[8] Thus, as in other ways, the centennial in its symbolic opening ceremonies turned its face from the new age and searched with Whittier for lost innocence in the American past.[9]

There were other indicators of the changing times at the nation's centennial celebration. A new dynamic and powerful type of individual appeared publicly at the fair who was destined to become, perhaps, the most dominant figure in shaping the character of the nation in the latter nineteenth century. As the platforms filled for the opening day ceremonies, the crowd of over one hundred thousand persons cheered the politicians Conkling, Blaine, and Hamilton Fish, the military heroes Sheridan, Sherman, and Porter, and President Grant (who combined both types). Frederick Douglass received a hearty applause when he finally reached the stage (after initially being detained by a skeptical guardforce) as did the Emperor Dom Pedro of Brazil, who had become something of a national celebrity since his arrival in the country.

Two other individuals, less easily distinguished in their plain civilian clothes, were nonetheless instantly recognized and loudly applauded by the crowd. J. Pierpont Morgan and Cyrus W. Field, already well known in 1876, represented a new type of American business giant, whose national and even international role was becoming increasingly more apparent in the last third of the century. Joining them, though physically behind the scenes as chairman of the Committee on Arrangements, was John Wanamaker, a Philadelphia dry-goods retailer who, as developer of the department store, would help effect a revolution in marketing as important in its way as Morgan's in finance or Field's in communications.[10]

Robber barons or captains of industry, public villains or popular heroes, despoilers of the nation's natural wealth or builders of the national economy, conspirators or opportunists—the business giant took his place alongside the machine and the rising West, as a new force in the national

life for which there were few models and no adequate, established patterns. Business affairs had heretofore been generally considered to occupy a low priority in any absolute scheme of values. Ideas on religion, politics, or war might be good literary material but "conceptions about making a living were not such stuff as books and articles were made of."[11] By 1876, it was no longer simply a question of understanding that new technological inventions and techniques were producing new industries, like steel and petroleum, or that older industries like beef packing and ready-made clothing were expanding.

The central fact of the new age that demanded acknowledgement and comprehension was that industry was becoming truly national in its scope and that this involved not merely larger businesses but a perplexing revolution in fundamental relationships. In 1860, there were 30,626 miles of railroad track in the United States and no transcontinental lines; in 1900 there were 258,784 miles and five transcontinentals.[12] Even such impressive statistics fail to indicate the shattering effect upon the protections and security which distance had once given to local producers and merchants. Neither do they indicate the new perplexities of management, the questions involved in dealing with armies of employees, or such new issues as the optimum size of an enterprise.

In the United States in the last third of the century, there were no ready answers or guides for such questions or for understanding such complexities. The fact that the business generation between the Civil War and the turn of the century —that of the Rockefellers, Vanderbilts, Carnegies, Morgans, and Fisks—were national figures and could be identified by the American public with certain enterprises or circumstances as no business generation before or since, indicates the general recognition of their new importance. That such individuals became symbols in their own time of both the greatest successess and failures of the society also shows the extent of the general confusion about their meaning.

In the 1880s men could still recall when a man with a good farm worth $1,500 or $2,000 was thought successful and where the richest man in town might be worth no more than

$5,000. After selling U.S. Steel at the turn of the century, Andrew Carnegie was reported to be receiving an income of $40,000 a day.[13] The public fascination with the titans of industry and the superrich in the late nineteenth century not only exposed the contrast between the many and the few, but cast the businessman in a new and unaccustomed role of social and cultural leader. The materially successful businessman seemed to be the one who understood the changes that were occurring, who could organize and control the new technologies. Didn't the very fact that he made money indicate his superior understanding?

It was precisely this general belief that men like J. P. Morgan held special knowledge of the mysteries of national transformation which made them the objects of both extreme hatred and near reverence, and it is also why the wealthy began to feel and act self-consciously as though they existed as a separate subculture within the society as a whole. Lacking an indigenous American pattern for their new social role, they sought to form their separate "high society" on the basis of conspicuous wealth and foreign cultural imitation, with results that seem today a ridiculous caricature. The fact that they were taken seriously at the time is a key to the confused condition of the society in general. "The timid ostentations of a possible three thousand men and women living in cramped, airless houses between two polluted rivers," Thomas Beer wrote of the famous New York Four Hundred "were advertised as though an aristocracy moved proudly through some customary ritual."[14]

In truth, most capitalists in the period between 1873 and 1895 were in as poor a position as any other group to assume the responsibility of authority and direction within the culture. Their situation was as insecure and precarious as nearly every other class.[15] Collectively, the achievements of businessmen during the period—the enormous material development of the nation—mask the actual failure of many businessmen on the personal level and the basic uncertainty that was felt throughout the business community. More than half of the years between 1873 and 1897 were ones of depression or reces-

sion, and the period was jarred by two of the four worst business panics of American history.[16] Prices, the measure of most direct importance to producers, farmers and merchants, generally fell throughout the period and, with few years excepted, business firms failed at the rate of one hundred or more for every ten thousand.[17]

Far from being as omniscient or omnipotent as many conventional interpretations suggest, businessmen themselves sought to discover the direction and meaning of the changes and dislocations they were experiencing. Most commonly, they resorted to the older tradition of the Bible and sought God's hand in the natural laws of trade, but the accumulation and defense of property (and profits which are easily convertible into property) became increasingly more important as security against fluctuating economic conditions.[18] The larger capitalists, of course, were able to weather and even profit by the periodic economic disturbances which destroyed the smaller businesses, but there is nonetheless, as Kirkland shows, sufficient evidence to conclude that the business generation as a whole "was more prone to seek security and reassurance than to welcome upheavals. Stability was its watchword."[19]

In their search for methods of diminishing uncertainty, businessmen called for new agencies to provide statistics which were "practical" rather than "political" and through which the "natural history of industry" and the laws of business might be found. They were instrumental in the formation of such groups as the Society for the Advancement of Social Science, founded in New York in 1865, and the American Social Science Association, founded in Boston in 1869.[20] Perhaps science, which had contributed so much to the perplexing changes which were transforming the country, might also provide the key or method for understanding and controlling the economic and social transformation.

A series of dramatic and often violent confrontations between labor and management added to the insecurity and self-consciousness of the business community and the nation as a whole, as well as being in themselves examples of insecurity. Beginning in the mid-eighteen seventies with railroad, steel, and mine workers' strikes and the terrorism of secret societies like the Molly Maguires, American life was punctuated by highly publicized expressions of discontent and disorder that seemed to many to forebode full scale class warfare and even revolution. The growth of labor organizations, the Knights of Labor and later the American Federation of Labor in the decades following the centennial, tended to disturb businessmen even more since unions complicated their management problems considerably and had been traditionally considered a conspiratorial interference with the natural laws of trade. Increasingly, business turned to the use of such methods as the lockout, yellow-dog contracts, black listing, hired detectives and union spies, and court injunctions.

Although it is probably true that the labor movement was itself born of a desire to stabilize and secure the workingman's position in the industrial order rather than to radically change it, apprehensive observers were obsessed with the vision of socialism, communism, or anarchism "marching forward to confiscate wealth and divide it among 'the rabble.' "[21] Adding further to the confusion of the major issues of the period was the accelerating rural-urban transformation of the nation.

Although Philadelphians felt that the centennial world's fair drew attention to their city, advertised its beauties, and brought it great credit, most Americans were still oriented toward a community life "where family and church, education and press, professions and government, all largely found their meaning by the way they fit one with another inside a small town or a detached portion of a city."[22] Visitors to the centennial city in 1876 were predisposed by the celebration to see Philadelphia as the city of the Liberty Bell and Liberty Hall rather than as the city of the Pennsylvania Railroad and the Franklin Institute. They saw the older, relatively stable, communal city of the eighteenth century, rather than the teaming, dynamic and confusing industrial city of the late nineteenth century. A great national migration movement toward the city, however, was already becoming significant.

By 1880 almost one-half of the people in the northeastern United States lived in towns and cities of four thousand or more, and by 1890 one-third of all Americans had become urbanites.[23] As Arthur Schlesinger has written, "in America in the eighties urbanization for the first time became a controlling factor in the national life,"[24] a new reality which, like the new technology, the captains of industry, and the emergence of the new West, demanded understanding, but for which there were few historical or intellectual precedents.[25]

The new American metropolis was not London or Paris, nor was it simply an extension of the older American cities like Boston or Charleston conceived in larger terms. Drawing thousands of new Americans from abroad and older Americans from the declining rural populations of the North Atlantic and the Midwest, the "supreme achievement of the new industrialism" concentrated the nation's people as it concentrated the nation's wealth and confused even the most traditional of American values—land.[26] In 1880, according to the census, the total value of farm land in the United States was no greater than the value of urban real estate. By 1890, urban real estate was worth twice as much as the farms and the estimated average wealth of an urban family was nearly three times that of a rural family.[27]

The rise of the industrial city might have proved less problematic had it not been accomplished in such a swift and chaotic manner. As with American industrial development, urban growth was characterized by the general absence of systematic planning or control. Municipal expansion and administration that was uneven, accidental, and often corrupt in the older cities of the eastern seaboard was even more pronounced in the newer cities of the Middle West. Chicago, Detroit, Milwaukee, Cleveland, the Twin Cities, and Columbus doubled or tripled their populations between 1876 and 1890.[28] Urban concentration not only gave urgency to a new set of problems—waste elimination, clean water supplies, traffic facilities and street paving, temporary and permanent housing, fire protection, crime, etc.—but, like the concentration of wealth, made the contrasts of American life more disturbingly visible.

If the new industrial city, rather than the wilderness, was beginning to capture the imagination and energy of the nation as a locus of new and exciting opportunity, the juxtaposition of urban values against the traditional rural communal standards made the contrasts of the emerging urban centers seem even more perplexing; and nowhere was this more pronounced than in Chicago, the wonder city of the Midwest.

5

The Representative City

Initially settled by a runaway slave and carrying an Indian name, Chicago was one of the new American cities of the nineteenth century which owed its rapid growth and eclectic character to the major movements and forces which shaped the nation during the period. The city's strategic location on Lake Michigan and the Chicago River assured it a place of singular importance in the waterborne commerce of the emerging Middle West as well as promised the important role of transfer point in the trade of a continental republic. Chicago, being incorporated in 1839, began its city life in the era of the canal but it achieved its most dramatic expansion and became of national importance in the era of the railroad.[1]

Apart from its favorable location, the site of the city had little to recommend it. A muddy swamp-land that produced a kind of wild onion (the Indians called it *Chegakou*) at the juncture of the great flat plains and the great flat lake, Chicago was conspicuously lacking in natural attractiveness. "In all the world," remarked one late nineteenth century foreign observer, "there is perhaps no site better suited for a prosperous city, no site less adapted for a beautiful one."[2] From its beginning, then, Chicago depended upon its practical and commercial potential, not upon any natural scenic or esthetic glories, and its extraordinarily rapid growth is thus a relatively accurate reflection of the strength of such impulses in nineteenth century America.

The rise of Chicago from 1837 to the end of the century divides itself neatly into two major periods of development. From 1837 until 1871, the city grew to be the dominant commercial center of the emerging midwestern section of the nation. By 1871, Chicago had surpassed the challenges of Cincinnati, St. Louis, and New Orleans to become the major city of the entire region and the greatest grain and lumber mart in the country.[3] Nearly three hundred thousand people had been drawn to the city with its varied opportunities, making it the most populous midwestern city and the fourth largest in the entire country. Most of the early settlers who originally built the city came from the older New England and southern states, but large numbers of European immigrants, especially Germans, Irish, and Scandinavians, also made their homes and identified their future prospects with the young city bustling with newborn meatpacking, iron, lumber, agricultural, and transportation industries. Chroniclers of Chicago's rapid growth often suggested that its "unusual and balanced combination of the best blood of New England and of the South" produced a fusion of the older national types through the bonds of industrial and commercial progress and, along with the steady stream of new Americans, enabled Chicago to avoid the extreme divisiveness and energy-sapping conflict in the era of sectionalism and the Civil War.[4]

By 1870, Chicago was recognized as a major American city only by the business and commercial communities. Nonetheless, it had in fact achieved economic dominance of the Midwest and was on its way to becoming the major transfer point of the nation.[5] The city's extraordinary growth, however, was not accomplished without high cost, several aspects of which were directly responsible for the catastrophe which separates the two phases of Chicago's development in the nineteenth century. Consistent with the tempo and temper of Chicago's early growth was the absence of adequate safety precautions in the city, its industries, and its building codes. Especially alarming was the nearly wholesale use of wood in the hasty construction of most of the city's commercial and residential structures, for there was always the singular danger of fire fanned by strong winds from the plains or off the lake and against which Chicago had no natural protective barriers. Although the danger had been recognized for years and the

outbreak of small fires had been a common occurrence, very little had been done to prevent a major disaster.

On the night of October 8, 1871, the inevitable, as one might say with perfect hindsight, happened. A small blaze broke out in a barn on De Koven Street near Clinton in the southwestern section of the city, quickly raged out of control in the area, which was like "a tinderbox," and in forty-eight hours swept a path of devastation east to the lake and north to Lincoln Park.[6] By the time the great fire had burned itself out, four square miles of the city had been gutted including nearly the entire downtown business sector, $200 million in property was destroyed, one hundred thousand people left homeless, two hundred and fifty bodies counted, and scores of others consumed beyond recognition. "The scene that one would have observed from a high point near Canal and De-Koven Streets was one of almost total destruction. Broken fragments of masonry walls stood up at infrequent intervals. Between them the ground was covered with blackened rubble. The so-called fireproof construction of the larger commercial and governmental buildings proved to be a tragic joke. In a heat of three thousand degrees exposed cast-iron members melted into a completely fluid state. Molten iron set fire to whatever the flames could not reach."[7] Of the approximately eighty-eight million dollars worth of insured property which was destroyed, not even half that amount was ever collected.[8]

As terrible as the disaster was, the city was by no means totally or permanently crippled. Much of the manufacturing and industrial area was not destroyed, the stockyards were untouched, and most of the larger and more costly railway freight terminals escaped the blaze. The fire was a human, personal tragedy of enormous proportions, but it left the city itself still in possession of its principal industrial and commercial resources. In addition, the great fire gave to Chicago as a city something that it had heretofore lacked in its superficially undistinguished development: it provided the city with an event which drew worldwide attention and sympathy, which gave Chicago something in her municipal history that was susceptible to romantic interpretation, and which could serve as a rallying cry and a test of the moral fibre and character of her people.[9]

Within forty-eight hours numerous small businesses reappeared in the downtown streets among the rubble. One realtor announced that he was reopening with "all gone but wife, children, and energy."[10] Relief supplies of clothes, food, and money began arriving from individuals and communities around the nation and from Europe, and within a week over five thousand temporary structures were built and two hundred permanent buildings underway. "Cheer Up!" exclaimed Joseph Medill from the editorial column of the October 11 *Tribune*: "In the midst of a calamity without parallel in the world's history, looking upon the ashes of thirty years' accumulations, the people of this once beautiful city have resolved that "CHICAGO SHALL RISE AGAIN!"[11]

Indeed, the booster spirit, the energy, and the enthusiastic faith in the city's future which had marked Chicago's early rise were not burned out by fire. On the contrary, the experience of the disaster seemed to kindle a new spark of municipal chauvinism and to initiate a new and even greater period of growth which would lead, some twenty years later, to Chicago's becoming America's second greatest city and one of the foremost cities of the world. 1871 marks a transition point in the history of the city, not only because it was an interruption in the material-physical rise of Chicago from a local to a regional to a national and even international trade center, but also because the city now added a new theme, that of regeneration, to its self-identity and its reputation, one that gave emotional color and a community spirit of pride to the process of rebuilding. The Great Fire of 1871 became a symbol for Chicago, something which might be pointed to in later years as an example of the city's courage, inner strength, and determination.[12]

Henry B. Fuller, a Chicago novelist and newspaper man who witnessed the rise of the city from the fire, wrote in the *Illinois Centennial History* (1920) that the disaster was only a check "which would serve but to liberate a new onrush of ambition and energy—one which was to lead, some twenty years later, to the triumphs of a World's Columbian Exposition."[13] And W. T. Stead, a social-gospel reformer and one of Chicago's most famous foreign critics, had to admit that Chicago was "the only American city which has had anything romantic about its recent history. The building of the city, and still more its rebuilding, are one of the romances which light up the somewhat monotonous materialism of modern America."[14]

Although the depression of 1873 slowed down the early pace of Chicago's rebuilding effort, the railroads had moved quickly to restore commercial service, to rebuild passenger stations, and to add new lines, so that by 1880 the "Phoenix City" (a nickname originally applied by Henry Ward Beecher) was prepared for a new cycle of commercial expansion and industrial development. Armour and Swift, for example, were both supplied with fleets of new refrigerator cars and were beginning to win the East over to eating western-dressed beef.[15] The State of Illinois, which had "made its appearance" at the Philadelphia centennial in 1876, "frankly and consciously as the 'prairie state,' proud of its productivity of the deep loam of its corn belt and its river bottoms" was reaching its peak years of agricultural and livestock development and the state's principal city, whose rise depended upon such staples, was regaining its position of dominance over the entire midwestern, Mississippi Valley region.[16] "Other places like Milwaukee, Kansas City, Detroit and the Twin Cities rose and flourished largely by its sufferance of favor," while the older cities, St. Louis, Cincinnati, and New Orleans (whose residents had thought they had heard the last of the windy city after the fire) "lay under tribute to the Lake City, and Denver and San Francisco were not too remote to escape its influence."[17]

Just as its economic expansion seemed to be only momentarily affected by the fire of 1871, so also was the growth of Chicago's population only slightly interrupted. By 1875 only New York, Philadelphia, and Brooklyn had more residents, and Chicago was growing at a faster rate. "Even in an era characterized by rapid urban expansion, a growth of nearly 268 percent in the twenty years following 1870 was breath-taking."[18] By 1890, Chicago had passed the million-person mark, and only New York was larger. Between 1870 and 1890 the rate of growth of the city of Chicago was considerably higher than that of the region, and the Chicago region grew at nearly twice the rate of the nation as a whole.[19] The population increase of the city was due not only to the concentration of more and more people within the old downtown areas of central Chicago but also to the physical expansion of the city through the annexation of equally booming adjacent townships. Indeed, during the decade 1880–1890 the population of the central district increased 57 percent (from 503,000 to 792,000) while that of annexed townships increased 650 percent (from 40,000 to 308,000).[20]

The ethnic and regional background of the city's population also exhibited significant changes in the period from 1870 to 1890. Chicago seemed now to draw less from the older eastern sections of the country, New England and the Middle Atlantic States, and the southern-born percentage of the population also declined. Instead, the city drew more and more from the middle western region and from the Old Northwest areas. With the resumption of large scale immigration to the United States after the Civil War, Chicago became even more cosmopolitan. By 1890, the foreign born were almost as numerous as the entire population of ten years earlier; nearly 78 percent of Chicago's population was either foreign born or the children of foreign born.[21]

The sources of older immigration had not declined (Germans, Irish, and Scandinavians), but to them were added significant number of "new" immigrants (Poles, Bohemians, Lithuanians, Greeks, Slovakians, Croatians, Italians, and Russian Jews). By the mid-nineties, Chicago was the nation's largest city for Poles, Croatians, Slovakians, Lithuanians, Greeks, Swedes, Norwegians, Dutch, and Danes, and yet the largest percentage of foreign born remained Irish and German.

The volume of immigration in the period perpetuated the unsettled racial and ethnic character of the city overall and, like the nation at large, significantly shaped the residential patterns of the city. More importantly, it also accelerated the trend toward racial and ethnic consolidation in many sections of the city. The newcomers were often poor, unskilled and insecure, and as they moved into areas vacated by the Germans, Irish, and Scandinavians, the sheer force of their numbers tended to give a permanent ethnic, racial, or socio-economic character to these areas.[22] While some historians, and doubtless many Chicagoans at the time, saw in this trend the casting off of unsettled pioneer ways and the acquisition of the "externals of a settled social order," others might have seen as an ominous sign the West Side tenement and tiny apartment complexes springing up after 1880, while the city's prosperous elite drifted southward, building their palatial mansions on Michigan Avenue between Jackson and Thirty-Fifth.[23]

The movement of residential areas outward from the downtown commercial section was but one aspect of the general physical expansion of the city in the 1880s and 1890s made possible by new developments in mass transportation (cable cars, elevated railways, and electric streetcars). During this period the city added 120 square miles to its limits.[24] Transportation improvements and the need for physical expansion out from the city's center encouraged also the growth of such factory towns as Waukegan, Elgin, Aurora, Joliet, and Chicago Heights, whose economic life remained wedded to the metropolis. One of the most famous of these, because it was built as an experiment in total commercial and social engineering, was the town of Pullman. Begun in 1880 as a pet project of George Pullman, the sleeping car king, the town attempted to provide a completely self-contained living-working community, and by 1884 had eight thousand residents.[25]

The physical growth of Chicago in the period was vertical as well as horizontal. Due to the rebuilding efforts in the central district, which had been gutted by the fire, and also due to the rapid expansion of the city in general, Chicago offered a "bonanza for architects" who "streamed in from everywhere."[26] Although new construction could be found in every sector of the city encompassing every conceivable functional type, it was in the commercial architecture of the down-town section that the newest changes and most arresting forms of architecture began to appear. The most immediately notice-able features of the new buildings were their great size and towering height. These were the years in which the skyscraper was created and in which the Chicago School of Architecture took form. Just as the innovations in mass transit permitted outward expansion of the city, the introduction of the elevator allowed for its vertical growth.

The commercial nature of the city, its rapid growth and the demand for downtown space, the need to quickly rebuild after the fire, the peculiar geological conditions of the city's subsoil, the newly passed city ordinances forbidding wooden construction and insurance underwriters' restrictions, new inventions like the elevator, and the energetic optimism and competitive spirit born of the open opportunities, all played their parts in the emergence of the new architecture. Thomas Robert Dewar, who visited Chicago in October of 1892, was most impressed by the great height of the new buildings, and when he asked a Chicagoan "whether it wasn't dangerous to build houses so high for fear of their falling" and causing great loss of life, the man cooly replied that "if they did fall, and people got killed, it would give others a chance, and they would start clearing and building again next day."[27]

Without question the years 1871 to 1900 were transitional ones for Chicago, years in which the city, while in the process of becoming a great modern metropolis, also retained some-thing of an attachment to its former turbulent frontier days before the Civil War when hard drinking sailors and lumber-jacks rioted all night in the gambling joints, saloons, and brothels along the river. Even as the city began to take on the more settled character of the older cities of the East, men con-tinued to carry knives and wear pistols in the streets. Not without some reason had Chicago earned the title of the wickedest city in the land before the great war.[28] The city's reputation as a wide-open, lawless, half-frontier town con-tinued into the nineties. Randolph Street between State and Clark still remained the gambling row and was known for

many years as "Hairtrigger Block."[29] " 'Hands Up!' It is the classic command of the Western robber, as he enters, revolver in hand, his first business to make sure that you have not yours. How many times has it been uttered in the suburbs of this city, the meeting-place of the adventurers of the two worlds? How many times will it yet be uttered?" asked the French novelist Paul Bourget in 1894.[30]

The U.S. Bureau of Labor estimated in 1893 that Chicago led the nation in the number of criminal arrests per thousand persons, and the journalist Julian Ralph was struck by the multitudes "swarming out pleasure bent" to theaters and bars at what was the Sunday evening service hour in New Eng-land.[31] The two leading industries of the State of Illinois in 1890 were meatpacking and liquor distilling, and while the former was produced for eastern use much of the latter was consumed in Chicago where there was a saloon for every two hundred men, women, and children.[32] Bearing the earmarks of a frontier town, rural community, and modern metropolis, Chicago presented a difficult, if not impossible, city to charac-terize. "As a society amalgamated into a settled ethnic or civil composite," remarked one writer in the nineties, "Chicago cannot yet be described."[33]

Increasingly more apparent after 1880, however, were the growing social and economic tensions resulting from the forces of change in the city's life. Chicago's politics, reflecting these conflicts, became dominated by the rise of city bossism, ethnic loyalism, and sporadic counter protests against mal-adminis-tration, municipal dishonesty, and social injustice. The rise and long careers of two of the most notorious and colorful of Chicago's precinct politicians, John "Bathhouse" Coughlin—Alderman of the extremely powerful First Ward which en-compassed most of the downtown business wealth and under-ground corruption—and "Hinky Dink" Kenna—the Bath's straightman and manager—illustrate in their slightly exag-gerated case the confusion of forces and conditions which chal-lenged and shaped urban politics in the late nineteenth century.

Even without the political abuses, the city as an institution, as Samuel Edwin Sparling pointed out as early as 1898, was chaotic and "chronically confusing" with its numerous independent administrative authorities (Cook County, the twelve townships, three park boards, the city council, the board of aldermen, etc.) each with its own varying degree of power over taxation and expenditure.[34] The rapid growth of the city after 1871 also made the situation ripe for political graft involving real estate, utilities (water, gas, electricity, etc.), construction contracts, and transportation facilities. As W. T. Stead wrote after a visit in 1893, "In an American city a street railway is worth more than a gold mine."[35] Or, as "Bathhouse" John once remarked about the opportunities in Chicago after the fire, "If there wasn't no fire, I might of been a rich man's son and went to Harvard and Yale—and never amounted to nothing!"[36]

As the city grew physically and demographically and expanded commercially under the impulse of the numerous new possibilities for economic enterprise, Chicago's less prosperous and seamy side grew as well, providing an ironic comment on the civic pride and optimism of her citizens. The stench from the manure and decaying animals near the stockyards was at times overwhelming and the Chicago River was polluted with "grease so thick on its surface that it seemed a liquid rainbow."[37] Foreign observers were often shocked and repelled by the smoke gushing from the overcrowded factories, the screeching and clanging of the trains and streetcars at all hours, and the crushing rush of downtown commercial life. "The dominant characteristic of the exterior life of Chicago is violence," concluded an Italian visitor in the early nineties, to which he added that "during my stay of one week, I did not see in Chicago anything but darkness: smoke, clouds, dirt, and an extraordinary number of sad and grieved persons."[38] A British journalist who travelled widely in the Americas between 1890 and 1893 remarked that few things could be more dismal than the sunless canyons "which in Chicago are called streets; and the luckless being who is concerned there with retail trade is condemned to pass the greatest part of his life in unrelieved ugliness."[39]

Within the ever more apparent slum districts the conditions (economic, social, and esthetic) reflected an even more sinister and bleak side of the city's life. By the 1890s nearly 50 percent of Chicago's people lived in dwellings housing more than ten persons and by 1893, Chicago's slum population, estimated at 162,000, like the city's total population, was second only to New York.[40] "Little idea can be given of the filthy and rotten tenements," wrote Agnes Sinclair Holbrook, a Hull House social worker in the 1890s, "the dingy courts and tumbledown sheds, the foul stables and dilapidated outhouses, the broken sewer pipes, the piles of garbage fairly alive with diseased odors, and of the numbers of children filling every nook, working and playing in every room, eating and sleeping in every door, and seeming literally to pave every scrap of 'yard.' "[41]

Irregular employment was common among the poor, many of whom were immigrants and found themselves unqualified or excluded by language from the work which was available. In sections like the Nineteenth Ward, where Hull House was located, prostitution and child labor were common. Chicago's garment industry, which employed between twenty-five and thirty thousand people in the mid-nineties and in which there was almost no labor organization or regulation, utilized the home sweatshop system to encourage competition among workers and to keep factory workers' wages down to the absolute minimum.[42]

The bleakness of city life which confronted many of Chicago's workingmen, women, and children, and the growing numbers of chronic poor began to take on a more hopeless character as the city appeared to consolidate itself economically and socially. Present deprivation can be tolerated so long as the future is reasonably promising, but when present conditions begin to seem permanent the situation assumes a much more desperate character. Chicago had known violence, of a personal nature especially, from its earliest settlement and had experienced periodic outbreaks of rioting by disgruntled workers and unemployed. During the depression that began in 1873, the city was shocked by a series of major strikes precipitated by wage reductions and layoffs which came to a violent climax in the summer of 1877. Striking railway switchmen, lumber workers, and North Side tailors joined with local vagrants, unemployed workers, and hoodlums to engage in pitched battles with scabs (strike breakers), police, hired Pinkerton detectives, and United States Army troops. Order was eventually restored at the cost of blood and broken heads, but the greatest damage was done to the city's confidence and optimism. Fear and hatred settled into the minds of both businessmen and laborers, and a pattern of violent conflict was established.

The labor movement gained momentum in the years after 1877, supported in varying degrees by a growing number of socialists, who were generally both moderate in their demands and hopeful that the accepted political methods were adequate to achieve their goals, and the more radical anarchists, who had become increasingly pessimistic about the possibility of standard, peaceful political solutions. Backed by the support of the newspapers and the wealthy businessmen, the police "formed the habit of brutally breaking up any meeting of workingmen."[43] When depression again struck in 1884 and one out of every four workers in Illinois was out of a job while interest rates and rents soared, neither business nor labor was prepared to exhibit restraint. By May 1, 1886, eighty thousand men were on strike, the national guard had been enlarged, all reserve police were called to duty, and it was reported that businessmen were forming private military forces. A riot between police and nonunion workers on the one hand and locked-out unionists on the other broke out on May 3, leaving two unionmen dead and several others wounded. The radicalization of the city was complete, and only time separated it from tragedy. Time ran out just after ten o'clock on May 4.

A worker's meeting had been called for the evening of the fourth at the Haymarket on the West Side to protest police brutality, to affirm solidarity, and to hear a speech by the anarchist Albert R. Parsons. Anticipating trouble, Mayor Carter Harrison, the chief of police, and a fully mobilized police contingent assembled in a nearby station house and waited. The mayor, after walking among the workers, and seeing that there were only three thousand instead of the predicted twenty-five thousand, concluded that the meeting was "tame," discharged the reserves and the chief of police, and went home himself. Inspector John "Black Jack" Bonfield, notorious for his efficiency at cracking heads, was left in charge of the remaining police force. The workers' meeting was nearing its conclusion and a light rain was beginning to fall when word was brought to Bonfield that the last speaker was advocating violence against the law and the public enforcers. Bonfield immediately marched 176 of his men over to the square and commanded the amazed crowd to disperse. Suddenly, a bomb exploded near the front rank of police, dozens fell to the ground, the crowd panicked, and the police began firing into the confusion. When it was over seven policemen were dead; sixty-seven others were wounded.

Chicago was hysterical. "Now it is blood," screamed the *Daily Inter Ocean,* while the police dragnetted the working class neighborhoods and raided suspected radical hang-outs. Having no evidence which might point to direct personal responsibility for the bomb throwing, the authorities seized upon anarchism itself, and anyone who advocated it, as responsible. Ten admitted anarchists were rounded up and indicted for murder, eight were tried and convicted, and on August 19 seven were sentenced to death. The "niceties" of due process were ignored in order to assure the conviction of the anarchists, whom the authorities and the general public believed were guilty.

The actual bomb thrower was never discovered, as the prosecution admitted, but several of the defendants (not all) could be shown to have advocated violent overthrow of the law, and that in itself was enough, according to presiding Judge Gary, to find them all guilty and justify the sentence. "Outside the courthouse, the crowd of more than a thousand persons cheered. The newspapers showed unbridled enthusiasm, declaring that the verdict would smash anarchism in Chicago, and declaring further that it would warn radicals all over the world that they could not come to America and abuse the precious right of free speech. In the entire United States, not one important daily newspaper was critical of the way Judge Gary had conducted the trial."[44]

It was quite obvious that the trial of the Chicago anarchists had very little to do with the discovery and punishment of the person or persons guilty of the specific murder of seven police officers. It was conflict, insecurity, and fear, that was the real crime (hadn't the promise of America meant escape from such problems?) and anarchism in general, personified in the seven who were convicted, was a conveniently simple and alien-sounding villain. Anarchism was the foreign snake which had crept into the American garden; kill it and prosperity and harmony would return once again. Little wonder, then, that the defendants received almost no public support. Even labor groups feared being tainted by anarchism if they showed any sympathy, much less outrage: "The anarchist idea is un-American, and has no business in this country," declared Terrence V. Powderly, leader of the Knights of Labor.[45] Not until 1889, after four of the anarchists had been hanged and another had committed suicide, would the Illinois Federation of Labor dare to say publicly that the Haymarket defendants had not received a fair trial.

Privately, during the trial and after, many individuals in Chicago and elsewhere questioned the justice of the Haymarket trial. An amnesty association was formed which drew the support of such notables as Henry Demarest Lloyd, Clarence Darrow, George Bernard Shaw, William Dean Howells, and Emma Goldman, and yet nothing positive was accomplished until Governor John Peter Altgeld pardoned the surviving three defendants in 1893, an act that even then —seven years after the incident—took a great deal of political courage and for which he received much abuse.[46]

In the years between the nation's centennial celebration of 1876 and the turn of the century, Chicago earned the title of "the most radical of American cities"; it was indeed "a laboratory for the study of social movements" as it was for economic and political movements.[47] During this period, the city also became conscious of itself, proud of its material achievements and its rise to national importance, fearful of its unresolved conflicts and disorder, and concerned about its crass ugliness and the deplorable living and working conditions of many of its citizens. Chicago had been known for its civic mindedness and pride since before the great fire, but the rise from out of the ashes served to increase the sense of municipal identity and a commitment to more than economic progress.

The awareness of social and economic and ethnic disparities and conflicts challenged the earlier complacency but by no means destroyed the underlying optimism. Rather, it led more and more toward an insistence that the first loyalty of all true Chicagoans—to distinguish them from loafers, foreign radicals, and troublemakers—must be to Chicago herself. The motto of what Julian Ralph called "Chicago's super-voluminous civicism" was: "We are for Chicago first, last, and all the time," and this meant that individuals or groups who seemed to have a primary commitment to anything else were suspect.[48]

Chicago's Germans were questioned as to whether their first allegiance was to Germany or America when they demonstrated against the 1889 Illinois law requiring English to be taught in all schools; the Irish were a continual source of suspicion because of their religious beliefs; there was a general hostility toward any ideological commitment such as socialism or anarchism (as in the case of the Haymarket defendants).[49] Curiously enough, even a full commitment toward capitalism or money-making in general, which was so much responsible for Chicago's rapid growth, came to be viewed as too narrow and limited.

Chicago's capitalists were required to show a civic mindedness above their personal allegiance to economic development. At one time, it would never have been questioned that there might be a distinction between these two aims, but in the growing self-consciousness born of the insecurity inherent in rapid change even Chicago's most successful and representative men and women after 1880 were required to affirm their civic commitment. A good example of this can be found in the rise in popularity of Chicago's numerous social organizations and civic clubs and in the increasing support given by the city's wealthy citizens to public cultural and philanthropic enterprises. Men's clubs like the Calumet, the Union League, and the Iroquois, and women's associations like the Chicago Woman's Club and the Fortnightly Club were all organized after 1870. For some individual members these may have merely provided an escape from the mundane and impersonal life of the bustling city; they all increasingly promoted, according to their own definitions, a higher quality of municipal life.

The effort toward civic improvement could be seen in the desire of the city's business and social leaders to outgrow vulgarity, to encourage the elevation of Chicago's cultural life, so that the city might be known for its libraries, museums, educational institutions, and galleries, and for its writers, artists, musicians, poets, and architects, as well as for its money-making. The city's industrial and financial giants were increasingly besieged with requests for philanthropic support for this or that activity. Even Philip Armour, who insisted that he had absolutely no other interest but making money, found himself establishing the Armour Institute in 1893, contributing to day nurseries, and presenting collections to the Art Institute.[50]

By 1892, Francis Fisher Browne's *Dial* could proclaim that "centers of social activity are thus forming, in which artists and scholars and educators will gather, at which ideas and ideals will prevail, and which, as an informal 'Academy' will set standards that shall mitigate and transform the grossness of our hitherto material life."[51] Other groups and individuals were less convinced that all Chicago's citizens needed was a higher cultural life, and they sought to reform the basic political and social conditions of the city. "The soul of man in the commercial and industrial struggle is in a state of siege," wrote Ellen Starr of Hull House. "He is fighting for his life. It is merciful and necessary to pass to him the things which sustain his courage and keep him alive (i.e., art, music, etc.), but the effectual thing is to raise the siege."[52] Other reformers like Frances Willard, Clarence Darrow, Eugene V. Debs, Graham Taylor, and W. T. Stead along with Jane Addams and Hull House (1889), the Municipal Voter's League (1896), and the Civic Federation (1894) sought to improve the city's basic social, economic, and political conditions. Even Stead, who found so much to criticize in Chicago (especially in *If Christ Came to Chicago*, 1894), also found Chicago's self-consciousness remarkable: "Far more than any city, excepting Paris, Chicago has a civic consciousness. Londoners live in London, but Chicagoans both live and believe in Chicago. The city has become to be, in a kind of way, a substitute for a deity."[53]

Chicago's history between 1870 and 1920 contains the major forces, conflicts, and directions of the national culture during the period. "Suffice it to say," concluded Thomas J. Schlereth in a recent article, "that none of the national struggles, problems, and achievements during these fifty years were missing from the region that James Bryce once called 'the most American part of America.' "[54] Chicago was a new American city of the ninenteenth century, a western city, which had grown "phoenix-like" from the great fire of 1871 to become the second city of the nation. Built upon commerce and business opportunity, its leading citizens were businessmen —not military heroes or politicians or descendents from old and venerable families. In the latter half of the nineteenth century, Chicago epitomized the major forces that were shaping the nation.

Part Three:
THE GREAT FAIR

The first astonishment became greater everyday. That the Exposition should be a natural growth and product of the Northwest offered a step in evolution to startle Darwin; but that it should be anything else seemed an idea more startling still; and even granting it were not—admitting it to be a sort of industrial, speculative growth and product of the Beaux Arts artistically induced to pass the summer on the shore of Lake Michigan—could it be made to seem at home there? Was the American made to seem at home in it?

Henry Adams

6

Genesis and Growth of the Idea

The successes of the centennial in 1876 introduced Americans to the concept of the world's fair as an appropriate institution for expressing national self-awareness and for encouraging patriotic pride. However, Philadelphia's limitations —financial, material, and symbolic—almost immediately stimulated discussions about the possibility of a second great fair in the United States. By honoring an event of more general international import, the next American fair would be a better demonstration of America's potential role in the world community and would not be hampered by a lack of funds or a hesitant Congress.

The centennial paid tribute to the founding and the continuity of the American Union; the international significance of the United States, though, was not altogether clear even one hundred years after the Declaration of Independence and eleven years after Appomattox. In the eyes of many Europeans, who tended to equate importance with longevity, the American nation remained an experiment. The European discovery of the New World, however, was an unquestioned milestone in the history of Western civilization. If the particular consequences of that event were somewhat ambiguous, the magnitude of its import was not. For the United States, which had been prone to view the Western hemisphere as its special province, Columbus could be seen as the original prototype of the American adventurer/hero who, like Boone or Crockett or Carson, blazed trails into an unknown wilderness so that others might follow and begin building the American Empire.[1]

Joel Barlow in his long poem *The Columbiad* (1807)

and Washington Irving in *The Life and Voyages of Christopher Columbus* (1828, revised in 1872) had earlier recognized Columbus' potential as an American symbol, and interest in the great explorer had grown after the Civil War with translations of European works, like Roselly de Lorque's *Life of Columbus* (published in New York in 1870), and new studies by American writers, like John S. C. Abbott's *Life of Christopher Columbus* (1875). In addition, small celebrations of the tricentennial of Columbus' landing had been held in 1792 in Baltimore, in Boston (by the Massachusetts Historical Society), and in New York (by the Tammany Society).[2] The next anniversary of Columbus' discovery of American would occur in 1892, just sixteen years after the Philadelphia World's Fair, and it would be the fourth centennial—four times more historically significant than a mere centennial.

Although it is probably impossible to determine the exact person responsible for first publicly proposing that America sponsor a great world's fair to celebrate Columbus' discovery of the New World, serious suggestions toward that end were advanced as early as 1876.[3] It was not, however, until the early 1880s that any widespread or promising support for the idea appeared to develop. In 1882, the Baltimore *Sun* advocated combining the celebration of the discovery of America with an international exposition.[4] At the same time in New York at the Cooper Institute, Dr. Carlos W. Zaremba, a citizen of Mexico, was proposing to Peter Cooper, Charles A. Lamont, and General John C. Fremont his idea for holding a Columbian world's fair celebration in Mexico City.[5] On February 16 of that same year, the Chicago *Times* carried a letter from Dr. A. W. Harlan, a Chicago dentist, proposing an international world's fair in 1892 to celebrate the discovery of the New World, in which the progress of the Western continent would be the leading feature. Chicago's growth, its central location, its communications and transportation facilities, and its cool summer climate would make it the most desirable location for a great fair. "It needs no argument to convince one of the value of world's fairs," Harlan added, "when they don't

come too often." By 1892 Americans will be ready to show their ancestors what the children of the New World are doing and "we cannot better do it in any other manner than by holding a world fair, and it should be held in our own Chicago."[6] Little further public interest in the matter seems to have been aroused until, on June 11, 1884, Dr. Zaremba invited the foreign diplomatic representatives in Washington to an informal conference to consider his plans for a Mexico City celebration and several weeks later confided his idea to George R. Davis and several other prominent Chicagoans then in Washington.[7] Shortly thereafter the scheme gained another major promoter in Alexander D. Anderson of Washington who spent thousands of dollars and several years promoting the idea of a grand Columbian exhibition which he supposed would be held in Washington. Anderson became secretary for the local board of promotion which eventually submitted the plan to Congress, lobbied the plan through the Committee on Foreign Affairs, and helped to arouse the interest of statesmen, officials, boards of trade across the country, and foreign ministers in Washington.[8]

During the next two years the idea gained more national attention through the involvement of the American Historical Society, an application by the city of Philadelphia to be considered for the site, the organization of a board of promotion in New England advocating the city of Washington, and several indications of interest by officials in the city of St. Louis. Dr. Zaremba brought several propositions forward to the American Historical Society in Washington, which then appointed a committee to confer with President Cleveland in the hope that he would call the attention of Congress to the question of the most appropriate manner for celebrating the fourth centenary of Columbus' landing.[9] Shortly thereafter, Philadelphia sent a committee to Washington to lobby for an appropriation to finance a celebration in that city. An editor of the New York *Independent*, Clarence W. Bowen, wrote from Spain that the King and Columbus' family (represented by the Duke of Veragua) where very interested in a Columbian celebration in the New World and had suggested that a replica squadron of Columbus' caravels be built and sailed to America from Palos.[10]

Following the appearance of Dr. Harlan's letter in 1882, the project received only casual editorial support from Chicago's newspapers; a genuine movement in Chicago evolved very slowly.[11] In the summer of 1885, Dr. Zaremba was in Chicago talking with Levi Z. Leiter, John P. Reynolds, Edwin Lee Brown, and John B. Drake trying to stir up interest in his plan for a Columbian celebration. Zaremba's direct personal efforts to organize Chicago were never successful, at best generating only lukewarm interest, but he did help to give the general idea of a Columbian celebration wider currency.[12] At the annual stockholders meeting of the Chicago Interstate Industrial Exposition in November, 1885, of which John Reynolds was secretary of the board, Edwin Brown introduced a resolution "that a great world's fair should be held in Chicago in the year 1892, the four hundredth anniversary of the landing of Columbus in America."[13] Once again, however, nothing tangible resulted. It would take more than the vague arguments of a few promoters to capture the interest of such a pragmatic-minded city in such an ill-defined and speculative project as a memorial world's fair several years in the future. Nothing quite so convinces one of the high value of some project as does seeing it ardently sought by others, and it was thus that the increasing interest by several American cities to become the site for the Columbian celebration ultimately drew Chicago into the competition.

Comments in the Chicago press had begun to appear by 1885 pointing out that if a great world's fair were to be held in a western city, St. Louis and Cincinnati would be Chicago's chief rivals. Julius S. Walsh, president of the International Association of Fairs and Expositions, was reported as saying that a meeting in St. Louis in 1884 had appointed a preliminary committee to sound out Congress and that a bill similar to that for the centennial would be formulated and a company formed if favorable action appeared likely.[14] With St. Louis showing signs of interest, the Chicago papers raised the emotional level of their editorials. St. Louis was labelled "our impotent neighbor," a mere "country town," compared to Chicago, with facilities that were far too limited to be seriously considered as a host to the world. A world's fair in Chicago, on the other hand, would be a "jumbo," for the "world is Chicago's oyster."[15] When several Cincinnati papers, in response to the "terrific stew" that Chicago and St. Louis were getting into, hinted that their city might also be interested, one Chicago paper asked "what can Cincinnati, the toothless, witless old dotard of American civilization accomplish?"[16]

By the spring of 1886, an organization of Washington businessmen had begun seeking the celebration there by actively petitioning various groups and organizations, including members of Congress, for their support. A board of promotion was also formed in New England to secure congressional action on a centenary celebration, and on July 31, 1886, Senator Hoar of Massachusetts introduced a resolution calling for the appointment of a joint congressional committee to consider the advisability of holding a world's fair, suggesting the erection of both temporary and permanent buildings in Washington.[17] Chicago papers reported the growing activities in the nation's capital but, if the Chicago papers are any indication, Chicago was more than ready to use the projected celebration as a vehicle for asserting her stature as the queen city of the West, but was as yet unwilling to challenge the East or the seat of the national government. In any case, any serious bid by Chicago for such a grand municipal project, as the Columbian celebration was increasingly envisioned, would necessarily require the united commitment of the newspapers, the voice of the city. It would also require the support of Chicago's social and political clubs, which represented the city's "wealth, intelligence, and business experience."[18]

Chicago's clubs had shown only sporadic and disconcerted interest in a Columbian world's fair for their city until May 1, 1888, when the Iroquois Club, one of the most influential, adopted a resolution stating that the four hundredth anniversary of Columbus's landing should be celebrated in Chicago, and a committee was appointend to open communications with other clubs and to invite their support.[19] As a result, Judge Shepard called upon all the great social and political clubs "to consider the advisability of holding an international fair in the city of Chicago, and to determine upon the best measures for carrying the plan into effect."[20]

A meeting was held on July 7, 1888, a resolution adopted which stated "that the representatives of the clubs of Chicago, in meeting assembled, form an organization in order to hold a world's fair in the city of Chicago to commemorate the discovery of America by Columbus four hundred years ago," and a committee (called the "Christopher Columbus Celebration Committee") designated.[21] A second meeting was held on July 14, but no specific plan was forthcoming. Nevertheless, a significant organizational step had been taken. The fact that the Chicago clubs were existing organizations, having functioning structures, was important. When committed to a common object, it was often said, "their action was conclusive of any public question."[22]

One of the basic requirements for any great world's fair was that it should surpass all previous efforts. Thus, it is not surprising that the movement toward a great American fair in 1892 would be temporarily halted during the fall of 1888 while France made preparations for opening the Third Paris Internationale in the spring of 1889. The French had already eclipsed the standard set by the American centennial with their great world's fair of 1878 (see Appendix A), and the early reports of their preparations for 1889 indicated an even more spectacular achievement.[23] Long before the opening day, which was May 9, 1889, American popular journals and newspapers began to be deluged with reports from Paris expressing admiration for the extensiveness of the French display, the elegance of the fair's buildings, the artistic spirit apparent everywhere on the grounds in the landscaping, flowers, and statuary, the striking effect of the ensemble, and the imposing magnificence of the Palais de Machines (which was the largest enclosed building ever constructed up to that

time) and the Eiffel Tower (which became not only the symbol of the fair, but later the symbol of Paris itself). Clearly, it would take an enormous concerted national effort for the United States to produce an exposition of this calibre. In addition, the financial success, the twenty-five to thirty millions of visitors, and the more than sixty-one thousand exhibits at Paris convinced many of the visitors and those who read about it that at Paris in 1889 the highest possible expression of the great world's fair idea had been created. "The brilliance of Paris in 1889," wrote George Berger, the Director General of the Fair, "makes one doubt the prudency of another fair before many years—at least no European country seems interested."[24]

The Great Paris Internationale of 1889 presented America with some serious questions concerning the proposed Columbian celebration of 1892. Should the country avoid the very likely international embarrassment of sponsoring an inferior world's fair by limiting its observances to other less conspicuous and symbolic productions, like the earlier proposed naval review or dedicatory monument (like the Jefferson, Lincoln, or Washington Memorials in Washington, D.C.)? Or if a world's fair was decided upon, the responsibilities and challenges accepted, what American city could possibly rival Paris as the site of such a celebration? Washington? St. Louis? New York?

One of the factors which became instrumental was the general feeling that the United States had not been adequately represented at Paris in 1889, that although American exhibitors had won more than their share of the individual awards, the American exhibit as a whole—in comparison to that of other nations, or in terms of what it might have been—was a discredit to the international reputation of the country and an injury to the national pride. Chauncey Depew, the famous New York orator and senator, "graphically expressed the general opinion of American visitors when he said that 'he entered the grounds with the stars and stripes flying, but came out with the flag in his pocket.' "[25] The response of the nation was not long in coming, and it came, significantly, from

New York City—the country's greatest city and the center of its financial and world commerce interests.

On July 17, 1889, while the Paris World's Fair was in full swing, Mayor Grant of New York called on several hundred of the city's prominent businessmen, industrialists, nationality and trades leaders to meet at city hall on the twenty-fifth "in response to a manifest feeling on the part of the community that the time had come when the initiatory step should be taken in the preparation for the occasion which had already been discussed."[26] The mayor's action met with immediate enthusiasm. A formal motion to proceed was carried unanimously and the mayor was authorized to appoint committees of twenty-five to address the questions of finance, permanent organization, legislation, and site and buildings.[27] Later that same day a special meeting of the New York Chamber of Commerce pledged its backing to the project and the New York press quickly joined in support. Tammany Hall and the New York Four Hundred seemed for once to be united on an issue of public importance.

The Third Paris Internationale served to raise the level of what America would be required to exceed in her proposed celebration of 1892, and it drew New York City into the contest over the major site for the Columbian World's Fair. The question remained, however: how could even the New World's greatest metropolis produce an international exposition that could possibly surpass the wonders of Paris? In an attempt to offer some kind of an answer, and following the formal commitment by New York, American visitors to Paris began searching for aspects of the French production which might conceivably be bettered. The material elements of the Paris World's Fair, the architecture, landscaping, and arrangement of displays, were so universally admired for their standards of taste and precision of execution, that to criticize them risked raising doubts about the cultural sophistication of the critic himself. The criticism of Paris, as it began to appear in American newspapers and magazines, thus centered upon the thematic or symbolic features of the French exhibition. The centennial of the French Revolution and the fall of the Bas-

tille, Americans were quick to point out, was not a matter of universal rejoicing. No European monarchy gave it official countenance.

Amos W. Wright in *Harpers Weekly* of August 10, 1889, happily quoted the British *Spectator* of June 1 which said that "to many it will seem as rational to celebrate this centenary as it would have been to celebrate the bicentenary of the Fire of London, on the ground that the city which arose from the ashes was cleaner and healthier than the city that was burnt."[28] There remained a certain degree of ill feeling among the European countries which such a celebration would do little to diminish, Wright pointed out. In addition, the progress and economic stability of the French nation was doubtful—there was a large national debt and the Canal Company and the Copper Syndicate had recently collapsed. An American world's fair honoring Columbus would have none of these disadvantages. The United States was prosperous and was at peace with the world and had no aggressive designs nor any enduring hostilities. The American people were a composite of the world, and the event to be commemorated had no offensive significance. On the contrary, it was one in which all nations could rejoice in celebrating. There was "nothing in which all mankind can more appropriately join in celebrating than the material addition Columbus made to the real estate and breathing room of civilization."[29]

Wright, like most easterners, had no doubt that New York was the most suitable place for the world's fair of 1892. It was the chief city of the Western World, the greatest mart of commerce and seat of manufactures, and possessed unequalled transportation and accommodation facilities. "The chief scene of the event of 1892 which is designed to commemorate the material growth and prosperity of America," said a *Harpers* editorial, "should be the great city, which is itself one of the most imposing monuments of that progress, and already the fourth city of the world."[30]

The events of the summer of 1889 critically damaged the hopes of Philadelphia and Washington to capture the American world's fair of 1892. Philadelphia would have appealed too much to the national spirit and not enough to the international or universal significance of Columbus' achievement, while Washington—outside of the government, which could not be expected to make the kind of financial commitment necessary—lacked the private resources required. A certain national input was indeed important, in order to secure the interest and cooperation of other countries, but private enterprise should take the lead.[31] Only New York, and perhaps Chicago, possessed the private resources on such a scale and so, as the newspapers in each of the two cities began to realize, the competition for the Columbian World's Fair of 1892 had been narrowed down to a choice between the established eastern giant and the younger western challenger. The ensuing battle that was waged in the editorial pages of New York and Chicago newspapers, one of the most bitter and vitriolic in American history, both stimulated national interest in the fair and became a source of national embarrassment. Of the two, Chicago's journalists seemed the less controlled while the New Yorkers debated whether or not it would be best to simply ignore the Lake City and in that way deny credence to its presumptuous challenge.

As early as June 28, 1889, the Chicago *Tribune* declared that New York "is not an American city—in its history, in its relations to the nation, in its attitude towards the government during the War of the Revolution and Rebellion, or in its social characteristics." The fair should be both a world's fair and an "all-American exposition" and New York is not a patriotic city, "not a national city and never was."[32] New York papers responded that Chicago lacked tradition, it was too new, while the great metropolis of the country was not only surrounded by a more heavily populated region but "had the embellishments of a cultured civilization to a greater extent than this raw new outpost, constantly boasting about its grain, lumber, and meat."[33] The *Tribune* called New York "the meanest city in America," which had no public spirit and could not be interested in an American celebration. "Chicago slaughters and packs its hogs. New York puts them on committees." New York is "too much on the make," too

profit hungry. The fair would probably fall into the hands of Tammany Hall and become the "national scandal of the century." New York would use the fair to absorb and destroy the trade of all the other eastern cities.[34]

As the New York papers debated the question of the most appropriate site in the city for the fair (Central Park, Riverside and Morningside Parks, Pelham Bay, and Port Morris were all suggested), the Chicago papers pointed out the inappropriateness of each one, insisting that New York's rotten climate made them all unsuitable. When New York predicted that a fair in Chicago would keep Europeans away, the Chicago press countered that if New York got it, visitors would not get to see the rest of the country and that "to come to the United States and not see Chicago would be like going to France without seeing Paris."[35] Chicago was the embodiment of American progress and spirit while New York was America's Liverpool. Not only was Chicago the best representative of American genius, industry, cosmopolitanism, and enterprise ("As all roads go to Rome, so all railroads go to Chicago"), it was also the standard bearer of the "great and breathing West."[36] "It is not Chicago versus the rest of the country. It is the West versus the thin fringe of people on the Atlantic seaboard."[37]

The fair was seen to be a potential unifying symbol for the West and the West, no longer divided, would be able to hold the balance of national political power. For too long, the *Tribune* said, "the American cow had been fed in the West and milked in the East; it is about time to move her hind legs farther West, so that some of the milking may be done here!"[38] Chicago stood not only for the West against the East, but for the farmer against the urbanite. An exhibition in Chicago would "go right to the heart of every farmer in the country."[39]

St. Louis could, of course, make many of the same regional and group-interest claims as Chicago, and the Chicago papers were occasionally diverted from their major concentration on New York to attack their southern neighbor. "St. Louis has no right to ask for the fair till it has been more thoroughly Chicagoized," quipped a *Tribune* editorial in October.[40] In particular, Chicago newspapers jumped on a St. Louis circular which implied that young Southerners who visited a fair in Chicago would be infected with Northern ideas. St. Louis was accused of attempting to dig up old sectional issues which the whole country wanted to believe were safely buried.[41] At the same time the *Tribune* argued that St. Louis was "out of the race," because her tributary population included too large a proportion of Negro field hands and poor whites who could never afford the time or money to support a fair in that city.[42]

While Chicago's newspapers were finding the proposed Columbian World's Fair an unusually popular issue by which to boost the relative virtues of their city and give vent to several of the growing regional and national antagonisms of late nineteenth century America, Chicago's civic leaders were also beginning to take the organizational steps which would make the midwestern metropolis' challenge to New York more serious than simply "windy city" rhetoric. On July 22, 1889, five days after Mayor Grant had begun the movement in New York, Mayor DeWitt C. Cregier of Chicago addressed the Common Council with an appeal for the appointment of a citizens' committee to direct a drive "to secure the location of the World's Fair in the City of Chicago."[43] The city council unanimously approved of the mayor's proposal and instructed him to appoint an initial committee of one hundred of Chicago's leading citizens, merchants, capitalists, and professional men. This committee was increased to two hundred and fifty shortly thereafter. On August 1, an executive committee was chosen from this group which included Andrew McNally, Lyman Gage, George R. Davis, George M. Pullman, Franklin H. Head, Edward T. Jeffery, Charles H. Schwab, Joseph Medill, and Mayor Cregier as chairman. Each member is said to have "chipped in" ten dollars to cover all preliminary expenses.[44] At the same August 1 meeting, Thomas B. Bryan suggested that a corporation be chartered under state law and a series of resolutions were passed, one of which stated that "the men who have helped build Chicago want the fair and,

having a just and well-sustained claim, they intend to get it."[45] A corporation was agreed upon with an initial authorized capital stock of $5 million divided into five hundred thousand shares at ten dollars each; an application was made to the Secretary of State at Springfield on August 12, 1889, and a charter promptly granted. DeWitt Cregier, Ferdinand W. Peck, George Schneider, Anthony F. Seeberger, William C. Seipp, John R. Walsh, and E. Nelson Blake were licensed to open subscription books for a corporation entitled "The World's Exposition of 1892, the object of which is the holding of an international exhibition, or World's Fair, in the City of Chicago, and State of Illinois, to commemorate on its four-hundredth anniversary, the discovery of America."[46] Stock was sold for the first time on August 14 (ten dollars a share; 2 percent payable on delivery of the certificates, 18 percent when Chicago was granted the site for the fair by Congress, the remainder to be paid in four equal installments at intervals of six months) and a delegation, composed of Jeffery, Octave Chanute (an engineer), D. Schlacke, and C. P. Darnley, was dispatched to examine and report on the Paris World's Fair.

From August of 1889 until April of 1890, every possible effort was made to generate widespread enthusiasm and financial support in the city and state and to convince Congress and the nation that Chicago was unquestionably the right place for the Columbian World's Fair. Promotional stickers appeared everywhere, real estate owners promised land free to the fair should it come, while "preachers, politicians, and salesmen preached the gospel of Chicago and the World's Fair," and missionary activities were extended to every state of the Union.[47] Clubs, groups, businesses, trade unions and professional societies and organizations came out publicly in support of Chicago's candidacy. Bills and circulars were printed and distributed by such diverse groups as the Ex-Confederate Association of Chicago, who argued that the fair would help the welfare of the whole South as well as that of the great West, and the Saddlery Hardware and Harness Makers Committee, which pointed to the benefits in work to all trades and encouraged all of the city's tradesmen to form committees and subscribe stock. Native sons of other states from Virginia to California now living in Chicago were encouraged to write the citizens of their former homes to get their support, while overseeing it all were the conspicuous efforts of the Chicago corporation's newly formed committees on "National Agitation and Cooperation."[48]

When the United States Congress assembled to begin the congressional sessions in December, 1889, the scene of the debate over the site of the fair shifted from the editorial pages of the New York and Chicago newspapers and magazines to Washington, D.C. Each of the contending cities had formed a resident Washington committee to lobby for its interests, and numerous bills were immediately introduced to both Houses. George R. Davis and Edwin Walker conducted the congressional campaign from the Chicago headquarters (Walker, subsequently solicitor-general of the exposition, was instrumental in drafting the final law which established the fair). On December 19, 1889, Senator Cullom of Illinois introduced an elaborate measure which in many ways was identical to the final act which was passed, and it, like the others, was referred to special committees. "Now was inaugurated a canvass of the Senators and Representatives which rivalled the eager maneuvers of a nominating convention."[49] The Senate Special Committee was the first to be established while the House Committee was not appointed by the Speaker until after a resolution was passed on January 7, 1890.[50]

It is interesting to note that the four cities under consideration—Washington, New York, Chicago, and St. Louis —were equally represented on the congressional committees, with the exception of St. Louis. The fact that Missouri was not represented on the Senate Committee gives some credence to the claim of Governor David R. Francis, who led the St. Louis delegation to Washington, that St. Louis was treated unfairly.[51]

The special committees of Congress began considering the arguments of the various contending cities in early January, with Washington's case being the first presented to the Senate on January 10, 1890. New York's claim was ably put forward by Chauncey Depew while Chicago's was led by Mayor Cregier and Thomas B. Bryan. The main arguments presented centered around two interrelated questions: which city was the most suitable in terms of representing the nation to the world, and which had the material and financial resources to make a great world's fair feasible not only in terms of constructing and managing the enterprise, but in terms of most comfortably hosting the millions of foreign and national visitors (hotels, restaurants, transportation facilities, etc.). Bryan argued that Chicago in its youth and rapid growth from frontier to metropolis typified the national character and that it also stood for the emerging American West which could no longer be ignored. "The conviction prevails in the West," he said, "that a denial now by Congress of the Fair to the only great section of the country that has helped others and waited patiently for its turn would be an act of injustice and sectional favoritism."[52] Mayor Cregier called Chicago the "metropolis of the West," pointed to its central location in the country and its railroad connections, and said that foreign visitors would be forced to see more of the country, if the fair were held there.[53] Edward Jeffery, just back from Paris, also spoke for Chicago, quoting building, manufacturing, shipping, and financial statistics to show Chicago's enormous growth and capacity to handle the crowds of people which would surely be attracted to a world's fair in the city.[54]

The hearings before Congress continued well into February before Representative Candler, chairman of the House Committee, announced that his committee would vote on the issue of deciding the city February 24. In view of the intensity of the debate, which had now been going on for nearly a full year, it was decided that a roll call of the entire House was necessary (the committee had completed its report on the world's fair except for inserting the name of the city).[55] People throughout the country, who had been following the course of affairs in Washington through the press, immediately saw that the House vote on the twenty-fourth would have a decisive impact on the Senate as well, and they waited at newspaper and telegraph offices as though a national election were being conducted.[56]

Prior to taking the vote, the House heard several speeches from its members, two of the strongest, according to a report in *Scientific American,* coming from William Springer and Abner Taylor of Illinois. Taylor asserted that "a great empire has grown up west of the Allegheny Mountains in the last century that the people of New York [the Empire State] seem to know but little about; and I desire that a fair shall be held in the West for the purpose of educating the people of New York to a knowledge of this great empire." Following the laughter and applause, he continued: "For the last half century this great empire has furnished the cow and the grass and the corn, and New York has done the milking. This empire now desires to do some of the milking herself; and by the noise from New York I should judge that they realize there that the weaning time has come." In conclusion, following more laughter, Taylor praised all the cities, but insisted that Chicago had the greatest advantages because of its location and in particular because it represented the spirit of the "prosperous and intelligent farmers" who have eliminated the word "fail" from their vocabulary.[57] Springer's speech followed roughly the same pattern, and the vote was called for. The question was to be decided by a majority, and not merely a plurality, so that the victorious city would need 154 votes. The results of the first count gave Chicago 115 votes, New York 70, St. Louis 61, Washington 58, and Cumberland Gap 1. Six more ballots were taken in which New York and Chicago slowly gained at the expense of the other contenders, until the seventh ballot showed that Chicago lacked only 2 votes to secure the verdict. The New York supporters, seeing that Chicago would likely go over on the next ballot, attempted to stall by a motion for adjournment, but were defeated 174 to 137, and on the eighth roll call Chicago received 157 votes— 3 more than the necessary number.[58]

The action by the House of Representatives on February 24, 1890, was not, of course, the end of the matter. It would still be some time before the two branches of the legislature would sort out their differences on the nature of the celebration to be authorized by the national government and present a final bill to President Harrison for his signature. But the House vote did prove, as expected, a deciding action on the choice of location. Chicago had won the prize—if she could prove that her claims, especially financial, were genuine. The municipal prides of St. Louis, and especially New York, were damaged by Chicago's selection, and the New York papers tried to laugh off Chicago's victory as a concession to Chicago's "wind": "Of course, some kind of a huge raree-show would be given on the borders of Lake Michigan, but its bigness would be equaled only by its crudity."[59]

More serious were the doubts which began to be voiced in the St. Louis and New York papers concerning the validity of Chicago's subscription list of stockholders and its $5 million pledge. These doubts eventually had their effect upon Congress, which then demanded more exact information from Chicago's local corporation. The Chicago Company was required to list and classify the subscriptions of stock received to date, a difficult and time-consuming job since the company had received twenty-eight thousand separate subscriptions, the capital stock from which was not fully subscribed until April 9. A committee consisting of Lyman Gage, Otto Young, Edwin Walker, Thomas B. Bryan, and George R. Davis was immediately sent to Washington to convince Congress that the Chicago corporation's subscriptions were sound. Appearing before the House World's Fair Committee, the Chicago group was surprised to be advised that $5 million wasn't enough for such an extensive production, that New York had pledged $10 million plus a suitable site, and that if the Chicago Company couldn't guarantee to match New York's new offer, then they would recommend that the House reconsider Chicago's selection.[60]

Under pressure to make an immediate response, the Chicago committee made the decision to pledge their city for the $10 million without conferring with the people back in Chicago.[61] Upon receiving this guarantee, and perhaps impressed by the confidence in their city as expressed by the

Chicago committee, Congress went ahead in March with the framing of the actual law which would authorize and establish the international exposition at Chicago. The President's signature would, however, await evidence that the promised $10 million was furnished.[62] The final world's fair bill, as reported by a joint committee of Congress and approved by both Houses, was signed by President Harrison on April 28, 1890. The act was entitled "An Act to Provide for the Celebration of the 400th Anniversary of the Discovery of America by Christopher Columbus, by holding an International Exhibition of Arts, Industries, Manufactures and the Products of the Soil, Mine and Sea, in the City of Chicago, in the State of Illinois."[63]

The process by which Chicago had been selected as the world's fair city was neither dignified nor efficient, and if it reflected more the unsettled and disordered state of American civilization at the time, this fact did not diminish the elation with which the news of Chicago's selection was greeted in the Lake City. Chicago had sought national recognition, and the world's fair victory was a positive sign that the nation's eyes would be turned toward the western metropolis to provide a new answer in the continuing quest for national self-determination, which was, after all, but another name for self-identity. Such an honor carried along with it a tremendous responsibility: Chicago now had to make good on its claim to be the best representative of the country to the rest of the world and, perhaps of more importance, to give a positive expression of the progress and unity of the American people for themselves.

The provisions of the world's fair bill of 1890 made it clear that in several quarters doubts still existed about the ability and appropriateness of Chicago to produce a world's fair of such wide symbolic dimensions. Not only was the Presidential Proclamation (stating the opening and closing dates, the precise location in Chicago, the regulations for the conduct of the exhibition, and inviting foreign nations to attend and participate) to await hard evidence that the grounds and buildings had been properly provided for and that Chicago's corporation had given satisfactory proof that the promised $10 million had been subscribed, but a national committee representing each state and territory was established to oversee and approve all significant decisions relating to the site, design, construction, and conduct of the World's Columbian Exposition. There were thus two different organizations, the local Chicago Company and the National Commission, who were charged with the responsibility for deciding what kind of a fair it was to be and for putting those decisions into effect. Even though the fair was scheduled to open one year later, in the spring of 1893 rather than 1892, time was critically short and the existence of the dual organization was bound to complicate and confuse the process of making it the great American world's fair that the country had determined it wanted and needed.

7
Organization

In closing its report of the congressional action of February 24, 1890, which gave the fair to Chicago, *Scientific American* remarked that if one were to judge the future by the spirit so far demonstrated by Chicago, "the fair will apparently drop down upon Chicago almost self-made, under the magic touch of her enterprising people."[1] Once the fair was assigned to Chicago, her boast had to be made good. Civic spirit and energy were important, perhaps essential, but by themselves could not provide the direction and concerted organization necessary to bring a great world's fair into being and assure its success. This process, requiring the involvement of a cross-section of American institutional and cultural life, reveals much about the character of America.

Throughout the debate over which city should host the fair, numerous general suggestions had been offered as to what kind, nature, and scope of enterprise should be produced and what it ought to accomplish. The Philadelphia Centennial of 1876, and especially the Paris World's Fair of 1889, provided useful models, but as of the spring of 1890 there was no general plan for the Columbian World's Fair of 1893. In addition, the very character of the early suggestions, arising as they did out of the competitive context of the city debate, made them seem narrow, biased, and inappropriate to the larger, primarily national meaning which the fair was expected to embody.

To General Francis A. Walker, who had been Director of the Department of Awards at the centennial, there was "something contemptible in inducing cities to bid against each other for the supposed profits of holding such an exhibition; something unworthy of the nation and the people in looking at hotel and restaurant keepers, theater managers, and retail shop keepers to 'put up the money' for celebrating the event that 'brought the New World into existence to redress the balance of the old,' and that set in train forces that have done more than all other causes operating within the same period to uplift humanity."[2] He went on to say that there should be three major thematic goals in planning and producing the fair. First, it should be a grand and dignified national celebration and not "a mere peddler's fair," one which would take advantage of the "grandest opportunity ever offered us to assert the oneness and greatness of the nation."[3] The centennial had been a "mighty force" making for national unity, especially following the Civil War, and the Columbian Exposition should begin where Philadelphia left off, adding further to such sentiments "especially in view of the ethnical and social diversity of our people and of the vast distances over which they are necessarily extended, in the present partial occupation of the soil."[4] These latter are elements of ultimate strength, but of present weakness, both industrially and politically. Second, America should appear as the leader of the people of all the Americas, and the conduct of the fair should reflect and further Pan-American solidarity. The anniversary to be celebrated, he pointed out, was "as much theirs as ours, though it is fitting that we should provide the setting."[5] And finally, it should be kept in mind that Columbus's discovery was the beginning of the social, political, and industrial regeneration of the world—an international event of greater positive significance to mankind than either of those celebrated by the centennial or the Paris expositions. In view of these general goals, General Walker concluded, the fair's dominant features should emphasize "education (especially historical and anthropological), public institutions, social organizations, charitable enterprise, and the arts of common life and domestic economy."[6]

P. T. Barnum, the great showman, while admitting he was no expert on world's fairs, offered his advice in March 1890: "Make it bigger and better than any that have preceded it. Make it the Greatest Show on Earth—greater than my own Great Moral Show if you can."[7] His advice was to make it as cosmopolitan as possible, to include as many examples of the diversity of human life and culture so as to help break down old myths and prejudices. The fair should be an exhibition of international novelty and diversity rather than one of national unity and solidarity as Walker had suggested.

The following month, April 1890, George Berger, the director-general of the recent Paris World's Fair, made his "Suggestions for the Next World's Fair" in response to the news that the United States was interested in hosting one. After expressing doubts about any nation attempting one so soon following the brilliance of Paris, but also acknowledging that "the Americans are the only people who could find justification for making an attempt so audacious, for the position of America is exceptional," he offered his first piece of advice: "Aim at novelty and at the extraordinary but without neglecting due order and method."[8] The simplicity of the formula was bound to satisfy everyone and no one.

But M. Berger had several practical suggestions for the plan of the fair which were based on his experience at Paris. First, the United States should choose a site which provided a large area "so far as possible in one piece" in order to separate the various classifications of buildings and architectural styles and to allow sufficient space for parks and gardens.[9] There should be a "monumental gateway" to give a vision of the whole, as at Paris, and the other major buildings should be balanced to the right and the left of the entrance according to the exhibits they house. For instance, the Fine Arts Building should be across from the Machinery Building so that "the visitor would thus be dominated, at the moment he entered the enclosure, by the sentiment of the splendor to which can equally attain the application on the one hand of the esthetic principle, and on the other of the mathematical principle—those two great principles between which has always oscillated the glory of nations."[10] Similarly, Agriculture should be balanced by Industry. Liberal Arts should be the largest building of the main group, symbolizing intellectual effort—"the foundation of all progress"—and while no particular style of architecture was recommended, Berger did expect that electricity would play a conspicuous part in the overall design.[11]

After February 1890, the doubts which had been cast upon Chicago's character and representativeness during the debate between the cities were transformed into a general fear that Chicago's conception of the fair might prove an embarrassment to the nation, that a people unaccustomed to the higher aspects of culture would make a cheap and vulgar display and belittle their opportunity by seeking only to make local capital. "Our reputation as a worthy member of the great community of civilized nations was at stake before the world, and Chicago has yet done little to give confidence in its ability or desire to make such a use of its great opportunity as would reflect credit and honor upon the public," wrote the architect Henry Van Brunt.[12] New Yorkers might have been expected to understand the higher elements of culture which were so greatly in evidence at Paris, and insure their inclusion in an American fair, but Chicago was known primarily for its materialism—its commerce and meatpacking—and a world's fair in that city might become, as one eastern newspaper predicted, "a cattle-show on the shores of Lake Michigan."[13]

It is thus easy to see why, in the early discussions about what kind of fair Chicago should or would hold, the example of Paris in 1889, as a symbol of the aesthetic ideal, was held up as a counterbalance to Chicago's well-known materialism, and why the Parisian model became the standard that Chicago had to follow, and yet surpass.[14] It also became apparent why Congress raised the acceptable financial commitment of the city from $5 to $10 million and framed the act creating the world's fair in such a way as to provide a formal, national check (in the form of the National Commission) upon the local Chicago Corporation's decision-making powers.[15]

It was perhaps not an unreasonable set of controls and conditons considering the expansive objectives and Chicago's reputation.[16] Through the mechanism which Congress created by the act, it was assured that there would be a national voice in determining the nature of the fair, as well as a local one.

On the other hand, if the primary object was to produce a fair which would express the coherence and unity of American culture, the creation of a second decision-making organization was certain to complicate and confuse such a goal.[17] Nevertheless, it was through this structure that the World's Columbian Exposition of 1893 would have to be conceived, planned, and executed.

In accordance with the provisions of the act, on May 26, 1890, President Harrison signed the commissions for the principals and alternates of the National Commission and an organizational meeting was called for the following month in Chicago. On June 27, the National Commission held its first meeting at the Grand Pacific Hotel. John T. Harris of Virginia was chosen to preside and, upon assuming the chair, delivered an address in which he said that the founding of America, the event for which the commissioners were to produce an appropriate celebration, was a leading step in the march for human liberty and enlightenment in the world. America was discovered by an Italian, but "it remained for the Saxon race to people this new land, to redeem it from barbarism, to dedicate its virgin soil to freedom, and in less than four centuries to make of it the most powerful and prosperous country on which God's sunshine falls" and the "balance wheel of the universe." Chicago, "this infant, yet giant city by the Lake" was a fitting site for such a memorial because "Chicago worthily typifies American life and progress in its phenomenal growth, restless energy, and indomitable will." Harris closed his speech with a plea for harmony between the National Commission and the directors of the Chicago Corporation: "Banish every thought of strife, partisanship and personal ambition," he exhorted his colleagues.[18]

Following the speech, the commissioners established a formal organization of committees and elected their officers.[19] Elected as president was Thomas W. Palmer, an ex-senator from Michigan who had amassed a fortune in lumber and had recently resigned as U.S. minister to Spain so that he might serve on the commission.[20] The remaining officers included railroad and bank men, publishers, ex-Civil War officers, and one ex-governor (of Connecticut). They resolved to consult with the surviving directors and committee members of the centennial world's fair, with Governor Richard C. McCormick (the commissioner-general of the American department at Paris), and with others who might have experience in matters such as the classifying of displays and the handling of foreign agents and exhibits. The most immediate concern, however, was the question of the best possible location within Chicago for the fair, but for this decision the National Commission (according to the April 25 act) had to wait for a recommendation from the Chicago Corporation. This latter body was also forming itself into what was hoped would be an effective and efficient organization.

The original Chicago group had been organized primarily to raise stock subscriptions, to overcome the criticism about Chicago, and to win congressional approval for their city. Once those immediate objectives had been met, there was a need for reorganization. Time was so short that the Chicago group began taking the necessary steps even before President Harrison signed the act establishing the world's fair. At the first general meeting of the company's stockholders on April 4, 1890, at Battery D on the Lake Front, a forty-five member Board of Directors was elected, who in turn chose their executive officers.[21] The organization of the local Chicago Company thus took a form common to other business corporations, with a president, vice-presidents, and chairmen of the major committees acting as the Executive Committee for the Board of Directors who were themselves elected by the stockholders. Thereafter, the Executive Committee met regularly once a week in the company's offices in the Adams Express Building until January, 1891, when it moved to larger quarters in the Rand McNally Building. All major recommendations or plans submitted by the standing committees had to receive prior approval by the Board of Directors or, if they were not in session, by the Executive Committee. All contracts let by the company had to be signed by both the president of the company and the secretary.[22]

The names of several of the major subscribers and early promoters of Chicago's fair were conspicuously absent from the list of officers of the new organization. Marshall Field, who had bought the largest block of stock as a good business venture (the fair would draw large crowds of customers to Chicago), Philip Armour, Gustavus Swift, George Pullman, and Cyrus McCormick as well as other Chicago business and financial giants apparently gave way to men who were more willing to spend the time working out the practical details of bringing the fair into being. Though it would be too much to conclude that the new company represented Chicago's civic sense as opposed to the old company's profit motive,[23] the new directors were drawn overwhelmingly from the ranks of Chicago's professionals (lawyers, bankers, etc.) and civil servants, and the salaries which were paid to the executive officers of the Company were based upon how much it was anticipated each individual's occupation would suffer.[24]

The new Chicago Corporation received its charter from the State of Illinois early in April, and by mid-May, 18 percent of the amount of previously subscribed stock was called in to cover the initial planning and organizing expenses. How the corporation was to raise the additional $5 million required by Congress was the problem of immediate concern. On June 12, a special meeting of the stockholders agreed to change the name of the corporation to the World's Columbian Exposition[25] and to increase its capital stock to $10 million. However, the method of raising the additional $5 million remained unclear (should the corporation simply try to sell more stock?) until, on June 14, the Common Council of the City of Chicago offered to increase the municipal bonded debt for the amount needed by the Chicago Company. This suggestion was immediately welcomed, but the offer was complicated by the Illinois Constitution which forbade any such indebtedness by the city. An appeal was made to Governor Fifer to amend the constitution to permit Chicago's proposal and, being sympathetic to the cause, he responded by calling a special session of the state legislature on July 23 to consider authorizing the increase. On the last of July, the necessary amendment was passed by the legislature (requiring only that the Exposition Company have $3 million of its original capital paid in before the city could begin to issue its bonds) and the governor signed the bill on August 5.[26] With this commitment by the municipal government of the City of Chicago and the support of the State of Illinois, the World's Columbian Exposition of 1893 became truly a joint, if not exactly centralized, project involving the interests of government—city, state, and national—as well as the interests of the private individuals who formed the Chicago Company.[27]

During the spring and summer of 1890, while the Exposition Company was reorganizing and the financial backing of the city was being established, the initial steps were also being taken toward a decision on the exact location of the fair within Chicago. The basic plan and scope of the fair, and its success or failure, would be determined in large part by the location and physical characteristics of the chosen site. The procedure for making a decision, as established by the congressional act, was for the Chicago Company to make a recommendation for the approval of the National Commission. There were several requirements in determining the site. The first was that it be extensive (the Paris exposition of 1889 covered 72 acres and the Philadelphia Centennial covered over 236 acres).[28] Second, the site should be available without great expense. And third, it should be conveniently located for ready access by the anticipated throngs of visitors.

Fortunately, in the years before the great fire Chicago had established a system of public parks which ringed the city: Lincoln Park on the north; Humboldt, Garfield and Douglas Parks on the west; and Washington and Jackson Parks on the south. Although not all of the parks had been developed by 1890, the land had been secured by the city against commercial development and all the parks were located near major lines of commuter transport. Chicago's park system was a major point of civic pride, something that Chicagoans could point to as a counter to the city's narrow materialism, the broadest view of which, as Mayer and Wade point out, was that the parks should be the people's cultural as well as recreational spots.[29] It seemed natural that at least some of the space needed for a world's fair could be obtained from Chicago's park system, and, indeed, in the early planning, nearly every park ground was suggested.

The extensiveness of such a great project, however, made the Chicago Park Board somewhat reluctant to offer the use of any of the park grounds which had already been improved by the city. From their point of view, the world's fair would be of greatest value to the city if it were constructed on hitherto undeveloped land and thereby make a permanent contribution. In addition, it was felt that the fair ought to be located along Lake Michigan, Chicago's one great natural attraction. For these reasons, two sites emerged as the best possibilities: a section of the Lake Front near the center of the downtown section of the city and the unimproved section of Jackson Park eight miles to the south. On June 28, 1890, the Board of Directors of the Chicago Company adopted a resolution recommending to the National Commission that three hundred acres of the Lake Front area to be used along with portions of Jackson Park and, on June 2, the National Commission accepted the dual site recommendation. The idea was that the lake front would be used for the major mechanical and artistic aspects of the fair while Jackson Park would be suitable for the livestock and agricultural displays.[30]

There were, however, major problems in obtaining and preparing the Lake Front site. Not only were there objections from property owners on Michigan Avenue and a general concern about having the major part of the fair located so near the already congested downtown section, but much of the Lake Front space would have to be obtained by the costly procedure of filling in the lake out to the breakwater. In addition, the federal government (the War Department), the state, the city, and the Illinois Central Railroad all had separate claims to the proposed site and an agreement would have to be reached among all those parties. And even if that obstacle were overcome, it was estimated that it would still take six to eight months to fill in the lake and a year to plan the buildings for the three hundred acres thus obtained.[31]

By the first week in August, authorization for the Lake Front project had been given by the state legislature and by the city council.[32] Negotiations with the federal government and the Illinois Central, however, were not proceeding as smoothly. The War Department had expended a considerable sum dredging out that portion of the harbor which was now proposed to be filled and did not, therefore, view the proposal with much favor. The plan also required that the Illinois Central railroad tracks be moved back from their present location along the Lake Front, and it was hoped that this might be done by offering the railroad compensation for the old property in the form of new land and rights-of-way. The railroad, however, demanded stiff terms for their cooperation, claiming ownership of a large part of the lake shore, and eventually took their claim to the Supreme Court (where the decision went against them).[33]

While the National Commission, the Chicago Company, and the various parties involved in the Lake Front proposal debated the merits of the dual fair site and tried to reconcile their divergent views, James W. Ellsworth, essentially in his role as a member of the company's Board of Directors, was proceeding by a different route to secure a decision on the site for the fair. Although not originally a promoter of the fair, Ellsworth, as president of the South Park Commission, had come to believe that the fair might be just the agency for finishing the improvement of Jackson Park which had been planned some twenty years earlier by the nation's most famous landscape artist and park designer, Frederick Law Olmsted.

Ellsworth talked to Olmsted in Brookline, Massachusetts, in July 1890, but Olmsted was reluctant to have anything to do with the fair, probably for the reason that almost nothing had been done to implement his and Calvert Vaux's plans for the south park system, and what had been done (mostly in Washington Park) had been done poorly.[34] However, Ellsworth was able to persuade Olmsted to come to Chicago and

report on Jackson Park, maybe partly due to the $1,000 retainer promised him.[35] Back in Chicago, Ellsworth convinced President Lyman Gage of the Chicago Company that it was worth the expense to have Olmsted and his partner, Henry C. Codman, brought to Chicago to give their advice on the most suitable site for the exposition.[36]

On August 9, 1890, Olmsted and Codman met with the fair directors and the members of the Committee on Grounds and Buildings, and inspected Jackson Park.[37] They also examined six other possible sites (two along the lake—Lake Shore and North Shore—and four inland) and none of them seemed especially promising. Olmsted, Codman, and John W. Root of the Chicago architectural firm of Burnham and Root (which had been acting as unofficial advisors to the Committee on Grounds and Buildings) agreed that the three proposed lake sites offered the only natural scenic advantage of the city and were therefore preferable to the inland sites. In spite of Ellsworth's retainer (which applied only to Jackson Park), Olmsted favored the northern lake shore site because the cost of preparation would be less and because it would offer visitors the best view of Chicago's commercial district. But when the railroads refused to consider laying the necessary special tracks to the northern site, the discussions returned to the south park system (Jackson and Washington parks).

In 1890, Jackson Park was a desolate, murky swamp of 586 acres, stretching a mile and a half along the shore of the lake about eight miles south of the business center of the city, and bordered on the west by the Illinois Central. A narrow strip of land six hundred feet wide and nearly a mile long, called the Midway Plaisance, connected Jackson to Washington Park on the west. The park commissioners had spent more than $4 million to reclaim the small area of the northern part of the park for public use, but most of it remained "a treacherous morass, liable to frequent overflow, traversed by low ridges of sand and bearing oaks and gums of such stunted habit and unshapely form as to add forlornness to the landscape."[38] The land had been formed by Lake Michigan into three sandbars parallel to the shore whose intervening swales were covered with a boggy vegetation "forbidding in the extreme."[39] The subsoil was water-soaked and undependable. Anyone attempting to construct a world's fair at Jackson Park, it was suggested, would be accepting a task of literally converting a "wilderness into a garden spot."[40] Olmsted's twenty-year-old plan, in fact, had envisioned a system of lagoons and waterways which would control and yet take advantage of the park's natural topography. Olmsted's recommendations, delivered to President Gage on August 12, basically expanded on this earlier plan and included a levee to hold off the lake and a picturesque lagoon surrounding a wooded island.[41] He planned to use only 112 acres of Jackson Park for the fair, the larger buildings of which would be built around the lagoon and the smaller buildings erected on the central island.[42] Although a final decision on the site, or sites, was far from settled, the company officials recognized the need for expert advice and officially appointed Olmsted and Company as consulting landscape artists on August 21. And on September 2, Burnham and Root were made consulting architects and A. Gottlieb consulting engineer.

Throughout the late spring and summer of 1890, as the Chicago Company and the National Commission began taking shape and the complexities of the project and the pressure of time began to be appreciated, the conflict inherent in the dual nature of the organization surfaced. Both groups had by midsummer selected a full set of officials, adopted bylaws and rules of procedure, and appointed a number of working committees which were nearly the same in each case.[43] Such duplication was not only wasteful and time-consuming, but inevitably led to suspicions and hostilities. The Chicago Company represented the bulk of the money to pay for the fair and felt that it should therefore have the major decision-making authority over its design and production. It viewed the National Commission as having a supervisory capacity only.

The National Commission, on the other hand, was extremely conscious of its national responsibility to Congress and thus saw itself as the superior authority over and above the local company, tending to view the company's funds as a "quasi-public fund, dedicated by the act of Congress."[44] If the Columbian Exposition were to be a true national celebration, then it would seem appropriate that a national body hold the controlling authority, and in fact the act of Congress establishing the exposition implied such an interpretation (see Appendix C). The act, however, did not completely delineate the areas of executive responsibility for the two organizations and left far too much to be worked out at a later time. The result was that each group charged the other with a lack of judgment, extravagance, usurpation of authority, and obstruction, revealing "all the jealousies, stupidities, and balkiness of which over-organized human beings are capable,"[45] and threatening to destroy the project before it had hardly begun. A *Harper's Weekly* editorial said that it had the impression that there were "a lot of people suddenly given a task to perform without any definite conception of how it was to be done."[46]

In an attempt to centralize its control and supervision, and perhaps to overcome the distrust and friction which had developed, the National Commission decided on a smaller, more permanent executive organization modelled loosely after the procedure followed at Paris in 1889. The plan called for the commission to elect an executive committee of twenty-six members (half Democrats and half Republicans) which would sit in permanent session in Chicago and would be able to act for the full commission when it was not in session. The executive committee would be led by a director-general, appointed by the National Commission upon the recommendation of the local Chicago Company but whose duties, powers, and compensation would be fixed by the commissioners.[47] Accordingly, at the second general session of the National Commission which began on September 15, the recommendation of George Davis of Chicago as director-general was received from the Chicago Company and approved by the commission.[48] An executive committee was also elected and James A. McKenzie of Kentucky, like Davis a former congressman, was appointed as Davis's chief assistant.

Among his first acts, the new director-general recommended to the commission the adoption of a plan for distribution of the administrative work of the exposition among fifteen major departments which corresponded to a preliminary classification of the exhibits to be shown (see Appendix D). This initial recommendation, based in part on the official reports of the centennial and the Paris expositions, became the basis of the plan which was finally adopted several months later.[49]

Friction and confusion between the National Commission and the Exposition Company continued. There was no doubt that the National Commission was responsible for controlling the exhibits and determining the classification plan. The Chicago Company was clearly responsible for recommending an appropriate site and constructing the buildings. However, by the fall of 1890, it became evident that these responsibilities overlapped considerably. The extensiveness, diversity, and categorization of the exhibits would influence significantly the type, size, and distribution of buildings, and these in turn would define the most appropriate physical site for the fair. On the other hand, the selection of a particular physical site would to a degree control the kinds and numbers of buildings which could be erected, and this would restrict the classification of exhibits which might be displayed within them.

While the National Commission deliberated over its organization, the directors of the Chicago Company, having voted on September 9 to go ahead with the dual site preparation (lake front and Jackson Park), became impatient with the commissioners' unwillingness to begin letting contracts for buildings and construction. The National Commission, in part reacting to the pressure from the company, was becoming at the same time less and less favorable toward any plan which split the fair into two sections eight miles apart, especially when there were major obstacles still unresolved (the negotiations with the Illinois Central and the War Department).[50]

The National Commission, reflecting the national suspicions about Chicago's character and being convinced of its responsibility to insure that the fair would properly present the best image of America to foreign nations and individuals, was obviously suspicious of the Chicago Company's motives in pushing for immediate action on the dual site proposal. Many members of the Chicago Company, on the other hand, viewed the National Commission as an unwieldy body of political appointees who knew nothing about bringing off such an enterprise as a world's fair, whose authority ought to be merely advisory, and whose hesitancy to act on the company's recommendations with dispatch threatened completion of the preparations in time for the 1892 deadline. At one point, the majority of the board which advocated major use of the lake front actually forced through a resolution to ignore the National Commission and go ahead with the letting of construction contracts. President Gage, however, threatened to resign until the resolution was cancelled, as he realized that such a decision would amount to a denial of congressional authority over the project.[51]

By November of 1890, it was clear that there would be no world's fair of any kind in 1893 unless some kind of general administrative policy could be worked out between the two organizations. That such a working arrangement did emerge by the end of the month, however, was not so much the result of the two groups—local businessmen and national politicians—learning to "cooperate in the work before them," (as the popular opinion then, as well as now, would have it)[52] as it was due to another much more practical consideration. In the congressional act creating the exposition there was no specific procedure or guideline for federal funding of the commission's administrative needs, and when the commission's expenses for the first two sessions alone exceeded $35,000, Congress balked at the prospect of continuing appropriations of this order.[53] Thus it was that, by November of 1890, the National Commission was effectively forced to redefine its function from that of the major authority of the Exposition to an advisory and judicial one, and to seek working accommodations with the directors of the Chicago Company. Congress had simply not appropriated the money for the commission to operate in any other way.[54]

In mid-November 1890, a joint committee was formed from both groups (the National Commission and the Chicago Company) to investigate and report on the jurisdiction of each group and to recommend a mutually agreeable administrative policy. The report of the committee was adopted by the company on November 24 and by the commission on November 25. It recommended that a third organization be established under the director-general to administer the fifteen departments.[55] Each department would have a chief and a staff and would be open at all times to the inspection of either primary group. The chiefs of the departments would be selected by the director-general, subject to confirmation by both the commission and the company, and would have charge of all correspondence with the exhibitors in their respective areas. Their salaries would be fixed by the director-general and paid by the Chicago Company, the company retaining the authority to raise or lower them. Only the director-general's salary would continue to be paid through the National Commission by federal funds.[56] In addition, the committee report recommended the establishment of a Board of Reference and Control within each organization consisting of the presidents, vice-presidents, and six other members. When brought together, both boards of Reference and Control constituted a Committee of Conference to which all disputes would be referred and whose decisions were final.[57]

The adoption of these proposals not only centralized the executive administration of the fair and provided a mechanism for handling the intergroup differences, but it also significantly cut down the size and extent of the power of the National Commission. After November 1890 the director-general and the Board of Reference and Control were in effect, the National Commission, and a full session of the commission was not scheduled again until April 1891. Although this arrangement did not by any means eliminate all the tensions and friction between the two major parties, it did sufficiently clarify the executive authority at this critical point to allow for an acceptance of the site for the exposition and the general plan for the physical layout and construction of the major buildings. Thereafter, any change in the plans for the fair's grounds and buildings were subject to the joint approval of the Board of Reference and Control and the company's Committee on Grounds and Buildings (which had been active during the entire period).[58]

8

The Site, the Plan, and the Design

The primary responsibility for recommending an appropriate site for the fair and for developing the plans for the site resided in the Committee on Grounds and Buildings of the Chicago Company. The committee had made and won approval for its initial recommendation as early as July 1890, and had already retained the advice and council of professional landscape designers, architects, and engineers. However, the complications surrounding the recommendation of the lake front and the conflicts between the Chicago Company and the National Commission had made it impossible to finalize the decision. "In September 1890," as Harriet Monroe recalled, "nothing had been determined and everything was demanded."[1]

In an attempt to coax some order out of the confusion, E. T. Jeffery, chairman of the Grounds and Buildings Committee (and also president of the Illinois Central) began in October to centralize his committee's planning and administration policy. Jeffery drew up a commission for Daniel H. Burnham to be named as chief of construction. All advisors and officials connected with planning the site and the design and construction of the buildings would henceforth report directly to the chief of construction, and he, in turn, would be the single individual directly responsible to the Committee on Grounds and Buildings.[2] This arrangement required that all previous consultants—Olmsted and Company, A. Gottlieb, and Burnham's partner, John W. Root—be formally discharged from their independent consulting positions to the committee, and then be reappointed to advisory posts subordinate to the chief of construction.[3] This plan was adopted by the Grounds and Buildings Committee and accepted by the directors of the Chicago Company and became officially effective on December 1, 1890. From then on, Daniel Burnham was the literal director of the construction of the world's fair.

The selection of Burnham to this extremely influential position was not an unreasonable one, given the situation. At the age of forty-four, Burnham was at the peak of his career as a partner in one of the most successful architectural firms in Chicago. Founded in the years just following the Great Fire, the firm of Burnham and Root, by 1890, had built roughly $40 million worth of buildings, several of which were among the most deservedly celebrated and important in Chicago.[4] Possessing a commanding presence, Burnham had a disposition that could be sympathetic and generous, stable and exacting, and a natural faculty for business and administration.[5] His abilities and personality provided an almost perfect balance to Root's exuberance and sometimes erratic brilliance.[6]

For more than a year before his appointment as chief of construction, Burnham had been advising the Committee on Grounds and Buildings and Root had been preparing plansketches for the prospective sites—even before Congress had given the fair to Chicago in February of 1890.[7] In addition, several members of the committee had direct ties or associations with Burnham, which would of course make it easier for them to work with him.[8] For these reasons, and for his demonstrated commitment to the project as well as his demonstrated ability to work with all of the diverse groups involved, Burnham seemed like a perfect choice. And he began, even before the appointment was made official, to exert considerable directing influence on the major planning decisions.

By the middle of October 1890, the debate over the choice of site or sites for the fair was coming to a head. The directors of the Chicago Company continued to advocate major use of the lake front, but the opposition of the National Commission and the difficulties involved in filling the lake and negotiating with the railroads were beginning to force a reconsideration.[9] A proposal was soon put forward to make only limited use of the lake front, by putting only five buildings there (Fine Arts, Electricity, Decorative Arts, Music Hall, and something called "The Fabulous Water Palace") and to use the South Parks for the major fair location. To most officials, this meant making major use of Washington Park, which though improved with roads, walkways, and planting, seemed to require less preparation for the fair than the wasteland of Jackson Park.

On October 27, Root was called upon to develop as quickly as possible a plan for the use of Washington Park, but the South Park Board refused to allow the fair to interfere with the existing trees, paths, and roads, and this made any possible plan for major use of Washington Park an impossibility.[10] Thus, by default rather than choice, the deliberations turned once again toward Jackson Park. This time, however, it was with the object of making it the central site, and not only for limited use as initially suggested by Olmsted. When the National Commission met in November, the proposal of Jackson Park was received with little favor.[11] Two days later, John Root, having consulted with Burnham and Olmsted, presented an argument before a joint committee of both the commission and the company (which included a number of visiting congressmen sent from Washington to report on the progress of the fair) in which he showed the extent to which Washington Park would have to be torn up to accommodate the fair. Jackson Park, on the other hand, was at present unimproved and had, in addition, the advantage of the lake. Jackson Park, Root concluded, "will associate the fair with the grandeur and beauty of the one distinguishing natural, historical, and poetic feature of this part of the American continent—its great inland seas." It could have a greatness that "no World's Fair hitherto has ever possessed."[12] Root's arguments were apparently persuasive for Burnham was directed, as chief of construction, to present a site plan for Jackson Park to the Board of Directors and the National Commission. This Burnham did on November 21, and it was on the basis of this plan that the World's Columbian Exposition was constructed.[13]

Union Stock Yards, 1889. *(Courtesy Chicago Historical Society)*

The Basin, July 30, 1891. *(Courtesy Chicago Historical Society)*

Directors, artists, and sculptors of the World's Columbian Exposition of 1893. Photograph probably taken in Winter, 1892.
From left-to-right: D. H. Burnam, Geo. B. Post, M. B. Pickett, Richard Van Brunt, F. D. Millet, Maitland Armstrong, Colonel Edmund Rice,
Augustus St. Gaudens, Henry Sargent Codman, George D. Maynard, Charles F. McKim, Ernest R. Graham, and Dion Geraldine. *(Courtesy Chicago Historical Society)*

Thomas W. Palmer, President of the
World's Columbian Commission

Mrs. Potter Palmer

Francis E. Willard, President of the
W.T.C.U.

George R. Davis, Director General
of the Fair.

Interior, Great Exhibition Building, Hyde Park. Published in London, England, in 1851. *(Courtesy Chicago Historical Society)*

Interior, north end of the Transportation Building, December 31, 1891. *(Courtesy Chicago Historical Society)*

Administration Building under construction, July 23, 1893. *(Courtesy Chicago Historical Society)*

Fine Arts Building, August 21, 1892. This building now houses the Museum of Science and Industry. *(Courtesy Chicago Historical Society)*

Construction at the World's Columbian Exposition, 1892, viewed from the southwest of the Manufacturers and Liberal Arts Building and the surrounding area. *(Courtesy Chicago Historical Society)*

Frame of the Horticulture Building.

Sculpture in foreground is—Lorado Taft's "The Sleep of the Flowers." Studio in the Horticulture Building, August 24, 1892. *(Courtesy Chicago Historical Society)*

The Edison dynamo.

Woodcutting machines in the Machinery Hall.

Interior of the Manufacturers Building

The Westinghouse engine.

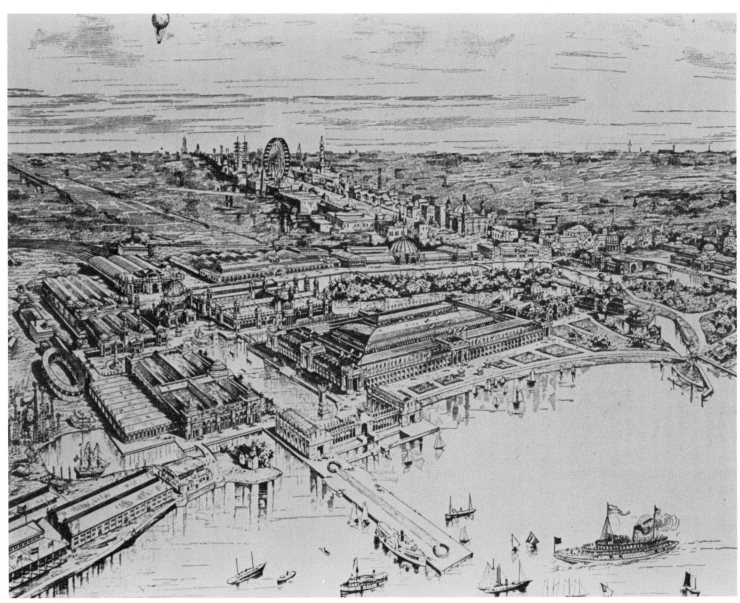

Bird's eye view of the Exposition, 1894

On November 25, 1890, the National Commission adopted a resolution stating that the commission was satisfied that the Chicago Company had completed the requirements of the congressional act of April 1890, and that a certified copy of the resolution be transmitted to the president of the United States. Upon receipt of this resolution, President Harrison issued a proclamation on December 24, 1890, announcing that a world's fair would be opened on May 1, 1893, in the city of Chicago and would not close before the last Thursday in October of that year. In the name of the United States government and the American people, the president offered an invitation to "all the nations of the earth to take part in the commemoration of an event that is preeminent in human history and of lasting interest to mankind by appointing representatives thereto, and sending such exhibits to the World's Columbian Exposition as will most fitly and fully illustrate their resources, their industries and their progress in civilization."[14]

The major features of the November plan for Jackson Park, which was officially adopted by both the National Commission and the Chicago Company on December 1, 1890, were primarily the work of four men—Burnham, Root, Olmsted, and Codman—and revealed the influence of Olmsted's twenty-year-old plan for Jackson Park and the recent Paris exposition.[15] Olmsted's earlier plan, which had of course envisioned the area as a public park, was based on the idea of making maximum use of the natural characteristics that the site offered. The water and the land came together in Jackson Park, and, while the result was not altogether a happy one in its present natural, swampy state, Olmsted saw that the water could be controlled and the land reinforced in such a way as to preserve the basic quality of the area and at the same time make it function for the fair's purposes. His suggestion of a large lagoon surrounding a wooded island, made initially in August, was incorporated into the November plan as one of the major elements. The second major element of the plan called for a great architectural Court of Honor surrounding a formal basin, with a system of interconnecting smaller canals and lagoons that would assure the buildings of a water as well as a land frontage.[16]

The inspiration for this idea was unquestionably drawn from the *cour d'honneur* of the French exposition and, while it is unlikely that Olmsted would have proposed it (so alien was a grand court from his way of thinking), "it could have been suggested by almost anyone else."[17] This element of the Jackson Park plan most directly evolved from the combined work of Root and Henry Sargent Codman, both of whom had begun in the fall of 1890 to make rough sketches which incorporated this idea.[18] Root seems to have recognized the need for an element of grandeur in the plan for the fair. He had studied the French exposition thoroughly, and one of his draftsmen had gone there.[19] Harriet Monroe quotes Root as objecting to the suggestion that the Columbian Exposition should not expect to rival Paris: "We have more space, more money, and we have the Lake; why should we not surpass Paris?"[20] In addition, Olmsted had delegated much of his authority over the Chicago project to his junior partner, Codman, while he himself was engaged with the Boston Metropolitan Park System. Codman had lived in Paris for several months during the exposition and had more academic training (he had studied in France) than Root, Olmsted, or Burnham.[21]

Though both Root and Codman had been working on the idea of a grand court similar to that at Paris, it was probably Codman's suggestion that the court basin and the waterways be formally treated with walls, terraces, and balustrades.[22] The rough outlines for the fair's principal buildings (size, shape, disposition, and number) were determined by all four men as well as the consulting engineer and were based on the general classification plan of exhibits. In general, the area of the buildings was to be one-third greater than at Paris and a "suitably dignified and expressive entrance hall to the exposition" through which visitors would enter was projected.[23]

The "brown paper plat" sketch of late November 1890, which became the basis of the final plan of the World's

Columbian Exposition, exhibited two major and ostensibly conflicting themes: academic formality in the grand court and basin and natural "sylvan scenery" in the wooded island and lagoon.[24] The introduction of the formal elements into the plan were certainly foreign to Olmstead's suggestions back in August, but at that time he had been influenced by the projected public use of the park after the fair had gone.[25] The site plan did contain an outline of the space to be occupied by the ten major buildings suggested by the classification plan for exhibits.[26] However, it did not offer any studies of specific designs and it made no recommendations as to the architectural style or styles to be employed. These questions would necessarily have to be answered before actual construction could begin. In the tradition of the great world's fairs, the selection and execution of the architectural design for the buildings was of the highest importance. Having chosen Jackson Park, which required so much preliminary preparation (reclamation and landscaping of nearly seven hundred acres of swamp) severely limited the time available to make those decisions if the fair were to be ready in the spring of 1893.

The responsibility for suggesting an architectural scheme seemed to fall naturally to Burnham and Root, who had been acting as architectural consultants to the Committee on Grounds and Buildings, at first unofficially and then with a formal commission. However, Burnham and Root were by no means the only influential and successful architectural firm in Chicago. Since the world's fair presented a unique opportunity for public exposure and honor, there were bound to be jealousies and resentments. During the summer it had been speculated that Adler and Sullivan and S. S. Beman[27] might be appointed the official architects of the fair, and it was even rumored that Richard Morris Hunt, a New Yorker and the dean of American architects, was being considered. In September 1890, when Burnham and Root were in fact appointed consulting architects, they alleviated this delicate situation by immediately announcing that they would not design any of the major buildings themselves, but would develop the general plan (the "brown paper plat" of November 1890)

and provide advice.[28] According to Harriet Monroe, "Root looked upon the Columbian Exposition as a great opportunity for his profession, and he accepted the post of consulting architect with the avowed purpose of concentrating upon his work the best American talent, and of making it an object-lesson to the people in the management of great building enterprises."[29]

On December 9, the basic plan for the site having been approved, a memorandum drafted by Burnham and signed by Burnham, Root, Olmsted, and Gottlieb was sent to the Committee on Grounds and Buildings.[30] The memorandum presented four options for the selection of architects to design the major fair buildings—free competition, limited competition, appointment of a single architect, or appointment of several firms—and argued, in the interests of achieving the highest quality and a "harmonious whole," for direct selection of a number of outstanding nationally recognized architects. Although it was not mentioned, the time limitation would have been a persuasive argument against adopting a competitive procedure. But of the greatest interest was the implied necessity for unity in the external scheme for the buildings, to counterbalance the multiplicity of the individual displays and exhibits that would be housed within. Several days later, Burnham received approval of his list of five recommended firms to design the buildings on the Court of Honor.[31] Since no Chicago firm was among those listed, there arose an immediate outcry by the local press and from the Chicago Company.[32] Ignoring the criticism, Burnham wrote letters to each of the five firms inviting their participation and proposing that they jointly decide the methods of artistic design. He also implied the desirability of a unified effect and assured them that they would have artistic freedom. Root, the consulting architect, would act only as liaison between them and the Committee on Grounds and Buildings. His personal views were not to interfere.[33] Burnham further proposed a meeting in New York within a week to discuss the details.

Shortly after receiving Burnham's letter, the eastern architects met in the office of McKim, Mead and White, with

Hunt presiding. While there was something less than enthusiasm for the project (only VanBrunt had cabled Burnham of his acceptance), they were able to accept with no particular opposition the use of the classical as the controlling style for the Court of Honor and a common height for the cornices.[34] When Burnham arrived in New York on December 22, he found the easterners lukewarm about a world's fair in Chicago. They seemed concerned about the distance and uncertain that Chicago would commit the necessary funds to do the job correctly. Discussions of the architectural style were of less importance in this situation than generating interest in the overall project and Burnham used all his "eloquence and enthusiasm (following a good dinner) to arouse in the New York and Boston men an active interest."[35]

Returning to Chicago, Burnham found himself still under fire for having gone out of the city for architects to do the main buildings. So, on December 27, he wrote another note to the Committee on Grounds and Buildings in which he said that "by this prior recognition of the profession at large you have removed all doubt as to Chicago's attitude toward the entire country, and have secured the cordial approval of architects everywhere and thus of the end for which your action was taken."[36] The debate continued for another week before, on January 5, 1891, Burnham's list of architects, which now included five from Chicago, was accepted by the committee.[37] January 10 was set as the date of the first conference of the Board of Architects and Burnham was given the authority to assign the particular buildings to the various firms.[38] The next day, Burnham got the acceptance of all the Chicago firms except for Dankmar Adler, "who appeared disgruntled and said he was undecided."[39]

On January 10, 1891, the first meeting of all the architects assigned the responsibility of designing the World's Columbian Exposition was held in the library of the Burnham and Root offices in the Rookery Building in Chicago. In addition to the ten invited architects, Olmsted, Codman, Gottlieb and Burnham were present.[40] The architects constituted themselves into an advisory board, chose Richard Morris Hunt as chairman and Louis Sullivan as secretary, and then went out to Jackson Park to view the site.[41] That evening, the Grounds and Buildings Committee gave a dinner for the eastern architects. When asked to speak, Burnham said that the exposition would be (following 1776 and 1861) the third great event in American history. "In both these crises men came to the front and gave themselves to the public. So the times now demand self-sacrifice. The success of this undertaking depends upon teamwork; if you work for the Exposition as a whole, it will be a great success."[42]

On Sunday, January 11, the visiting architects were entertained by John Root at his home. On the following morning, the Architectural Advisory Board discussed Root's sketch of the exposition plan, adopted it as the general scheme, and agreed that the buildings in the Court of Honor would be controlled by the "classic motif."[43] Hunt was unable to be present due to a bout of rheumatism and Root, who had caught cold the night before, was also absent. Hunt recovered quickly and became a major influence in the architecture of the world's fair. John Root, however, developed pneumonia, and his genius was lost to the enterprise. He died three days later, on January 15.

Although shocked and saddened, the architects continued their discussions for the week following Root's death. The Committee on Grounds had instructed the chief of construction to provide the plans and estimates for the buildings at Jackson Park (there remained only twenty-one months before the opening ceremonies were to take place), and so, when Burnham rejoined the deliberations two days before the architects adjourned, he apportioned the work among the architects and gave them a month in which to prepare their sketches.[44] The architects were each paid $10,000 for the preparation of their drawings and for supervising the execution of their designs. They were to be concerned only with the artistic design, not with the engineering, and they were to have their plans ready prior to the end of February 1891.[45]

When the architects once again assembled in Chicago in late February to present their tentative sketches, the easterners brought with them Augustus Saint-Gaudens, perhaps the leading sculptor in America, as an advisor.[46] Saint-Gaudens was subsequently asked by the Grounds and Buildings Committee to be the official advisor on sculpture.[47] In the course of the discussions of the plan and arrangements of the buildings, Saint-Gaudens suggested that the eastern end of the Court of Honor (nearest the lake) be bound together architecturally by a single statue of the Republic backed by thirteen columns representing the original states. All the architects agreed.[48] On February 24, 1891, the architects and Saint-Gaudens met with the Grounds and Buildings Committee to present and explain their designs and receive approval to begin construction. Lyman Gage presided over the meeting at which, as Burnham later wrote, everyone "realized that the artistic honor and dignity of the country were intrusted to their hands. All were thrilled by the instinctive feeling that this was an historical occasion."[49] As Burnham recalled:

> One by one they put their drawings on the wall. Hunt, crippled by rheumatism, sat on the edge of the table and told about his Administration Building with its dominating dome expressing the leadership of the government. The scheme as a whole began to take hold of us. Then came Post. George Post had a dome four hundred and fifty feet high. When they saw the dome, a murmur ran around the group. George turned about, saying, "I don't think I shall advocate that dome; probably I shall modify the building." Charles McKim had a portico extending out over the Terrace. It was extremely prominent. He did not wait as George had done, but explained that the portico had merely been under consideration and that he should withdraw it to the face of the building.
>
> Thus was the feeling for unity manifested, and the willingness of these two men to subordinate their individual ideas in order to produce a single harmonious effect illustrates the spirit which made possible the artistic success of the Fair. Where these two led, all others were willing to follow. . . .
>
> So the day went on. The winter afternoon was drawing to an end. The room was as still as death, save for the low

voice of the speaker commenting on his design. It seemed as if a great magnet held everyone in its grasp. Finally, when the last drawing had been shown, Mr. Gage drew a long breath. Standing against a window and shutting his eyes, he exclaimed: "Oh, Gentlemen, this is a dream." Then opening his eyes, he smilingly continued: "You have my good wishes; I hope the dream can be realized."

> All day long Saint-Gaudens had been sitting in a corner never opening his mouth and scarcely moving. He came over to me and, taking both my hands, said: "Look here, old fellow, do you realize that this is the greatest meeting of artists since the fifteenth century!"[50]

Thus, in Burnham's memory at least, was desire for harmony shown by these American artists, all of whom sensed the importance of the fair as an opportunity to demonstrate that not only could such arch individualists as artists cooperate in a public enterprise, but that the honor of the nation in the eyes of its own people and the world could be served by nothing less. Burnham was especially captivated by the idea of bringing the greatest of American artists in a variety of fields together in a jointly conceived and executed national production and he proceeded, once the designs had been approved by the Board of Directors and the National Commission, to bring that ideal into a reality.

Following the death of Root, Burnham needed a new chief designer, not only for the fair, but for his private practice as well. Out of respect to Root, no other individual was ever appointed to the official position of consulting architect, but Burnham did ask several of the easterners to suggest a suitable replacement and eventually, on the advice of Professor Ware of Columbia, he interviewed a young New Yorker, Charles B. Atwood, who had studied extensively in France. Burnham was much impressed by Atwood's severely academic approach, offered him the job in his private firm and subsequently appointed him designer-in-chief of the exposition. Burnham recalled that Atwood was "a great user of books, and certainly referred to the measurements made by the scholars," and there is a story of McKim spending a full day comparing

Atwood's drawings to book plates only to finally exclaim, "Damn him, he is right every time."[51] Although not originally appointed as an architect of any of the fair's great buldings, through his position as designer-in-chief Atwood came to have a major influence on the overall architecture of the exposition, designing in all more than sixty of the fair's buildings.[52] Overall, the most impressive aspect of Atwood's work was his conscious control over finish, which for a temporary exposition was remarkable indeed.[53]

Henry Sargent Codman, Olmsted's main representative during the design and construction of the fair, was, like Atwood, a major influence in the overall design of the fair as it finally emerged. Burnham was especially fond of **Codman**, who, he thought, possessed a superior knowledge of formal landscape settings. Codman was responsible for designing the formal treatment of the canals and channels (most of which were done after Root's death) which became popularly regarded as Venetian, and for "the colossal garnishments of the Court, emulating Baroque Rome."[54]

Formal, academic, monumental were the descriptive themes which came more and more to control the design of the World's Columbian Exposition. In the plan of the Jackson Park site, in the architecture and artistic decoration of the buildings, and in the landscaping, unity and consistency on these principles seemed more and more the values to be prized. Thus it is not surprising that when the question arose as to what color scheme or schemes ought to be employed in the Court of Honor, it was settled along the same lines. As Burnham remembered it, the eastern architects were at Jackson Park discussing the question when a collective inspiration came: "Let us all make it perfectly white."[55] The director of color, William Pretyman, appointed earlier by Burnham "on account of his great friendship with Root," was out of town at the time, so Burnham made the decision to paint the Court of Honor white without consulting him.[56] When Pretyman returned to the city, he was indignant at the interference and resigned. Burnham replaced him with Frank Millet, a well-known eastern artist and writer.[57]

Beginning in the early spring of 1891, the planning of the Jackson Park site, the designing of the buildings, and the refinements of landscaping, decoration, and painting proceeded simultaneously with the physical construction of the fair. The initial dredging and filling operations had been started in mid-February, but by March 1891, the major work of construction, landscaping, and building of canals had all yet to be done. The excavating and grading called for by the plans required the removal or relocation of more than one million square yards of earth.[58] The inlet from Lake Michigan had to be enlarged and shaped and waterways dredged in all directions to provide water frontage to all the major buildings. A large lagoon had to be formed into the great court around which the major buildings would be grouped, and all sixty-one acres of waterways had to be faced and made sound. The ground upon which the buildings would rest had to be raised to provide effective drainage and an adequate water supply and sewage system laid out. The beach front of the park required a mile and a half of paving and a pier fifteen hundred feet long to receive water-borne traffic had to be built out into the lake.

The grounds necessitated a loam cover in preparation for the planting of grass, flowers, and shubbery, and an extensive system of streets had to be created. Ninety thousand feet of railroad tracks were needed, first for moving building materials to the site, and later for transporting the exhibits. An electric plant had to be built to provide power three times the amount used in lighting the city of Chicago and ten times that of the Paris exposition of 1889.

The Chicago Company alone was responsible for erecting more than fifty structures, including the major exhibition halls, covering a total of about one hundred and fifty acres and requiring an estimated seventy-five million feet of lumber and twenty thousand tons of iron and steel.[59] In addition, plans had to be drawn up and the ground prepared for the additional structures that would eventually be erected by the federal government, the state governments, foreign governments, exhibitors, and concessionaries, and which would ultimately swell the number of buildings in Jackson Park to nearly three hundred in all.[60] All but the finishing touches had to be completed by October, 1892, in order to allow sufficient time for the receiving, placement, and preparation of the exhibits before opening day in May of 1893.

To many people, these difficulties might have seemed appalling, but to the officials of the Chicago Company and especially to the chief of construction, it was simply a typical Chicago problem, one that will, determination, and hard work would solve. The project became a challenge, just like that of the Great Fire, a test of whether or not the spirit of 1871 was still alive in 1891. Daniel Burnham was convinced that it was and that all that was necessary to bring it to the surface was to subordinate individual selfishness to the overall ideal, as the architects had done in agreeing as they did on a unified scheme of design. Like a general leading his troops (the military metaphor appears again and again in Burnham's and his assistant's descriptions),[61] Burnham enlisted his "army of earthworkers" in a "peaceful campaign" which, by late June of 1891, had the grounds ready for the foundations of the major buildings.[62]

In March, M. E. Bell, the assistant chief of construction, complained that the fair was taking too much of his time away from his work, and so Burnham replaced him with Ernest R. Graham. In August, when Gottlieb, the consulting engineer, resigned over Burnham's continual correction of his work, the chief of construction brought in his own engineer, E. C. Shankland.[63] If there had been confusion in the administration of the fair, Burnham was going to make sure that in the area of his responsibility, at least, there would be a unity of direction and purpose and "a concentration of human energy and intelligence" as great as the exposition itself.[64] Not being satisfied with supervising the construction from his offices in the Rookery Building downtown, Burnham built a shack, a kind of command post, on the grounds itself where he met with the numerous visiting architects, painters, sculptors, engineers, and builders.[65]

Armed with the plan of the exposition, Burnham was the supreme authority in Jackson Park during the period of construction between March 1891 and May 1893. Willis John Abbot described Burnham as a "wise despot," who "forced every building—secondary or major—to have some correlation to the general type of the greater structures."[66]

Burnham's enthusiasm and dedication, his view of the building of the fair as a great civic duty, must have carried over to the sometimes seven thousand workers in Jackson Park, and he encouraged a feeling of unity and purpose in every way possible, including bringing Theodore Thomas and his orchestra out to the grounds to play Bach and Beethoven while the construction moved on.[67] The subordinate artists and construction workers must have been inspired to have accomplished what they did in so short a time, as the conditions in Jackson Park were at times abysmal. Working in the bogs and swampy quicksands, men and horses sunk leg-deep, wagons tipped over and nearly disappeared, and plank-roads had to be laid out before any vehicle could safely proceed with its load of lumber, soil, or shrubbery.

The winters of 1892 and 1893 were unusually severe, temperatures sometimes falling to twenty below zero, with heavy snow storms that crushed the unfinished buildings and thaws that flooded areas recently prepared. "Storms; 'cold spells'; 'wet spells'; deluge from the skies, hell underfoot, challenged the gritty men who had sworn to put it over."[68] And still the work went on.

Accidents were numerous (seven hundred injuries and eighteen deaths were recorded in the year 1891 alone). Pay for the workers was low and often delayed in coming, and there were "strikes galore," none of which halted the progress.[69] In later years, Burnham always expressed great pride in the workers who built the fair, in their "unity of purpose, self-sacrifice, and the quality of workmanship without due compensation."[70] Seven months before the opening of the fair, Frank Millet forecast that "the exposition will show not only what has been done, but what can be confidently predicted as the outcome of the persistent and well-directed energy."[71] The building and constructing of the fair was expected to be an object-lesson and a symbol for the nation as significant as the completed fair or any of the displays therein.

Ground was broken for the first major building (Mines and Mining) on July 2, 1891. Soon the skyline of Jackson Park became silhouetted by the framework of the other great buildings, giving the appearance of a city slowly emerging from the swampy meeting of the plains and the great lake. It was specifically the need of the world's fair's planners to produce large, temporary and removable or convertible buildings in a limited space of time which made it possible to attempt a bold and artificial effect of harmony and balance. As Frank Millet admitted, and everyone else recognized, that goal would be "impossible to carry out in a permanent form."[72] The world's fair that arose in Jackson Park was a sketch in lines of iron, which took advantage of the newly developed techniques of iron and steel manufacture (much of which had been recently pioneered by Chicago architects in buildings of the downtown business district). The exteriors were coated with a new plasterlike, all-purpose substance first used at Paris, called "staff."[73] The knowledge for constructing buildings from a basic iron, steel, and wood framework permitted the erection of large, yet strong, skeletal structures in a minimum of time. The use of "staff" allowed an "architectural spree" in the making of "an object-lesson of practical educational value equal to its impressive character."[74] In other words, while there was a strong contrast between the real strength of the steel skeletons and their artificial covering, the massiveness and scope of the buildings permitted by the new techniques could be matched by the use of "staff" to provide a harmony and accuracy to the most noble and ancient designs.

By the spring of 1892, construction had progressed to the stage at which the finishing decorations for the buildings and grounds could be planned and the work contracted. Frank Millet, the director of color, was given charge of assembling the artists and he did so in the same manner as Burnham had done, making appointments rather than inviting competition, based on the recommendations of the architects and Saint-Gaudens. Most of the decorative sculpture and mural painting was to be added only to the external features of the buildings and other fair structures. The insides of the buildings, with the exception of Hunt's Administration Building, were to be left unfinished in the interests of saving both time and money. The artists were expected to cooperate with the architects in producing works which would further the spirit of harmony, grandeur, and order, and to see the exposition as an opportunity to demonstrate what could be accomplished by the arts working together. Originality and variety were to be held within these bounds.

Nevertheless, Millet and Saint-Gaudens were able to enlist many of the most well-known and talented artists and sculptors in America, including Phillip Martiny, Lorado Taft, Gari Melchers, Kenyon Cox, and Elihu Vedder.[75] Two of the larger sculptural works had been commissioned earlier when it had been decided that the Court of Honor should be balanced at either end by an appropriate symbolic monument. Daniel Chester French,[76] who had achieved his first success at the Philadelphia Centennial with the showing of his "Minute Men at Concord," was chosen to execute a giant statue of the Republic for the northeast end of the basin, while Frederick MacMonnies was commissioned to sculpt the Grand Columbian Fountain to stand at the southwest end in front of the Administration Building.[77]

The ideal of bringing together the best of American artists and architects to work in harmony on the great enterprise, and to give them a relatively free hand within the limits of the overall plan, was noble in itself and certainly unique in American history. However, there were consequences involved in turning to the artist as if he were a cultural physician trained in the science of healing cultural maladies. Some of these were esthetic and some were financial. The financial costs of such a procedure had to be anticipated and satisfied, by and large, by the Chicago Company.

9

Finance and Promotion

The Chicago Company had, of course, encountered difficulties with finances before—just in satisfying the requirements of the congressional act—but, following the spring of 1891, when the actual bills for dredging and filling Jackson Park were being received and the initial contracts for the construction, building and decoration were being let, the inadequacy of the original financial resources became increasingly apparent.[1] Lyman Gage, in his "Report of the President of the Chicago Company" for its first year, estimated that the Company's total expenditures would amount to $17,625,453 and that its resources would be: from the sale of stock $5 million; from the city of Chicago, $5 million; from gate receipts, $7 million; from granting concessions, $1 million; and from salvage, $3 million—amounting in all to $21 million. He re-

garded, at this time, the estimate of resources a conservative one and that of the expenditures "liberal beyond expectation."[2] However, not only were these first estimates grossly inaccurate, but the subsequent budgets, up to the time the fair closed, were also unable to reliably predict the actual cost of the project.

There were two major reasons for this. First, time limitations forced the Chicago Company again and again to let contracts before actual receipt of the funds with which to pay for the work. Operating on credit, the fair's finances were dangerously near insolvency until the late summer of 1893. The need for haste also led to costly mistakes which later had to be corrected and which added to the total cost. Second, and of greater importance, however, was the continual confusion of responsibility for executing the details of the overall plan for the fair, only the general idea and spirit of which had been established in the spring of 1891.

Since the specifics of the general plan were being worked out while the fair was being built, it was no wonder that the budget committee was unable to keep up with the changes. The problem was not simply, as Neufeld suggests, that the artists, whose "only consideration was aesthetic," continually made changes in decoration or design without worrying about financial costs; it also involved the continuous changes which were made to accommodate the growing demand for exhibit space. The Chicago Company was charged with the responsibility for building and executing the design of the fair, but the National Commission was to determine the general scope and specifications, meaning in particular the allotment of space to the exhibitors. Changes in the number and type of exhibits, which continued up to opening day, were at least as responsible for the budgetary confusion as was the ambitiousness of the artistic features of the plan.[3]

By August 1891, the directors of the Chicago Company determined that their initial financial resources were not sufficient to insure that the World's Columbian Exposition of 1893 would surpass all previous fairs and, at the same time, adequately present America's total cultural progress and enterprise. Since the National Commission was committed to the same end, and since it was charged with the responsibility for the general scope and plan for the fair, the company reasoned that the federal government should come to the aid of the fair by granting an appropriation sufficient to defray the increasing costs of fulfilling the goal.[4] On September 2, 1891, E. T. Jeffery, chairman of the Committee on Grounds and Buildings, reported to the directors of the Chicago Company that either some of the proposed features of the fair would have to be abandoned or additional funds secured. He recommended that Congress be petitioned for assistance, since "we believe that the people of the United States have an interest in this Exposition that justifies us in asking the cooperation of the National Government to complete what we have so well begun."[5]

Jeffery's proposal was approved by the Chicago Company, which decided that the aid requested should be in the form of a loan, and was forwarded to the National Commission, which also approved it and sent it to Washington. Congress convened in December 1891, and both the House and the Senate appointed subcommittees on the fair, but the request of the Chicago Company was not officially delivered to Congress until February 24, 1892, when President Harrison communicated the annual report of the National Commission. By this time, financial matters had assumed such a serious state that the Chicago Company had determined that it needed a direct Congressional appropriation, a subscription rather than a loan, to back up the fair's credit. The president, in his message, said that the United States was committed to the enterprise in part because of having invited other nations to participate and that, although he could make no specific recommendations, he was favorably disposed to federal support.[6]

Congress, however, was by no means so willing to demonstrate its responsibility for what it had conceived (in financial terms) as purely a local, private matter, and so when a bill for the appropriation was subsequently reported, it met with extreme opposition, which revealed not only a hostility toward the appropriation itself, but also a distrust of Chicago, the Chicago Company, and the fair as well.[7] Subcommittee investigations, visits to Chicago by congressmen, interrogations of the fair's administrators, reports, and debates had by July 1892 accomplished nothing. Congress was prepared to adjourn when a new bill was introduced in the Senate which seemed to promise a satisfactory resolution.[8] The bill proposed that instead of a direct appropriation, the secretary of the Treasury be directed to coin $5 million in souvenir Columbia half-dollars to be given the Chicago Company for resale upon the presentation of financial estimates and vouchers of indebtedness certified by the president of the Chicago Company and the director-general. A filibuster ensued in the House to block passage of the bill before adjournment, so a new bill was quickly drawn up cutting the amount to $2.5 million in souvenir coins and, as a concession to those suspicious of Chicago's moral character, stipulating that the world's fair be closed on Sundays.[9]

The act was approved on August 6, 1892, and was received in Chicago with less than unqualified joy. Not only was the amount half what the fair directors felt they needed, but the stipulation of the Sunday closing made it questionable whether the gift would reimburse the company for the prospective receipts from Sunday visitors.[10] The donation was finally accepted by the exposition officials, however, and it did allow for the completion of the work. The company's credit was improved so that it issued another $5 million worth of 6 percent debenture bonds (which were taken by banks and wealthy citizens in various parts of the country) and the decision was made to sell the 5 million Columbian souvenir half-dollars for one dollar each, thus making up the difference between the amount asked for and that granted by Congress.[11] Time was growing short. The buildings were to be ready for the October 21, 1892, dedication services and the congressional appropriation, even as backhanded as it was, permitted the achievement of that immediate goal.

The National Commission had adopted a classification of exhibits so extensive that the company's directors could not possibly operate within the $10 million originally thought sufficient. This classification plan was one of the major difficulties encountered in providing an accurate budget, as well as being a primary influence in the Chicago Company's decision to petition Congress. In addition, it was not until late 1891, months after the actual construction began, that the commission finally appointed a full set of directors for the fifteen major departments, who were responsible under the director-general for deciding the exhibits to be displayed.[12] By January 1892, however, Julian Ralph could report in *Harper's Monthly* that all the departments now had directors and that staffs were either complete and operating or being assembled.[13]

Most of the department chiefs had previous exposition experience or were experts in their departmental areas.

The Presidential Proclamation of December 24, 1890, announced to the world that a great fair would be held in 1893. However, it became apparent early on that to many nations Chicago was an unknown city, while to many people, at home and abroad, Chicago was associated only with buffalo hunts, wild Indians, and pig slaughtering. Therefore that same month, December, 1890, the Department of Publicity and Promotion was established under the directorship of Moses P. Handy, a highly successful eastern newspaperman, with the job of circulating information about Chicago's exposition, awakening interest world-wide, and encouraging participation of governments and private citizens. Handy, one of the first departmental chiefs chosen, had a modern understanding of the importance of the press in molding public opinion and creating an appealing image, and he set out to work immediately to form a staff of writers chosen for the most part from Chicago journalists. A list of five thousand foreign and thirty thousand U.S. and Canadian newspapers was put together and to this was added the names of the state legislators, state and territory officials, Senate and House members and prominent men and women in the United States. Circulars were also sent to every diplomatic and consular representative requesting the names of important foreigners.

Once assembled, the mailing list (which had over fifty thousand domestic addresses alone) became the vehicle for circulating a weekly informative and descriptive exposition newsletter, written by Handy and his staff. In order to gain the cooperation of the newspapers, Handy insisted that the newsletters contain articles of high journalistic quality, which would interest not only prospective exhibitors and visitors but also attract the attention of those who would never find it possible to come to Chicago. To relieve foreign newspapers of the need for extensive translation or editing, the newsletter was written in standard newspaper form and printed in Chicago in fourteen languages, and the department provided special articles on request. Handy's idea was to provide press releases which would help the exposition while at the same time help the newspapers which printed them, and the plan worked so well that only three months after the department was formed, he could report with some claim to fact that he "was in communication weekly with all the civilized and many of the only partly civilized people of the globe."[14]

In addition to the newsletter, the Promotion Department issued pamphlets, guides, handbooks, and through its bureau of engraving distributed hundreds of thousands of lithographic views of the grounds and buildings.[15] For a long period, the department was producing over one hundred thousand words of printed matter a day.[16] In addition, to evaluate the publicity which the fair was beginning to receive, Handy kept a file containing copies of published articles on the fair, covering every state, territory, and nearly every foreign country. Publishers were requested to send copies of their issues which mentioned the fair and for a time the Promotion Department had the largest newspaper mail of any address in the United States. By January of 1892, the department had over a hundred scrapbooks of newspaper articles and was receiving clippings amounting to a four hundred and fifty page book every day.[17] There was little money for elaborate entertainment of visiting correspondents, but the department did furnish translators, conducted tours, and answered questions. A special briefing room for reporters was established complete with sheets of clippings from the foreign press to show the increasing international interest.[18]

There had been publicity bureaus at other great world's fairs in the past, but the extensiveness and efficiency of the Promotion Department of the Columbian exposition was something quite new. R. E. A. Dorr, Handy's chief assistant, estimated that one-third of all that was printed about the fair by the newspapers, at home and abroad, was written by the department itself and this pervasive influence carried over to books and magazine articles as well.[19] Not only did the department spread the word about the fair and help to generate interest in the Columbian celebration, but the profes-

sionalism of Handy and his staff was in itself a strong influence in changing minds about the sophistication of Chicago and its proposed great fair. Handy must also be given much of the credit for helping to establish the pre-opening day image of the fair as a major symbol of American culture (unified, mature, progressive) and character (idealistic, unselfish, persevering), and as an educational object-lesson not to be missed by anyone who harbored doubts.

While the Department of Publicity and Promotion was taking charge of advertising the exposition by means of pictures and the printed word, other departments and elements of the fair's administration were cultivating personal contacts in foreign lands. Representatives and consuls of the State Department in foreign countries were contacted to publicize the fair and these regular foreign agencies were supplemented by dispatching special commissioners to the most important areas. At the request of the director-general, a detail of army and navy officers was sent early in 1891 to Latin America and a similar group of civilians were accredited to visit the Far East, Africa, and the Middle East.

Director-General Davis invited the foreign ministers residing in Washington to come to Chicago to have the project explained at first hand, and a number of them accepted the invitation and were royally treated. Later in 1891 and 1892, two groups of world's fair officials visited the countries of northern and southern Europe, spending in all several months contacting official, commercial, and industrial groups. Considering the relative obscurity of Chicago, the great distances over which the exhibitors would have to transport their displays, the inconsistency of American tariff regulations on foreign goods, and the short period of time since the last great world's fair, it was not surprising that international interest in the Columbian World's Fair was slow in developing. Up to June 15, 1891, less than twenty foreign governments had communicated their acceptance of President Harrison's invitation to participate,[20] and of these only Germany, Turkey, and Japan seemed in any way enthusiastic.[21] Interest did increase, however, and by January, 1892, the demands by foreign governments for space had exceeded the amount made available by the director-general and Great Britain, France and Germany had begun squabbling over the space allotted them.[22]

Also by 1892, state appropriations for displays and buildings had exceeded $3 million and twenty-nine of the forty-four states and four territories had legislated funds for that purpose.[23] The western and midwestern states were the most rapid to respond to the enterprise, but Pennsylvania also was quick to make a large appropriation. In March of 1891, the national commissioners representing Pennsylvania had argued persuasively in their state legislature that Pennsylvania should take a leading role to demonstrate her appreciation of the other states' exhibits at the centennial. "We are now well satisfied," they told the legislature, "that the World's Columbian Exposition to be held in Chicago in 1893 will far excel all international exhibitions that have preceded it, and must result in great good to the country at large. The western states are making special exertions to be well represented, and are appropriating large sums of money for that purpose."[24] In addition, a number of corporations, independent manufacturers, and special groups (as diverse as the American Dairymen and the Pacific Slope Association of San Francisco) had begun to make applications for exhibition space. By appealing to the competitive commercialism and nationalism of countries, states, private groups and manufacturers, the Promotion Department and the Columbian exposition ambassadors were beginning to have their desired effect. General popular interest in the project was also growing significantly as the size and ambitiousness of the exposition became more clearly understood. Aside from the novel architectural and artistic plan for the fair, two special features which had not been originally planned for the celebration began to receive widespread attention and even enthusiasm, especially from those individuals and groups who had previously been put off by the commercialism and materialism of world's fairs in the past.

The first of these unusual features was proposed in an October 1889 article in *Statesman Magazine* by Charles C. Bonney, whose idea probably stemmed from a similar, though limited, trial at Paris in 1889. Bonney suggested that the world's fair of 1893 should include a series of world-wide congresses on government, law, finance, labor, religion, education, literature, and other subjects of international interest, at which leading world figures and experts would participate. Several of the officials of the provisional Chicago Company were immediately attracted to the idea. A general committee was formed which included Bonney as chairman, Lyman Gage as treasurer, and Walter T. Mills (editor of *Statesman*) as secretary, and a statement of purpose was drafted, printed and mailed to various countries in the world. The announcement stated in part that "the crowning glory of the World's Fair should not be the exhibit . . . of the material triumphs, industrial achievements, and mechanical victories of man, however magnificent that display may be," but that something "higher and nobler" is demanded by the "enlightenment and progressive spirit of the present age."

A series of world congresses would help to "bring about a real fraternity of nations," by establishing personal acquaintances and friendships among the "leaders of the intellectual world."[25] The announcement further included suggested themes such as: the fraternal union of literature, religion, science and language of different peoples; economic, industrial, and financial problems of the age; educational systems; international law and war; the prevention of pauperism, insanity, and crime; the encouragement of productivity, propriety, and virtue.[26] The plan for the congresses sought to include the traditional use of the world's fair as a place for individual, organization or group meetings as well as assemblies of a more general nature. Two kinds of congresses were therefore proposed—special congresses for existing societies and their members, and popular congresses open to the people of the world as represented by those attending the fair.

The announcement met with immediate interest and approval within the United States and abroad. As the requests for participation or for more information, as well as suggestions for additional subjects, were received by the World

Congress Organization, it became obvious that it, like so many other areas of the exposition, was in need of expansion. At first it was thought that the congresses, because of their international character, would fall under the act establishing the exposition and would therefore be supervised by the National Commission. However, President Harrison was doubtful about its propriety and so on October 30, 1890, the World's Congress Auxiliary was formed as a separate organization distinct from both the National Commission and the Chicago Company.[27] The official announcement was issued by the U.S. government, along with the Presidential Proclamation of December 1890. Further official recognition came as a result of a report by the Senate Committee on Foreign Relations in May 1892, which agreed that the auxiliary was the proper agency for international congresses. In June the State Department authorized its diplomatic and consular officers to invite participation by the governments to which they were accredited.[28]

Organizing the congresses proved to be a major undertaking, involving the cooperation of both the national government and the Chicago Company. Two hundred and fourteen local committees were appointed to contact eminent figures in various fields around the world, an advisory council of over fourteen thousand nonresident members was established to help decide what subject areas should and should not be included, and eventually a system of committees was organized to work out the final plans for the actual congresses.[29] The main purpose of the auxiliary, as explained by Bonney in January of 1892, was not simply to present diverse examples of the intellectual, spiritual and moral development of nineteenth century civilization alongside the exhibits of material progress. It was also "to bring all of the departments of progress into harmonious relation with each other, to the end that utmost attainable completeness and amity may characterize the World's Congresses of 1893 without materially impairing the distinctive characteristics of the various contributions to the marvelous progress of the nineteenth century."[30]

The notion that the World's Columbian Exposition would go beyond the usual nationalistic, commercial, and industrial emphasis and attempt to unify the material and nonmaterial aspects of culture was of course useful to the Chicago Company as a counter to Chicago's reputation and the belief that Chicago would produce a "cattle-show." In addition, the general interest in this aspect of the fair indicated an even wider hope that it would do more than merely summarize the material achievements of civilization.

A second novel aspect of the fair which drew considerable attention to the entire enterprise in the months prior to opening was that women were to play a conspicuous and responsible role in a world's fair for the first time. Though the first American world's fair in New York in 1853 was an all-male show, women had made their appearance by attempting to conduct informal conventions on temperance, women's rights, and antislavery themes. Lucy Stone, Antoinette Brown, Lucretia Mott, and Susan B. Anthony all came to the fair hoping to get a hearing for their messages. The crowds, however, were hostile and insulting and the New York mayor and police chief made no effort to protect the women's right of free speech. "A gathering of unsexed women," shouted the *New York Herald,* reflecting the general response toward these advocates of equal and independent roles for women in American life.[31]

The centennial at Philadelphia in 1876 was also initially planned without considering participation by women, but the managers were harassed, largely by Elizabeth Cady Stanton and Susan B. Anthony, into allowing a women's pavilion to be built. Mrs. E. D. Gillespie of Philadelphia, the great-granddaughter of Benjamin Franklin, took charge of assembling examples of the products and accomplishments of women and the pavilion was generally well received and patronized by the fair's visitors. While women's products were being treated as a novelty in the woman's pavilion, and had received no real government recognition, Susan B. Anthony and several other women attempted to gain a hearing for their views on women's rights. They asked for and were denied representation on the platform of the Fourth of July ceremony. They had hoped to be allowed to read the Women's Declaration of Independence issued by the Seneca Falls Convention of 1848. The management refused to permit either the reading of the declaration or to allow the women to present a copy to the chairman of the ceremonies. Nonetheless, on July 4, Susan B. Anthony, Matilda J. Gage, Sara A. Spencer, Lily D. Blake, and Phoebe W. Couzins marched through the crowd to the platform and, after waiting for the Declaration of Independence to be read, presented their declaration to the chairman. There was nothing he could do but accept it; the women marched out, handing out copies as they passed, and later outside read and explained their message to a friendly crowd.[32]

In 1889, when Miss Anthony learned that once again there were plans for a great world's fair in America, she became determined that this time women's participation would be officially sanctioned and supported by the national government and that if this were done it would benefit women in the United States in general and the suffrage movement in particular. Knowing that women's suffrage was hardly popular with the Congress and that some women whose social prestige would be needed might be frightened off if suffrage were mentioned, she began quietly working behind the scenes in Washington. Contacting some women there whom she could trust, she encouraged them to hold organization meetings in their homes and invite the wives and daughters of Washington officials. Working discreetly, Miss Anthony helped create a lobby in Congress for women to be placed on the fair's governing commission with men, and when in January, 1890, it was announced that a world's fair bill was being considered, she drafted a petition to that effect and obtained the signatures of 111 women, the wives and daughters of Supreme Court justices, cabinet members, congressmen, and military officers.[33]

When the act creating the world's fair was finally passed, it created the National Commission of men and authorized them to appoint a number of women to a "Board of Lady Managers." At the time, this concession to women was thought to be largely complimentary. The women were not expected to take an active part and no particular responsibilities or rules for their selection were stipulated.[34]

Subsequently, the National Commission appointed to the Board of Lady Managers 115 women representing the various states and territories and at their meeting in Chicago on November 19, 1890, the women chose Mrs. Potter H. Palmer as their president and Miss Phoebe Couzins as secretary. At the same meeting, they agreed that women's exhibits should not be segregated from the main displays at the fair (as they had been at the centennial) and they adopted a resolution to petition Congress for a definition of their responsibilities, which at the time appeared to be merely advisory, adding the request that they be allowed to do some "useful work."[35] From this first meeting on, increasing attention was focused both in the United States and abroad on the role women would play in the Columbian exposition.[36]

Largely through the efforts of Mrs. Palmer, Susan B. Anthony, Frances Willard and others, influential women and women's organizations in the United States and in Europe were contacted and asked to cooperate in sending exhibits demonstrating the accomplishments of women in every area.

In view of the immediate interest in this aspect of the fair, the directors of the Chicago Company decided that there should be a Women's Building erected at Jackson Park to serve as a place for exhibits and as an administrative home for the Women's Department. And in February of 1891 the fair's Board of Architects agreed that the Women's Building should be designed by a woman architect. Twelve designs were submitted and Sophia G. Hayden of Boston (who had studied at M.I.T.) was awarded the contract for her Italian Renaissance design, and eventually the building was erected across the lagoon from Olmsted's wooded island.[37]

From January of 1891 to the fall of 1892, the Women's Department contacted notable international women, women's clubs and organizations, and attempted to interest them in the World's Columbian Exposition as an agent for reforming current attitudes about woman's work and woman's place in the progress of the century. During that same period, the

World's Congress Auxiliary labored to generate enthusiasm for the idea of taking advantage of the fair as an intellectual and educational opportunity for the exchange of knowledge, and Handy's Promotion Department increased its campaign to convince foreign governments, state officials, and private manufacturers of the commercial advantages and importance of a good representation. There was one group, however, which needed no convincing whatever to become excited about the opportunities of a world's fair in Chicago.

Long before the Columbian Exposition was formally announced in December 1890, the Chicago Company had begun receiving scores of requests from people who looked upon the world's fair as a grand chance to make a fortune in six months. Amusement vendors, restauranteurs, circus acts, musical troupes, and speculators with all sorts of extravagant ideas for making money wrote letters or came in person to apply for space on the grounds of the exposition.[38]

The managers of the Chicago Company had expected from the beginning to allow for an amusement and concessionary side to the Columbian World's Fair. The Paris exposition of 1889 had found that by charging individuals for the privilege of operating their concession or entertainment on the fair grounds, a substantial amount of money could be received which would help defray the costs of the entire fair and permit the lowering of general admission prices. The Chicago Company counted on large receipts from this source to repay the original investors in the project, but as the plan for the fair developed—with its emphasis upon formal grandeur and classical idealism—it became a real question what to do with the show-business element. After the basic plan and design of Jackson Park was adopted in early 1891, none could conceive of placing a carnival in the Court of Honor or violating the peace of Olmsted's Wooded Island with a rowdy circus. Still, on the other hand, none could deny that amusement features of world's fairs were popular, drawing great crowds, and financially advantageous. Out of this quandary, a solution emerged almost at the last minute which became the basis for one of the most memorable and significant aspects of the World's Columbian Exposition.

Largely as a result of the influence of G. Brown Goode, who was called in as an expert advisor from the Smithsonian Institution, the classification system adopted by the National Commission in the fall of 1890 included a new department whose main responsibility was to insure that the educational value of the exhibition would surpass any previous attempt to show the progress and development of human civilization. All the exhibits of historical and cultural interest—archeology, anthropology, the progress of labor and invention in various countries and societies—whether isolated or collected, were in theory the responsibility of the Department of Ethnology.[39] Professor F. W. Putnam of Harvard was asked to direct the department's efforts in searching out and assembling exhibits from around the world.[40] At the same time, Thomas W. Palmer, president of the National Commission, was beginning to advocate the use of the Midway Plaissance—the undeveloped strip of land connecting Jackson and Washington Parks—as a location for collecting and displaying "the rare human exotic" exhibits of social and cultural interest. This kind of thing had of course been a mainstay of travelling circuses and carnivals for many years, and the exhibitions of troops of natives from the French colonies had been especially popular at the Paris exposition.

There was, at this time, a fine line of distinction between serious educational exhibits of authentic foreign and primitive cultures and exploitive exhibitionism meant to shock or horrify for its commercial value. As originally adopted, Palmer's suggestion for the use of the Midway was to have included only the former, educational type of ethnic exhibit and it was placed under the control of Professor Putnam to conduct on a "dignified and decorous basis."[41] By early 1892, however, the Chicago Company was feeling pressured to secure its financial situation and the prospect of losing revenues by ignoring amusement concessions began to seem short-sighted. Although no official declaration was ever made, it was finally decided to

View from the roof of the Manufactures and Liberal Arts Building. *(Courtesy Chicago Historical Society)*

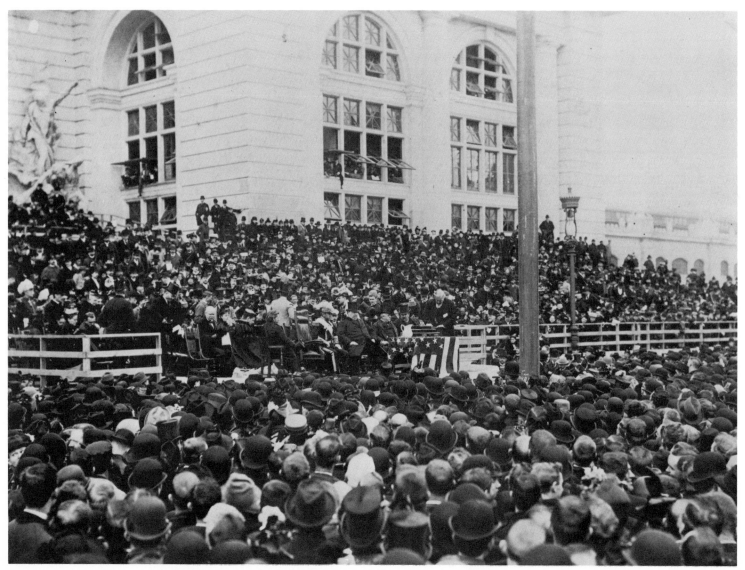

President Grover Cleveland at the opening of the World's Columbian Exposition. *(Photograph by C. D. Arnold; Courtesy Chicago Historical Society)*

Chicago Day at the World's Columbian Exposition, 1893. *(Courtesy Chicago Historical Society)*

View across the west end of the main basin showing MacMonnies Fountain and Obelisk. *(Photo by C. D. Arnold; Courtesy Chicago Historical Society)*

Manufacturers and Liberal Arts Building with the Rostral Column and electric fountain in the foreground. *(Courtesy Chicago Historical Society)*

Fine Arts Building, south facade. *(Courtesy Chicago Historical Society)*

Looking east across the Main Basin. *(Courtesy Chicago Historical Society)*

Missouri Building. *(Courtesy Chicago Historical Society)*

Facade and Golden Doorway of the Transportation Building, designed by Louis Sullivan. *(Courtesy Chicago Historical Society)*

Detail of the Golden Doorway, Transportation Building. *(Courtesy Chicago Historical Society)*

Sweden Building. *(Courtesy Chicago Historical Society)*

Midway view with the Ferris Wheel in the background. *(Courtesy Chicago Historical Society)*

Partial view of the Ferris Wheel. (*Courtesy Chicago Historical Society*)

Grand Basin and Colonnade.

Naval Exhibit, (fake) battleship *Illinois.* *(Photograph by C. D. Arnold; Courtesy Chicago Historical Society)*

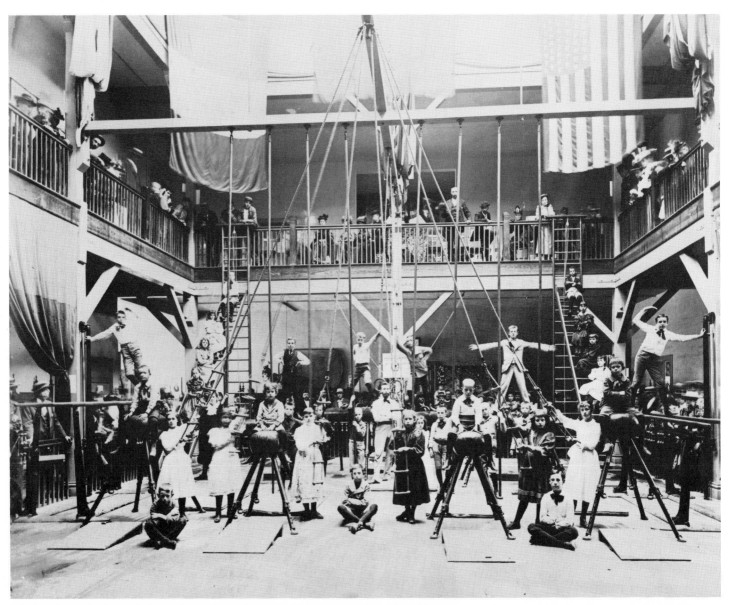

Interior of the Childrens' Building Gymnasium. *(Photograph by C. D. Arnold; Courtesy Chicago Historical Society)*

include a number of carefully selected amusements in the Midway section, and a young San Francisco entrepreneur, Sol Bloom, was hired to take charge of concessions.[42]

Bloom was only twenty-two at the time, the son of Polish immigrants and possessing no formal education, but he had established a reputation for himself in San Francisco as a young man who could turn any venture into a profitable enterprise. Shortly after taking the job, and being placed under Chief of Construction Burnham instead of Putnam, Bloom discovered why there had been no progress on the Midway: "To have made this unhappy gentleman [Professor Putnam] responsible for the establishment of a successful venture in the field of entertainment was about as intelligent a decision as it would be today to make Albert Einstein manager of the Ringling Brothers and Barnum and Bailey Circus."[43] By the summer of 1892, a substantial number of Midway concessions had been chosen (most of which had to give the appearance of having some cultural, historical or educational value) and the actual physical work of construction was underway.[44] Under Bloom's leadership, the Midway at the World's Columbian Exposition became one of the most successful and famous (our word *midway* comes from it) amusement areas of any of the great world's fairs.

10

Dedication Day

The act of Congress establishing the exposition at Chicago had stipulated that the buildings be dedicated "with appropriate ceremonies" on October 12, 1892, but New York City was intending to celebrate its own anniversary on that date, so a subsequent bill postponed dedication until the 21.[1] Chief of Construction Burnham reported in mid-summer that the main buildings would be sufficiently advanced by that date to permit formal acceptance by the National Commission, and in early October, President Palmer of the commission received a report from an independent committee of architects which certified that the buildings were ready. The arrangements for the dedication program were made by the National Commission's Committee on Ceremonies and the cost ($250,000) was borne by the Chicago Company.[2]

Activities began at noon on October 20 with a grand civic and military parade in which nearly one hundred thousand people marched under the supervision of the chief marshall, Major-General Miles of the U.S. Army. All local business was suspended, and the streets were cordoned off and patrolled by 1,200 Chicago policemen, the buildings were gayly decorated with flags and streamers, and all Chicago seemed to turn out to watch the parade and listen to the military marching bands. There was a definite festal feeling, one observer recalled, in which "Chicago indulged to the full its somewhat irrational passion for bigness."[3]

Beginning at nine o'clock on the following day, October 21, a grand procession of dignitaries escorted by a contingent of federal troops made its way to the great Hall of Manufactures and Liberal Arts which had been readied for the actual dedication ceremonies. President Harrison was unable to attend, his wife being fatally ill, but Vice-President Levi P. Morgan represented him. Also present were the justices of the Supreme Court, former President Hayes, General Schofield (commanding general of the U.S. Army), various cabinet officers and members of the Diplomatic Corps, senators and congressmen (including Senator John Sherman), twenty carriages of commissioners and consuls of foreign governments, and thirty state governors and their staffs.[4] Following a lunch for seventy thousand people provided by the Chicago Company, the ceremonies at the Manufactures Building were opened by John K. Paine's "Columbian Hymn," which was sung by a five-thousand-member chorus and played by Theodore Thomas' five-hundred-piece orchestra.[5] Bishop Fowler of the Methodist-Episcopal Church offered the invocation and was followed by a succession of speeches by George Davis (the director-general), Mayor Hempstead Washburn of Chicago, Harlow Higinbotham (president of the Chicago Company), Mrs. Potter Palmer (president of the Board of Lady Managers), Thomas W. Palmer (president of the National Commission), and Vice-President Morton. All of the speakers praised the builders, architects, and artists and the organizers and officials who had contributed to the building of the fair, their spirit of cooperation and their dedication to the enterprise.

The speakers predicted that the fair would be a great force for world peace and for the advancement of knowledge and liberty and would in particular show the world the maturity of American culture, artistic as well as materialistic, and demonstrate to the country the sophistication, civic-mindedness, and representativeness of Chicago. "The ceaseless, resistless march of civilization westward, ever westward," said director-general Davis, for example, "has reached and passed the great lakes of North America, and has founded on their farthest shore the greatest city of modern times. Chicago, the peerless, has been selected for the great celebration which today gives new fire to progress, and sheds its light upon ages yet to come. Established in the heart of this continent, her

pulse throbs with the quickening current of our national life. And that this city was selected as the scene of this great commemorative festival was the natural growth of predestined events."[6] Chicago had asked for, received, and built the fair not from a narrow ambition "born of local pride and selfishness" but from a sense of national destiny and public spirit.[7]

Mrs. Palmer, whose presence on the platform constituted an unprecedented recognition of women, took advantage of the opportunity to say that the honor was appropriate since it was a woman, Queen Isabella, who transformed Columbus' dream into reality and since it was the progress of science which had liberated women from the "never-ending tasks that have previously been hers." Woman could now take her rightful place alongside man in education, art, and industry. "Even more important than the discovery of Columbus which we are here to celebrate," she concluded, "is the fact that the General Government has just discovered woman."[8]

Of the nearly twenty-five acres of cheering, handkerchief-waving people who congregated in the great building, only a handful were able to hear the speakers on the program. Still they stayed on while the program was carried out line by line. The reason was, perhaps, as the *Chicago Record* reported, that "nearly every man in the assemblage of 150,000 had a personal interest in the spectacle because he had sacrificed directly or indirectly to promote its success. The thousands of singers who had given their time and energies free, the Exposition stockholders, 30,000 of them in all walks of life, the private citizens whose taxes made up Chicago's contribution, the residents of every state and territory . . . all these felt that it was their Fair."[9]

Following Mrs. Palmer's address, Harriet Monroe's lengthy "Columbian Ode" was read (parts of it being sung by the chorus), and the dedicatory oration was delivered by Henry Watterson of Kentucky.[10] Watterson reviewed the history and character of the American people, praising their energy and their practical spirit. What the nation needed most, at the present time, he insisted, was a "moderation of public sentiment," a respect for duty and a renewed obligation to "union"—the basic theme of America. "We have had full enough of the dramatic and sensational," he concluded, "and need a season of mediocrity and repose."[11] Chauncey Depew of New York carried this same theme to a wider sphere in his "Columbian Oration." "This day belongs not to America, but to the world," he said, for all nations are invited to come to America to witness the "flower and fruitage of this transcendent miracle," the United States.[12] "The time has arrived for both a closer union and," he warned, "greater distance between the Old World and the New. The former indiscriminate welcome to our prairies, and the present invitation to these palaces of art and industry mark the present period. Unwatched and unhealthy immigration can no longer be permitted to our shores. We must have a national quarantine against disease, pauperism and crime. . . . We cannot admit those who come to undermine our institutions, and subvert our laws."[13]

It was near evening when the final closing prayer was offered and the crowds began to disperse. A great amount of work was still to be done to prepare the world's fair for opening day the following spring, but there was also great confidence that it would fulfill the expectations that it would be the largest and most comprehensive world's fair ever. And yet, if the dedication day speeches were any indication, there was a feeling that the fair would symbolize the end of an old America as much as it would the beginning of a new one, for, as President Palmer noted, "there are no more continents to discover."[14]

11
Final Preparations

The winter of 1892/1893 was even longer and more severe than the preceding one. Snow covered the grounds and buildings at Jackson Park from December through March, and the surface of Lake Michigan was frozen over. The heavy weather frustrated efforts to complete the final painting and landscaping, and many of the statues and monuments had to be boxed or covered with tarpaulins to prevent them from being damaged. Extreme temperatures and the weight of snow weakened the roofs of many of the exhibition halls and, at one point, brought down large sections of the roof of the giant Manufactures Building. Understandably, exhibitors were reluctant to allow their goods and displays to be put in place until they could be assured that the leaks were repaired and that the roof was water tight.

Apprehension that the fair would not be ready by May 1 became serious as March wore on. It was not until almost the first of April that the buildings were secured against the weather and exhibits began arriving in the large numbers expected. Director of Works Burnham now had more than twelve thousand workers at Jackson Park laboring around the clock (thanks to the electric light).[1] All they needed was a week of good weather, he assured the company's officials, to have the fair prepared for opening day.[2] But April was equally uncooperative, bringing rain, hail, and high winds that raised havoc with the lighter buildings on the Midway and left Jackson Park a sea of mud and debris with barely a week to go until opening. Only with great difficulty was the fair ready at all for the opening ceremonies on May 1, and it wasn't for two months after that date that all buildings and exhibits were in place and the landscaping completed.

The financial picture looked equally bleak in the early months of 1893. In February, the Chicago Company was shocked by a congressional decision to withhold $751,000 of the amount appropriated in souvenir coins until the company gave security that it would pay the cost of the judges and awards. The company, which had sold bonds on the basis of the $2.5 million appropriation, refused to pay the costs claiming that not only would it violate the terms of the bonds but that the expenses of judges and awards were clearly the responsibility of the National Commission.[3] The deficit thus caused in the fair's resources came at a very critical time, but fortunately the Chicago Company was able to convince the railroads (who expected to do a handsome business during the fair) to take an additional $1,000,000 in bonds.

On April 1, President Higinbotham reported to the annual meeting of the stockholders of the Chicago Company that the company was in a position to meet the projected amount necessary for the completion of the work on May 1, and that the directors felt "encouraged to hope that the Exposition about to be opened in our city will prove the crowning glory of our century, and leave a lasting, permanent, and excellent impression upon our time."[4]

According to the act establishing the exposition, the inaugural ceremonies were not restricted to activities in Chicago, but were to begin officially with an international naval review on the Hudson River. On April 17, 1893, nine foreign nations accepted the American invitation and sent warships to rendezvous at Hampton Roads, Virginia, prior to proceeding to New York.[5] The naval review was held on the twenty-sixth, with President Cleveland and numerous foreign dignitaries in attendance. Receptions and ceremonial entertainments followed, and a great military and naval parade concluded the New York celebrations on April 28.[6]

At noon on April 30, while President Cleveland, the Duke of Veragua, and other dignitaries were en route to Chicago, a ceremonial brunch was held in the Music Building on the fair grounds at which Daniel Burnham presented the buildings to the directors of the Chicago Company. Olmsted, Sullivan, and Theodore Thomas were among the artists and designers present, and the guests included that legendary western showman, Buffalo Bill (his Wild West Show was being set up just outside of the grounds). After speeches and cigars, Burnham brought out the silver loving cup that he had recently been given by the New York Society of Artists, filled it with claret, and passed it around. Each of the guests was cheered by the others as he drank, including Buffalo Bill who had to remove his great white sombrero to drink from the tankard.[7] For Burnham, the recognition of the leaders of eastern culture was a personal triumph. The loving cup symbolized that New York had finally accepted Chicago and its fair, and would henceforth give its "whole-hearted and enthusiastic support."[8] Even before the gates were opened, the World's Columbian Exposition had begun to bring Chicago the acceptance and recognition of the older sections of the country which many of its leading citizens wanted so badly.

While officials, builders, and artists struggled to make Jackson Park ready, Chicago itself worked "as it never had . . . since the days following the great fire" to make the city the greatest exhibit of the fair.[9] Chicago's citizens loved pageantry and spectacle and "opportunities for advertising and display were seldom missed."[10] A world's fair with all its attendant excitement and color was therefore a natural catalyst for the energies of the entire city and tended to bring to the surface the contrasting self-images of Chicago.

For a year prior to opening day, the world's fair had been the major topic of public interest in the city; only the nomination of John Peter Altgeld for governor and the presidential election of 1892 diverted attention from the preparations for the big show of 1893. New buildings were erected downtown, transportation facilities were expanded, and new boarding houses, restaurants, saloons, and gambling houses sprang up everywhere in anticipation of the throngs of visitors. Gamblers, sideshow operators, saloon keepers, pimps, pickpockets, "madams," confidence men, realtors, merchants, and concessionaires flocked into the city "anxious to stake out a claim before the rush of gold struck the city."[11] General Miles started a bicycle race to New York to advertise the fair, and the city's publishers contributed hundreds of books, atlases, guides, and histories to the cause. During the summer of 1892, the city council defeated Alderman Madden's proposal to restrict the number of saloons in the residential districts, letting "it be known that Chicago would be a wide open town in 1893,"[12] and that those who came to the city secretly hoping to find the wicked and overgrown frontier town would not be disappointed.[13] The coming of the world's fair allowed Chicago to indulge itself in a holiday from the serious issues that daily faced the city and to feel once again that it was free and young and reckless. So, in the spring of 1893, when an election was scheduled, the city wanted for its mayor during the fair the man who would best typify that expansive spirit. That man was Carter Harrison.

Harrison had come to Chicago originally from Kentucky, and he and the city had grown up and left their imprint on each other. Carter Harrison loved Chicago, so much so that he once said that he must take it as his bride, all of it for better or for worse—and the city returned the favor by electing him to four terms as its mayor (1879–1887).[14] There had always been something of the Old West about him, something "dashing and democratic, big and magnificent, some fire a little too hot to keep within rigidly conventional confines."[15] By 1893, Harrison had become a tradition and it seemed only right that he should be in the mayor's chair when Chicago achieved its greatest triumph.[16] But, at the same time, there were many people in Chicago who thought the ex-mayor represented too much of the city's past, that he was too liberal (he was known to be friendly toward labor and had testified in 1886 to the peacefulness of the Anarchists) and permitted too many corrupt and lawless individuals to influence him.[17] The law and order and the moral forces in the community, including most of the newspapers, backed the conservative Republican Samuel W. Allerton in an election that was one of the bitterest in the city's history.[18]

In the end, Carter Harrison had the support of many of the Chicago people actually working at the fair because they knew his image and personal charm would be good publicity for the exposition and would help attract visitors. He won the election and took office a few weeks before opening day.[19] And, in a sense, both those who favored Harrison's election and those who opposed him were correct. He did prove to be an extremely popular and effective representative of the city to visitors during the fair, and he did allow wide open gambling and prostitution and permit the Bathhouse Johns and Mike McDonalds to continue to prosper.[20]

Carter Harrison symbolized Chicago's old free-wheeling, optimistic spirit of individualism and frontier boosterism, but many people believed that philosophy inappropriate and ineffectual for a city which had reached maturity. A new spirit was demanded, both by the conditions and the times, in which the chief element was a wider interest in the cultural aspects of city life and the development of a new sense of civic pride and responsibility. The world's fair of 1893, especially as its symbolic and artistic features became known, was thought to be both a reflection of the new Chicago spirit and a great instrument for spreading the message. "It is probable that the Columbian Exposition of 1893 will be the birthplace of this new phase of greatness of Chicago," James Dredge, a member of the British Royal Commission to the exposition, told a London audience in January 1893, "for it will be full of every possible object lesson, and will bring home to the inhabitants of the city, more forcibly than any other event could do, the fact that there is more in heaven and earth than had been dreamed of in their philosophy."[21] One has the feeling, Dredge further told his listeners, that true greatness will come to Chicago once "her inhabitants give themselves leisure to realize that the object of life is not that of incessant struggle; that the race is not always to the swift; but rather to those who understand the luxury and advantage of repose, as well as of sustained effort."[22]

Beginning in the spring of 1891, the World's Columbian Exposition was seen by many Chicagoans to be a great educational force for building public spirit on a new basis, as significant in its way as was the opening of Adler and Sullivan's civic Auditorium in 1889, or Theodore Thomas establishing the Chicago Symphony in 1891, or especially the opening on October 1, 1892, of the new University of Chicago.[23] Indeed, the two great undertakings of 1892, the "big show and the big university," had more in common than a certain similarity in the styles and personalities of their major builders—Daniel Burnham and William Rainey Harper—or that the fair's buildings were dedicated in the same month as the university opened its doors, or even that the fairgrounds and the university were located side-by-side. "The conjunction of the two events might be felt as marking saliently a stage in the forward movement of the state," wrote Henry B. Fuller, "and might well be accepted as the climax of an almost unequalled progress, through twenty years, in the general complex of civil life."[24] The "White City"—the world's fair—rose "pari passu" with the "Grey City"—the university—and both enterprises were seen as a corrective for the confusing problems of the "Black City" through education, cultural uplift, law and order, and a new kind of public spirit.[25] The fair and the university were both examples of pride in urban citizenship and the belief that Chicago held the promise of a golden future. "When the people of the world come to Chicago," wrote Henry Demarest Lloyd, "let us show them as our supreme treasure, outshining the magnificence of palaces, a citizenship with which we vindicate our rights like freemen."[26]

Beginning shortly after the original architectural scheme was made public, the idea quickly gained currency that the World's Columbian Exposition, the "White City," would be an experiment or laboratory for solving not only the questions of civic architecture and esthetics but also the growing urban problems of transportation, finance, power, health services, fire and police protection, and housing administration. Thus, in its operation as in its construction, the fair attempted to become a model, an idealized demonstration of the reconciliation of the practical, material needs of a large city with the equally essential human desires for beauty, comfort, and entertainment.

The moving of people from the city out to the exposition, and back again, was a major consideration from the earliest plans for the fair. Chicago had, of course, superb railroad connections to all parts of the nation—that fact had been an essential argument in favor of awarding the fair to Chicago in the first place—but the problem of transporting people to Jackson Park required a good deal of planning. By the time the fair opened there were seven different alternatives available for visitors to reach the fair from the central city ranging from a leisurely coach route down Michigan Avenue, to the Illinois Central Railway, to the scenic water route along the lake via the steamers of the World's Fair Steamship Company. A railway terminal station (modeled by Atwood after the Baths of Caracalla in Rome) was planned and built at the rear of the Administration Building so that all of the thirty-five railroad lines serving Chicago would have direct rail connections to the fair.[27] By May 1, it was estimated that by using all available means of transit, three hundred thousand people could be taken to Jackson Park and returned to the downtown area each day.

Transportation for visitors within the fairgrounds (685 acres) had also been carefully thought out. An electric railway made a thirteen mile trip around the grounds every three-quarters of an hour and had a capacity of sixteen thousand people. In addition, there were several varieties of water transport available along the two and a half miles of lagoons and canals. There were electric launches that carried thirty passengers each and made a prescribed course around the grounds, stopping at every major building or, like express buses, stopping only at a few. There were smaller boats which could be hailed like a cab, or rented by the hour, and there were the romantic Venetian-style gondolas, built in Italy and manned by experienced Venetian gondoliers. Lifeboats and safety equipment were stationed at various points and at least one lifeboat patrolled the waterways at all times. Responsibility for controlling the water traffic and for developing safety rules and regulation was placed in the hands of an officer delegated by the U.S. Navy.

Private vehicles, horsedrawn or otherwise, were restricted from the grounds, including bicycles, and all except the most perishable supplies had to be delivered either before the fair opened in the morning or after it closed at night. Those items which had to be delivered during operating hours were done by exposition personnel only. Thus, visitors were relieved of the commercial noise usually associated with city life. In addition, all advertising was carefully regulated to eliminate the usual harassment by hawkers and peddlers and the litter of handbills. Concessionaires and exhibitors were warned that if their advertising materials were found strewn about the grounds, their distribution permits would be cancelled. All signs had to be approved in advance by the administration and only one newspaper was allowed to be sold on the grounds, *The Daily Columbian,* which was produced by the exposition's Department of Publicity and Promotion.[28]

Contracts were sold by the exposition for the right to operate restaurants on the grounds and to sell such items as seltzer water, cigars, ice cream, popcorn and peanuts (shelled only).[29] Guards were instructed to receive complaints and to report on the cleanliness of the concessions and the entire park was swept each evening. For the first time at any fair, a Bureau of Public Comfort was established to act as a kind of ombudsman for the general needs of the fair's visitors. Through the bureau, medical and emergency hospital service was available, waiting rooms and toilets were maintained, and a Rooming Department provided hotel and rooming house information and secured accommodations for out-of-town visitors in previously screened facilities. The Bureau of Public Comfort also had supervision over the Columbian Guards, an attempt to provide a model for city policemen, who were drilled in a military fashion, sworn in as South Park patrolmen, and given the responsibility for supervising safety precautions and general security.[30] The guards were assisted by a secret service of some two hundred detectives appointed by the police chiefs of various American and European cities and led by "Blackjack" Bonfield of the Chicago Police.[31]

Providing pure water for drinking and other purposes had caused problems in previous world's fairs, and Chicago itself had had its own history of difficulties in drawing water from the lake. But the sanitary engineers decided upon a Pasteur-Chamberland filtering system for the fair, and it proved highly successful.[32] Also effective was an experimental procedure for sewage and garbage disposal (the Engle System). Sewage was first treated chemically at the cleansing station to reduce it to solids—the purified effluent was run off into the lake—and then the solids were burned under pressure in a single Engle furnace with the capacity of one hundred tons a day. Tests with the system also indicated that by careful sorting and reuse of the ashes of combustion as fertilizer or road cover, it could effectively pay for itself.[33]

Fire protection was provided by a special department trained by Chicago professionals, and included a seventy-five-foot fireboat which was stationed on the lagoons. The danger of fire was a particular concern because of the large numbers of people, the temporary nature of the buildings, the fireworks, and the extensive use of electricity. Hydrants were located throughout the grounds and in the main buildings, and 1,800 hand extinguishers were distributed. During 1893, the Fire Department answered ninety-two calls and the total loss by fire (with the exception of the Cold Storage Building disaster)[34] was only $1,730.[35]

The mechanical and electrical power needed to run the intramural railway, the fair's electrical system, the sewage system, and other general requirements, and supply individual exhibitors (like the Otis elevators in the Transportation Building) and concessionaires, was provided by the exposition boiler, engine, and generating plants. Twelve underground tanks stored the fuel oil pumped in pipes from Lima, Ohio, by Standard Oil.[36] Although the various exposition halls and buildings were engineered and designed with their expected general power requirements in mind, the most novel feature of the fair in this regard was the extensively integrated plans for the use of electricity. Paris in 1889 had been the first world's fair to be lighted by electricity, but at Chicago the architects were asked to design their buildings specifically with an eye toward the artistic possibilities of artificial illumination. The result was that, following May 8 when the exposition was first illuminated at night, the fair provided a revelation to its visitors of the enormous potential of electric lighting, not only to illuminate but to enhance visual effects. "Words almost fail the beauties of the fantastic illuminations with which the wizards entwine the graceful outlines of the White City," said the front page of the *Chicago Herald* on May 9.

The novel use of electricity at the exposition was a technical innovation of great importance as well. On May 23, 1892, the Westinghouse Company was given the lighting contract for their bid, which was much lower than that of Edison's General Electric Company. George Westinghouse lost money on the project, but in the long run his working demonstration of the practical use of alternating current (by which method power could be transmitted more safely at greater distances than by the older direct current) led subsequently to his being awarded the contract for the first great hydroelectric plant at Niagara Falls. "Very few of those who looked at the machinery," wrote Westinghouse's biographer, "who gazed with admiration at the great switchboard, so ingenious and complete, and who saw the beautiful lighting effects could have realized that they were living in an historical moment, that they were looking at the beginnings of a revolution."[37]

The first month of the fair's operation was devoted to the preparation of the grounds, installing exhibits, and finishing the work on the Midway Plaisance. May was rainy, and attendance was so small that a general fear arose that the exposition would fail to attract people in the large numbers anticipated. All the great expectations for the fair as an educator and an object lesson would fail if the people didn't come, and, in addition, the authorities had been counting heavily upon the influx of resources from the gate receipts. The fair had received an increasing amount of criticism, some of it exaggerated, in eastern newspapers for not being completed on time and several papers had predicted bankruptcy, while in Jackson Park the waiters had gone on strike and the Columbian Guards were threatening similar action if their salaries weren't raised.[38]

To make matters worse, the first shock waves incident to the financial panic of 1893 were felt in Chicago almost simultaneously with the opening of the fair. On May 9, the Chemical National Bank in Chicago failed, and two days later the Columbian National Bank, a branch of the Chemical National operating on the fairgrounds, also failed. The exposition bank held the deposits of many exhibitors, and a number of them were foreigners, so that its failure presented a serious threat to the success of the fair itself. President Higinbotham of the Chicago Company immediately contacted several of his wealthy friends (George Pullman, Lyman Gage, et al.) to guarantee the foreign deposits, and although he was successful, the entire experience and the increasingly bad economic news from around the country made the fair's managers very uneasy about the financial condition of the exposition.[39] Orders were given to reduce the expenditures of the fair wherever possible in the construction and installation efforts, and in the work force. In an attempt to increase gate receipts a Department of Functions was established and Frank Millet— who, among his other contributions, was quick to see the need to make the fair a festival as well as an object lesson—was put in charge. Millet began immediately to develop special crowd pleasing attractions, like parades, swimming matches, boat and canoe races, parachute drops, and fireworks displays, and to advertise special dates in honor of various cities, states, and nations.[40] One of the casualties of this shift toward popularizing the fair was the elaborate program of musical events which had been planned by the exposition's musical director, Theodore Thomas.

The most popular form of music in America between the Civil War and the turn of the century was the amateur military-style band,[41] and Thomas had included an almost daily series of free band concerts on the grounds by some of the most popular bands in the country. Patrick S. Gilmore and John Philip Sousa brought their bands to the fair, joining Liesegang's Chicago Band, various state and city ensembles, the Sargona Band of Spain, the Imperial Band of Austria, two German bands, and the Royal Scottish Pipers among others.[42] The band concert programs consisted of marches, waltzes, popular tunes, overtures, and melodies transcribed from the orchestral works of Berlioz, Weber, Beethoven, Brahms, Tschaikovsky, and Wagner.

But the military bands were primarily meant to entertain, in Thomas's view, not to "edify," and he therefore arranged an impressive schedule of concert orchestra and choral society performances including eminent soloists and conductors from America and abroad. These performances were to be held in the Music Hall at the north end of the Peristyle in the Court of Honor, which had been designed and built "to be used by musical talent and connoisseurs of the art rather than by the mass of people who will visit Jackson Park," and a fee was to be charged.[43] Thomas's hope was that these latter events would show the world the achievements of American musical development and at the same time expose Americans to the achievements of other nations.[44]

Trouble began almost immediately after the fair opened. Ignace Jan Paderewski, "whose leonine hair caused the ladies to swoon and whose virtuosity was acknowledged by all," was scheduled as the solo pianist for the inaugural concert on May 2.[45] Paderewski insisted that he could play on no other instrument than a Steinway, and, although the contracts with foreign artists appeared to give them the right to name their instruments, the music instrument manufacturers exhibiting at the fair argued before the National Commission that only exhibited instruments should be used in performances at the fairgrounds. Steinway and Sons were not exhibitors, and the National Commission ruled that Paderewski's Steinway should be removed from the Music Hall. Thomas, supported by Daniel Burnham and James Ellsworth of the Chicago Com-

pany, felt bound to support the artist, and the concert was given before a packed house. Paderewski "tossed his tawny mane in triumph," played his Steinway—now the most famous musical instrument in the country—before an audience of swooning women, and left "to the fluttering of a thousand spoken 'divines.' "[46]

The underlying reasons for the episode remain somewhat obscure. The whole incident had the appearance, as Bloom later remarked, of a publicity stunt for Steinway and for the music concerts, and it had been rumored that the Chicago Company was considering dropping the concerts to cut expenses.[47] It is even possible that some of the fair's managers had sought to use the Steinway issue as an easy excuse for cancelling Thomas' expensive program. But in any case, Theodore Thomas's public reputation and character were injured, and the exhibiting piano makers, several members of the National Commission, and the Chicago newspapers began calling for his resignation. In August, when falling attendance added the final blow, Thomas resigned his position and sadly admitted that his attempts to present "high brow" music at the fair had failed.[48] Americans, it seemed, would accept uplift in almost everything else at the fair except their music.

The disappointing gate receipts in May (subtracting the opening day figures, the daily average was only thirty-one thousand) also revived the conflict between the national authorities (the National Commission) and the local Chicago Company over the question whether or not the fair ought to be open on Sundays. The Sunday controversy eventually drew the state and federal courts into determining the superior authority over the fair's operation.

As a result of accepting the souvenir coin appropriation from Congress, the Chicago Company had agreed originally, if reluctantly, to keep the fair closed on Sundays. Toward the end of May, however, the directors decided to reverse their former position and open the gates. The former restriction, they argued, had been made void by Congress subsequently withholding the funds for judges and awards, and, in addition, Congress did not have the right, constitutionally, to make such a religiously based restriction in the first place. To further complicate the issue, on May 14, Charles W. Clingman filed an appeal with the state courts for an injunction restraining the exposition officials from closing the fair on the grounds that it infringed upon his property rights as a stockholder in the Chicago Company. When the company's resolution was brought before the National Commission it met with extreme opposition, "several of the Commissioners advocating applying to the General Government to send in troops with which to close the Fair."[49] Instead, District Attorney Milchrist applied to the federal courts for an injunction restraining the fair's officials from opening the gates on Sundays.

Acting on its executive decision and the state injunction granted to Clingman, the Chicago Company opened the fair on Sunday, May 28. The major buildings were left open, but (although the admission price was kept at fifty cents) much of the machinery was shut down and many of the exhibits were covered. On June 8, however, a temporary injunction was granted by the federal courts to District Attorney Milchrist, and the Columbian Exposition found itself under two different injunctions, one to open on Sunday and one to close. An appeal was made to the Circuit Court of Appeals and on July 17, the court, led by Chief Justice Fuller, overturned the lower court's ruling and cancelled the injunction granted to Milchrist on the basis that, since the Chicago Corporation had spent in excess of $16 million toward the enterprise, its authority was superior to that of the federal government.[50] The national government's right to intercede, to control the operations of the fair, was denied. But this unusual episode was not over yet.

Following the Sunday, May 28, opening, Sunday attendance dropped and the fair's officials continued to receive protests from all sections of the country, many religious groups boycotting the fair altogether. By the end of June it began to be apparent that Sunday opening was not going to make up for the congressional appropriation of $2.5 million, which would have to be paid back, and so the directors of the Chicago Company ordered that the gates be again closed, starting on July 23.[51] On July 24, however, Judge Stein of the Illinois State Courts summoned the director-general and the Chicago Company's directors to appear before him to answer for contempt of the court's injunction granted to Clingman. Director-General Davis was fined $250, Directors Hutchinson, Gage, McNally, Kerfoot, and Lawson were fined $1,000 each, and the company was ordered to reopen the gates on Sunday.[52] Judge Stein's action made it impossible to close on Sunday and, although the average attendance remained between 50 and 60 percent less than on other days, the exposition remained open on Sunday thereafter.[53] The entire episode was, as President Higinbotham latter wrote, "a unique and disagreeable experience," but it was also a clear expression of the intensity of religious interest in the world's fair and, more importantly, a reflection of the confusion about what was the proper role of religion in American life in the last decade of the century.[54] Many Americans felt that, in fact, the confusion and conflict of the period was the result of the decline of the traditional control of religion and morality, and they looked anxiously toward the fair to provide a symbolic reaffirmation of both the sacred and the ideal dimensions within the cultural life of the country.

12
The World's Congress

Long before the fair was given to Chicago, orthodox religious elements in the society had campaigned against opening the gates on Sunday. A world's fair was essentially, they argued, a secular event and as such should, like all secular events, show respect for the Sabbath. But as the object of the fair—to celebrate Columbus and demonstrate the comprehensive advancement of American civilization—and the lofty character of the plans for its construction became more widely understood, a much more complex and intense attitude began to emerge. A world's fair that truly represented American civilization ought to show the religious dimension as much as, if not more than, the secular dimensions of the society. Indeed, it began to be argued that the world's fair (with its expectable emphasis on technology and scientific progress) in Chicago (known for its materialism) presented an opportunity that should not be missed for reaffirming the traditional belief in the religious meaning of the American experience and for furthering the older religious values at a time when they seemed to be swiftly eroding.[1]

On July 10, 1892, Reverend John H. Barrows, an associate editor of the religious reform magazine *Our Day* and a member of the World's Congress Auxiliary of the fair, addressed a crowd of sixteen thousand members of the National Convention of the Societies of Christian Endeavor at Madison Square Garden in New York on the subject of "The Religious Possibilities of the World's Fair." "The Discovery of the New World," he said, "was a chief event in the social and in the spiritual progress of humanity, and the pulpits and schools of

America have an unequalled opportunity of showing what God has wrought through the four marvelous centuries since Columbus sighted the West Indian Island from the deck of the Spanish caravel. The Exposition will not only furnish an unparalleled spectacle to the eye, it will also provide for the mind an unequalled feast."[2] Not only on Sunday, he continued, but throughout the week there will be "tent preaching and open-air preaching" near the gates of the exposition, and the Hotel Endeavor, the Sunday School, Women's Temperence Union, YMCA and YWCA, and the tract and bible societies are organizing to proclaim the gospel during the fair. Most important, he announced, will be the religious congresses, which will be held from the end of August through September and which will provide "an immense opportunity of showing, not only to the people of Christian lands but to the representatives of non-Christian nations, the splendid vitality and vigor of the missionary spirit which is the grandest feature of this grandest century since Jesus commissioned His disciples to evangelize the world."[3] In this age of materialism when the sins of Christian people are so apparent, Barrows offered his conviction that "the divine way of building up the Kingdom of Christ in America is to engage with fresh ardor in efforts to Christianize India and Africa, Turkey and China,"[4] and over every closed gate on Sunday, he wanted to see inscribed in gold "the immortal statue wherein is wrapped up the Christian future of America and the world: 'Remember the Sabbath day to keep it holy.' "[5]

Traditional American Christianity was self-consciously engaged in a period of serious testing, and while, as Barrows had argued, the world's fair of 1893 offered great opportunities for missionary conversion of the world, others saw Chicago itself as a symbol of those elements in American society most in need of regeneration. On March 13, 1893, Joseph Cook delivered his 234th Boston Monday Lecture on the "Perils and Promises of the World's Fair: Crime and Christianity in Chicago," in which he listed the main evils he expected visitors to encounter there: harlotry, drunkenness, gambling, robbery, murder, anarchy, greed, and Sunday desecration.[6] Chicago

is the war "front," he said, to which we ought to send, along with Dwight L. Moody, the successors of Luther, Edwards, Whitefield, and Finney to set the city ablaze with "evangelical truth." There will be meetings, preaching, and "temperance propaganda," he assured his audience, "and best of all, as we now expect, there will be an exhibition every Sunday of the American Sabbath."[7] As these two examples show, behind the pressure for Sunday closing of the world's fair there existed a certain sense that traditional American Christianity was in a state of siege in which, more than ever, the older rituals had to be insisted upon. And the test was taking place not just because there was a world's fair nor because it was being held in Chicago, but because the Columbian Exposition in Chicago represented the West and it was in the West, as one writer put it, that "our great energies find their opportunity, there are cities built in twenty-five years— and destroyed in two days, there will be Armageddon."[8]

Other Christian moralists in American society also felt that Christianity would be tested at Chicago in 1893, but they were less sure that the best response was to retreat into the rigidity of older formalities. For them the crisis in religion was due at least as much to the inability of American Christianity to respond to the changing social and cultural conditions of the society as it was to the new conditions themselves. Differing very little from the traditionalists in their belief in the applicability of Christian ethics, or in their sense of American society as in need of regeneration (or uplift, as it was popularly phrased), they nonetheless felt that the times demanded new tactics and a new acknowledgement and response to the social realities of American life.[9] For these generally younger, more "realistic" church and civic leaders, the world's fair was itself seen as an agent for the transformation of society. Reverend Frederick A. Noble of Chicago's Union Park Congregational Church saw the exposition as an expression of a religious idea. "We call this a Columbian Exposition," he said in a sermon on April 30, 1893. "It is. But it is more—it is a Divine Exposition." God is behind it all, the fair is a "great theological institute."[10] If the world's fair was to be truly a

Administration Building, at right, Electrical Building at left. *(Courtesy Chicago Historical Society)*

Boone and Crockett Club Exhibit, Wooded Island. *(Courtesy Chicago Historical Society)*

U.S. Government Building.

The Statue of the Republic.

The Electricity Building.

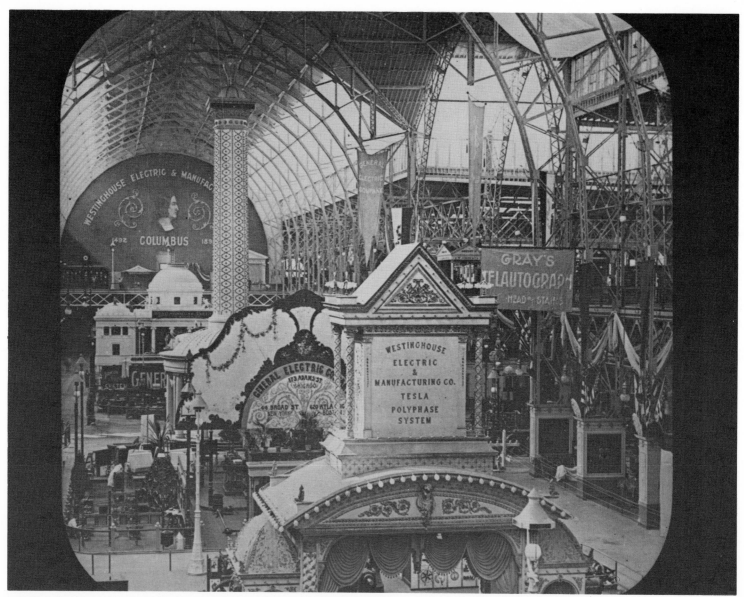

Interior of the Electricity Building, Westinghouse exhibit. *(Courtesy Chicago Historical Society)*

The Agriculture Building.

The Manufacturers and Liberal Arts Building.

Transportation Building.

The Grand Canal, looking north.

View across the Court of Honor, east to west. *(Photograph by C. D. Arnold; Courtesy Chicago Historical Society).*

The Machinery Hall.

Interior of the Manufactures and Liberal Arts Building. *(Photograph by C. D. Arnold; Courtesy Chicago Historical Society)*

Hoo-den Building on Wooded Isle. *(Courtesy Chicago Historical Society)*

Looking west across the Main Basin at night, Administration Building in background. *(Courtesy Chicago Historical Society)*

Wreckage of Exposition, after closing. *(Courtesy Chicago Historical Society)*

"Divine Exposition," then it made very little sense, it was argued, to close it down on the Lord's day. In fact, it would unfairly discriminate against the working classes who would be able to come only on the weekends.

In a pamphlet printed early in 1892, the Reverend Henry C. Kinney, a missionary at the Chicago stockyards who had been involved with workingmen in New York and Chicago for eleven years, charged that Sunday closing would debar millions of working people from visiting the fair and that it would be both unjust and inhumane. "I claim that a vast majority of the Christian leaders know nothing of the working-man," he wrote. They don't know his real life or real needs.[11] "The greatest mistake of all, of course, is that made by the national part of the management," said *The Dial* in November, 1892, "when it was decided to close the exhibition one day of every week, and that on the one upon which, above all others, it is desirable that the gates should be open."[12] The thinly disguised attitude that lay beneath these arguments for keeping the fair open was that the working classes were in the greatest need of spiritual and educational lessons. Mrs. M. G. Van Rensselaer, a New York architectural critic, in an article in *Forum* praising the fairgrounds' beauty, harmony, and unity, expressed it most clearly: "This is the place that those self-styled Christians who do not believe Christ's distinct assertion that the Sabbath was made for man, not man for the Sabbath, desire to have closed on the one day of the week when our mind-hungry, beauty-starved, ignorant, but eagerly ambitious masses could best make use of its civilizing and uplifting ministrations."[13]

The Sunday issue was settled finally, not by traditionalists or social gospel reformers, but by the courts. Nevertheless, the expectations and attitudes toward the exposition continued to reflect the insecurity within the religious community and the general belief that the fair would mark in some way the beginning of a new era, a reestablishment of Christian values and ideals. Beginning almost as soon as the world's fair opened in May 1893, the term "New Jerusalem" began to be used to describe the visitor's first impressions, especially of the grand and formal Court of Honor.[14] "Words fail. The magic splendor of that sight can never be excelled on earth. Will the new Jerusalem be fairer?" asked a kindergarten teacher from Kankakee.[15]

Professor William James of Harvard, a student himself of religious phenomena, on returning to Boston from abroad during the late summer of 1893 heard of the popular reaction to the fair. "Everyone says one ought to sell all one has and mortgage one's soul to go there," he wrote to his brother Henry in England, "it is esteemed such a revelation of beauty. People cast away all sin and baseness, burst into tears and grow religious, etc. under its influence!"[16] Why the exposition, and especially the Court of Honor, should have had this affect was perhaps best explained by the architect Henry Van Brunt, designer of one of the court's buildings: "When the visitor enters the great Court, he will find himself cloistered as no scholar was cloistered before. No philosopher or disciple of the Academy ever walked and meditated in such porches. The great Basin in the midst, with its tributary canals, the terraces and balustrades which surround it, the statues, the monumental fountains, the vases, the bridges, the standards, the rostral columns, the gardens, the kiosks and shelters, are arranged to show that order is heaven's first law."[17] For many Americans, order and harmony were so little a part of their daily experience that even an artificial and archaic symbolic manifestation of those qualities seemed "heavenly."

Religious interest in the World's Columbian Exposition was not, however, focused only upon the "divinely" classical Court of Honor and the Sunday question. The World's Congress Auxiliary, whose official motto was Not Matter, But Mind; Not Things, But Men, had organized a Department of Religion under the direction of Reverend Barrows and other representatives of Chicago's largest demoninations, and had assigned them the last month and a half of the fair to hold their conferences. Beginning on August 27 and continuing until October 15, forty-five general divisions of the department representing nearly every religious denomination in the United States held separate congresses of their members. The culminating event, however, and one of the most extraordinary of the entire program of the World's Congress Auxiliary, was the World's Parliament of Religions, which began on September 11 and lasted seventeen days.

It seemed a fitting end to the World's Columbian Exposition to bring the representatives of the world's great religions together in a grand ecumenical conference which would proclaim to the world that the united forces of religion stood rallied against the disintegrating material forces of the age. Nearly three thousand men and women representatives of the world's religions assembled in Chicago in September to hear Barrows announce their purpose: "We are not here as Baptists and Buddhists, Catholics and Confucians, Parsees and Presbyterian Protestants, Methodists and Moslems; we are here as members of a Parliament of Religions, over which flies no sectarian flag, which is to be stampeded by no sectarian war-cries, but where for the first time in a large council is lifted up the banner of love, fellowship, brotherhood."[18] The ideals of peace, harmony, international brotherhood, and religious tolerance were admirable, perhaps even remarkable, goals to be held up in the latter nineteenth century. Several American Christian leaders, however, had expressed grave concern about inviting representatives of "heathen" sects to speak about their faiths on American soil, and, indeed, there were those who felt that the whole parliament had injured Christianity and encouraged agnosticism.[19]

The underlying purpose of the parliament was not so much to spread knowledge of the different beliefs of the world's religions and develop a toleration and respect for those differences as it was to demonstrate, by presenting a unified front, the continuing relevance of religious leadership in human progress. "There is a general unanimity of applause," Dr. Barrows had said a year before the parliament opened, "that religion shall in some conspicuous way, in this age of materialistic pride, assert its kingship over human life."[20] "It was an unspoken but sublime protest against materialism," George Dana Boardman told the Philadelphia Conference of Baptist Ministers on October 23, 1893. "It was

not one form of religion against another," but an attempt "to array (if possible) all religions against the irreligious."[21] "No wonder," he concluded, "that at our closing session we felt that the day of Pentecost had come again, and that we sang Handel's Hallelujah Chorus."[22]

The Department of Religion was just one of twenty different departments of the World's Fair Congress Auxiliary which, it was hoped, would be collectively "associated in history with the greatest intellectual uplift of the ages."[23] In all over seven hundred thousand participants were drawn to the newly completed (and classically designed) Art Institute on the lake front to reaffirm the continuing role of ideas in human affairs.[24] The aim of the auxiliary, wrote the president and chief organizer Charles C. Bonney in 1891, was to promote "the progress, prosperity, unity, peace, and happiness of the world," and the controlling purpose was to "bring all of the departments of progress into harmonious relation with each other, to the end that the utmost attainable completeness and unity may characterize the World's Congresses of 1893, without materially impairing the distinctive characteristics of the various contributions to the marvelous progress of the nineteenth century."[25] The congresses, which were, as Neufeld emphasizes, an extraordinary organizational achievement, were to give all varieties of thought the equal right and equal opportunity to be heard, and yet to be governed by strict regulations that forbade open debate, volunteer addresses, or random discussions. "Controversy was prohibited and the passing of resolutions of approval or censure was forbidden."[26] All differences of opinion or conflict of ideas was apparently expected to be contained, controlled, and subsumed within the overriding concern for harmony and peace. "A new age has dawned," declared Bonney at the opening on May 15, 1893. "A new leader has taken command. The name of this leader is Peace."[27]

Although the themes of peace, harmony and control through educational uplift pervaded the world's congresses overall, individually considered they brought together a remarkable number of American thinkers, educators, reformers, writers, and social leaders, and it is unfortunate that a complete record of the papers and proceedings was never assembled. Nevertheless, from the records which do exist it is possible to gain some sense of the major questions which were addressed.[28]

The Department of Education held its congresses during the last two weeks in July, the most interesting of which was the three day International Congress on Education under the general supervision of the National Education Association. William T. Harris, U.S. Commissioner of Education, was in charge, and the various sessions were presided over by the presidents of Michigan University, Johns Hopkins, MIT, Princeton, and Clark. The congress heard presentations on all levels of education, from kindergarten to the university, on instruction techniques and teacher training, educational publications, and the application of "rational" and experimental psychology to education. The most important topic considered seems to have been the place of industrial, technological, and business education. Professor Woodrow Wilson of Princeton presented a paper entitled "To what Extent Should an Antecedent Liberal Education be required of Students of Law, Medicine, and Theology?" in which he argued in favor of general, liberal education and deplored the loss of synthesis in knowledge. "This new ignorance," he said of the specialization tendencies in higher education, "which likes knowledge piecemeal and in weak solution, has created a feudal system of learning."[29] The trend toward technical education had been growing in America for several years and reformists had argued that the American curriculum didn't train individuals to live in the "real" world. Another reason put forward at the congresses, according to Neufeld, was that 1893 and the Columbian Exposition signalled the entry of America into the competition for world markets and Americans needed to keep ahead.[30]

Technical education was also seen as a way of attacking the current problems of poverty and unemployment. A major focus of this question centered on the controversy over requiring Greek and Latin for the bachelor's degree in American universities. President Jordan of Stanford and Charles Francis Adams argued for eliminating such requirements, while several others feared that the current trend would lead to the growth of specialization and applied science as opposed to liberal education (art, philosophy, and science).[31] The congress also heard papers by such eminent American educators as Josiah Royce of Harvard, James McCosh of Princeton, Timothy Dwight of Yale, Seth Low of Columbia, and G. Stanley Hall.[32]

Another revealing confrontation took place in the Congress of Authors on July 13, when Hamlin Garland, whose grim tales of contemporary rural life had begun to make a name for him, read a paper on "Local Color in Fiction," which challenged an earlier paper by the very popular romance writer Mary Hartwell Catherwood. Eugene Field, writing in the Chicago *Daily News*, found the realistic/romantic conflict interesting and amusing enough to devote several of his columns to it. Both Garland and Mrs. Catherwood responded to Field with good humor, but Mrs. Catherwood exposed Garland's weak spot, his denial of tradition, in her insistence that the high authority of the past be cherished and recaptured in order to give America a model for developing the necessary forms for a cultured society. Garland couldn't share her adulation of seventeenth century France, but he was sensitive to the need to find the meaning of "Americanism," and his writing after 1893 came more and more to reflect his desire to recapture and recreate in romantic terms an American pioneer past. The Congress of Authors was the beginning of what Larzer Ziff has called the "domestication" of Hamlin Garland.[33]

A similar note of disagreement was sounded in the Congress of Architects in August. The congress, as might be expected, was dominated by discussions and expressions of admiration for the achievements of the exposition, and Burnham and Olmsted provided the key addresses. But at the last session, Louis Sullivan spoke on the use of polychrome in the design of buildings, "a subject which, in the face of the whitewashed *cour d'honneur*," as Hoffman notes, "posed basic questions." Sullivan argued that form could emerge organically from simple geometric figures and that Americans, as Americans and not Greeks, should develop their own styles and avoid what he called the "pure perversion" of classical imitation.[34] If the World's Columbian Exposition marked the beginning of the "domestication" of Hamlin Garland, for Sullivan it marked, as he himself later bitterly saw it, the beginning of his professional and personal decline.

Other congresses held during the summer of 1893 also reflected a desire to find a controlling principle or method for the profound insecurity of the period and for finding a suitable replacement for the old order whose end was symbolized by the fair itself. In the Philosophy Congress, for instance, while John Dewey spoke of the need for "Reconciliation of Science and Philosophy" and Josiah Royce delivered a paper on "The Twofold Nature of Knowledge," one speaker declared that "we must educate the masses or go to the wall."[35] At the Congress on Evolution (which heard a paper by Herbert Spencer), James A Skelton, in a speech which paralleled the famous address by Frederick Jackson Turner (to the Historical Congress) on "The Significance of the Frontier in American History," said that "this westward march of empire and freedom during the ages comes to an abrupt end.... The Columbian Exposition of 1893 celebrates both the beginning and the end of the Columbian epoch of characteristic modern Western Civilization and the beginning of a new epoch, in which the race is again to be tested."[36]

Henry George, Hamlin Garland, and Edward Everett Hale in the Social and Economic Department sessions spoke for profit sharing, single tax, and public ownership as possible ways of creating a new, more equitable social order, and in the process revealed their hostility to the rise of giant private corporations and monopolies. The need for civil service reform, more uniformity and codification in the law, and greater control over municipal administration were cited as pressing issues in the Congress on Government. In the congresses organized under the Department of Moral and Social Reform, there was a perceptible emphasis upon the need to apply new

social science principles to bring order and effectiveness to the organization and administration of social and charity work. And yet the attitudes expressed toward society's poor and unfortunate seemed split between fear or hatred and paternalistic affection, and suggestions such as encouraging the poor and unemployed to save more money were loudly cheered.[37]

A problem of immediate and pressing public concern focused unusual interest on the Labor Congress, which held its sessions during the week of August 28. Although the influx of people, money, and activity in Chicago had mediated somewhat the effects of the depression of 1893 for local workers, the public was becoming alarmed about the growing number of visibly unemployed tramping the streets. On the afternoon of the twenty-sixth, a fight broke out between police and a score of unemployed workers who had attempted to parade past city hall. Joseph Medill's *Tribune*, which was always careful to distinguish the orderly, decent American workers from the troublemakers, declared that Mayor Harrison was too permissive to be able to handle the present dangerous situation. "It is astonishing," said an editorial, "in view of what happened in 1886, that he, in his insane craze for the praise and cheers of loafers, tramps, black-flag anarchists, and red-flag socialists should have allowed the busy thoroughfares of the business center of the city to be blockaded and occupied by processions of anarchists, agitators, and ruffians pretending that they wanted work."[38] In response to such public pressure, Mayor Harrison directed his police chief to restrict further parading by workers, and more trouble occurred when the police so informed a large crowd which had assembled on the lake front on the twenty-eighth.

In the midst of this charged atmosphere, the Labor Congress opened its first session on the morning of August 30. Local labor leaders had been urging that the sessions be held out-of-doors to accommodate more people, and Mayor Harrison had given his permission for a meeting that afternoon on the lake front. Two hundred members of the Chicago Carpenter's Union had volunteered to assist the police in preserving order during the rally. The afternoon session of the Labor Congress was therefore shifted to the lake front, where twenty-five thousand union and nonunion workers gathered to hear Henry George, Samuel Gompers, Bishop Fallows, Clarence Darrow, Kate Field, Eva Valesh, and Thomas Morgan speak against the evils of concentrated wealth, monopoly, and unemployment.

Henry George argued for the single tax, Gompers advised patience, perseverance and public works, Bishop Fallows urged greater unionization and the use of the ballot as a means of reform, and Morgan said that violence was hopeless. Only Eva Valesh of St. Paul went so far as to suggest that the present economic system was intolerable and that violence might result. Overall, however, the speakers at the rally on the thirtieth (as in all the sessions of the Labor Congress) expressed cautious optimism and advised peaceful reform, and the effect upon both the public and the workers of the six-day congress seemed to be to diffuse, for the moment, what had appeared a dangerously explosive situation.[39] The immediate seriousness of the situation and the need for reform were made abundantly clear during the congress, and many suggestions for correction or improvement were offered, but even more obvious was a deep-seated cultural insecurity which made it possible to advocate reform only in terms of assurances that basically the culture (however one chooses to define it) was all right. Although there was evidence of a growing recognition and concern over social problems, especially those related to the deteriorating economic condition of the society, the Labor Congress failed to attract as many people or as much attention outside Chicago as did the Congress on Education or the sessions of the Department of Religion. Actually, the great Parliament of Religions had only one near rival in the summer of 1893, and that was the World's Congress of Representative Women, held as a division of the unique Department of Women's Progress.

The participation of women as a separate group within the World's Congress Auxiliary followed closely upon the official acceptance of an important role for women in the fair as a whole, symbolized by the Board of Lady Managers of the exposition. As a complement to the material exhibits of woman's progress which were being organized especially for the Women's Building, a number of the national women's clubs and organizations began to apply to President Bonney of the Congress Auxiliary for permission to hold their meetings as part of the world's congress. Bonney was agreeable not only to women holding separate congresses but also to their participation in any of the other congresses being planned which would be "suitable," and he assigned the first week after opening day to the Department of Woman's Progress.[40] Subsequently, over twenty separate women's groups (the YWCA, and DAR, the National Council of Women, the American Federation of Women's Clubs, and the Order of the Eastern Star among them) were authorized to hold meetings of their national membership during the week. The culmination of the department's activities was the general World's Congress of Representative Women, which began on May 15 and lasted throughout the week and which was intended to set forth the progress of women in education, industry, literature, art, moral and social reform, government, and religion.

May Wright Sewell, president of the National Council of Women of the United States, was chosen as chairman of the congress, and through her efforts and the cooperation of the International Council of Women, which decided to hold its 1893 meeting at the fair, an advisory council of 528 women representing twenty-seven different countries was established (209 of whom served as official representatives of established women's organizations).[41] Eighty-one meetings were held in the Art Institute and the Women's Building during the week, and at times there were as many as eighteen sessions in simultaneous progress. Three hundred and thirty women read papers or addressed the congress, whose total attendance exceeded one hundred fifty thousand people (on several occasions more people tried to hear the proceedings than the rooms assigned could accommodate).[42] Women's position, history, and potential in industry, government, science, education, and literature and the arts were discussed, and the evils of the double standard, prostitution, impurity, and intemperance were pointed out. Lucy Stone, in one of the last addresses of her life, spoke on "The Progress of Fifty Years" of the American woman; Jane Addams presented a comparison between household work and factory work as an occupation; Elizabeth Cady Stanton argued "The Ethics of Suffrage"; and Susan B. Anthony talked of the disparity between "Woman's Influence and Political Power."[43] Throughout the congress the dual themes of reform and women's solidarity were continually stressed, not only to better the conditions and opportunities for women, but as preconditions to solving the country's and world's problems. Nevertheless, at the time, the women's activities, the Parliament of Religions, and the world's congresses were as the French commissioner saw them, outstanding efforts of the World's Columbian Exposition in the realm of ideals.[44]

13
The Exhibits

While the nation's magazines and newspapers gave primary attention to the moral and educational aspects of the fair's architecture, decoration, women's activities, and congresses, and while visitors marvelled at the grandeur and harmony of the visual display, many novel and significant individual exhibits, which would have provoked considerable critical attention at earlier world's fairs, were generally overlooked. To the general visitor, the sixty-five thousand exhibits collected at Jackson Park were so numerous as to be overwhelming and so most people "preferred to view the scene of beauty by day or night from the outside, and to glance hurriedly at what was within."[1]

Rather than in the extensive display of agricultural machines or mining equipment, the first public exhibit of the work of the nation's new agricultural experiment stations (created by the Hatch Act of 1887), or Gifford Pinchot's Biltmore forestry exhibit,[2] representatives of the American agrarian tradition felt a general pride in the more than forty-five acres of exhibits devoted to them, and in the heroic pioneer farmer and domestic animal sculptures prominently placed about the grounds. The most popular exhibits in the giant Hall of Agriculture were not the model agricultural schools, or the agricultural implements of the big farming corporations, but an eleven-ton cheese from Ontario, a 1,500-pound chocolate Venus de Milo from New York, and Brinker's cotton bale exhibit—where miniature cotton bales done up in silk and satin and brass could be purchased as souvenirs from the old ex-slaves who had grown the cotton in 1863.

This pattern seems also to have been true for the exhibits in the Manufactures and Liberal Arts Building (where the American Bible Society and the charity displays were more often noted than Yerke's telescope, the printing presses, or the Roebling Wire Company [builders of the Brooklyn Bridge] exhibit), in the Electricity Building (where Edison's kinetograph, a primitive "talkie," was obscured by the impressive seventy-foot-high tower of light bulbs), or in the Transportation Building (where the Town of Pullman's "Ideal of Industry" exhibit drew more attention than the Otis elevators). Machinery Hall, with its collection of gas engines, turbines, dynamos, and textile, meatpacking and woodworking machinery was simply too complicated and extensive to have received anything but a generalized interpretation as "progress."[3] In the Palace of Fine Arts, the seventy-four galleries of sculpture and paintings (over nine thousand) from Europe and the United States made it nearly impossible to locate any particular work, in spite of the division into nationalities and the extensive cataloging. "Sculpture, painting, drawing, carving, engraving, are all collected in the art galleries to bewilder with wild admiration the hasty visitor," wrote Mulj Devji Vedant, an Indian visitor, ". . . till, 'tired with all these, from these he will be gone' to find himself the same lonely man."[4] Discerning any new movements in the arts was impossible in this situation. The small collection of French Impressionists was overwhelmed by the academic tone of the grand military, historical and mythological romantic allegories, "the inevitable Madeline Lemaire, the inescapable Detat-Ponsan, the 'Wasp's Nest' of William Bouguereau, lent by Charles Yerkes."[5] Significantly, the "declared" masterpiece of the exposition was not found within the Fine Arts Palace at all; it was the building itself.

The most severely Greek of any of the buildings on the grounds, topped with a giant "Winged Victory," the Fine Arts Palace appeared to the English journalist George Warrington Stevens "surely as divinely proportioned an edifice as ever filled and satisfied the eye of man."[6] Before his death, John Root had begun planning the art building, but afterwards it was given to Charles Atwood, whose design, although pleasing Burnham and St. Gaudens, was publicly criticized as being plagiarized from a French artist's 1866 *Prix de Rome* project. Atwood defended himself by arguing that "in my design I recurred to the model of the Erechtheum" and even "sent a man all the way to Boston to measure the plaster cast of the Erechtheum in order that I might follow it without any mistake."[7] "It produced nevertheless," said French Commissioner Bruwaert, "an excellent effect, and for an American who has not yet had either the time or the money to go to Europe, the surprise and the pleasure are equally great."[8]

The state exhibits, which were assembled for the exposition and which were displayed in individual state buildings, tended to emphasize historical, archaeological, and anthropological themes as well as particular state products and industries. The efforts of state women's committees were especially conspicuous in decoration and furnishing (the construction of the Arkansas Building was entirely designed and supervised by women of the state), and exhibits of women's progress, state education, and artistic accomplishments were also common. The Louisiana Building contained a Creole kitchen, antebellum style, complete with "snowily turbaned and aproned colored cooks and waiters, and superintended by young ladies of Caucasian blood, representing the beauty and hospitality of that Grand Commonwealth."[9] Most of the state buildings followed the neoclassical style, or traditional colonial, but several had a local or national historical character. Florida's, for instance, was a reproduction of Old Fort Marion in St. Augustine; Virginia built a replica of Mount Vernon; and Massachusetts followed the design of the John Hancock home on Beacon Hill.

The United States Government presented an impressive display which, including a large "modern Renaissance" Government Building (judged a disaster by most critics), eventually cost $1.25 million.[10] In addition to the exhibits by the various departments of the government housed in the main building, the Smithsonian Institution, an army field hospital, a weather observatory, and a model lifesaving station were allotted space on the grounds. Most popular of all, however, was the replica of the battleship *Illinois* constructed on pilings in the harbor and fully equipped and manned by uniformed sailors.[11] The Bureau of Indian Affairs and the Ethnological Bureau prepared extensive exhibits for the Government Building on Indian customs and life in North and South America, in which visitors could see contrasted "the red man as a savage wrapped in a blanket, and his child in the dress of civilization, endeavoring to master benignant mysteries."[12] Richard Henry Pratt, founder and builder of the experimental Carlisle Indian School in Pennsylvania, had rejected in 1891 an official offer to take charge of the exhibit because he considered it "contrived by the two government bureaus [as] calculated to keep the nation's attention and the Indian's energies fixed upon his valueless past, through the spectacular aboriginal housing, dressing, and curio employments it instituted."[13] He urged the commission to avoid "anything like an aboriginal and wild west feature," pointing out that Buffalo Bill would already do that, and when it looked like the exhibits were planned to show the Indian as unsuitable for full citizenship, he decided to have Carlisle make its own exhibit, demonstrative of the Indian as a fully capable American citizen.[14] Pratt believed, and perhaps correctly, that the heavy emphasis on ethnicity in the anthropological displays on the main fairgrounds, and especially on the Midway (not only Indians, but Eskimos, Egyptians, Africans, etc.), was designed to demonstrate the primitiveness of nonwhite (nonEuropean) cultures so that there would be no confusion about who was and who was not inherently a true, "civilized" American.

The importance of the question of ethnicity, or race, appeared not just in the divergence of opinion about the American Indian's image or in the frequently expressed demand for a selective immigration policy based on race or ethnic background, but also in the debate and final policy concerning participation in the world's fair by black Americans. When the initial suggestions for an exposition of Ameri-

can progress were first being discussed, black leaders and many white supporters viewed the fair as an opportunity to show, through representation in the administration and in the exhibits to be displayed, how far Afro-Americans had progressed since emancipation. Black spokesmen were split at first, just as the women had been, between those who thought that there should be a separate building or department for Negro exhibits and those who wanted the exhibits spread throughout the other departments without distinction by color. The question that was raised, integration versus separation, is of course a major continuing issue in the Afro-American experience, but in the 1890s—at least so far as the World's Columbian Exposition was concerned—the dispute was settled not by black Americans, but for them.

Disregarding the numerous petitions sent both to him and to Congress, President Harrison refused to appoint any blacks to the 208-member National Commission. Similar applications sent to Director-General Davis to appoint a capable black American to some representative capacity in the exposition were also denied. Exclusion of Afro-Americans from any directive responsibility also extended to the Woman's Department, where petitions by two different groups of black women for recognition by the Board of Lady Managers were ignored.[15] Not only were black Americans refused participation in the directing energies of the exposition, they were also quietly denied positions in the construction, administration, or operation of the fair except as menials. Only one black ever received a clerical position, and none was allowed into the prestigious Columbian Guard.

With the realization that there was little hope for active participation by blacks in the world's fair, appeals were made to Congress for an appropriation to finance a comprehensive statistical exhibit of the economic and educational growth of the American Negro, and fair officials were petitioned for space to present Afro-American exhibits. Congress never acted on the requests and the directors of the fair remained firm in their decision that all such displays had to be submitted to state committees. Since these were composed of whites, it meant the "effective exclusion of Negro exhibits."[16] In the end, the only Afro-American exhibit at the World's Columbian Exposition was that provided by Hampton Institute, which was included as part of the U.S. Department of Education's display in the Manufactures and Liberal Arts Building.[17]

In a remarkable pamphlet published privately during the fair by Ida Wells, F. L. Barnett noted the extreme irony in the world's fair officials designating August 25 as "Colored People's Day,"[18] and Frederick Douglass asserted that "to the colored people of America, morally speaking, the World's Fair now in progress is . . ∴ a whited sepulcher."[19] America was posing before the world as a highly liberal and civilized nation, he said, and has brought a greater variety of mankind here than ever before. But "as if to shame the Negro, the Dahomians [an African tribe exhibited on the Midway] are also here to exhibit the Negro as a repulsive savage."[20] Whether or not the ethnic exhibits assembled along the Midway tended to convey a genuine cosmopolitanism, as the original planners had hoped, or actually encouraged viewers to look upon people of color as irredeemably barbaric and degraded in the scale of human evolution, as both Pratt and Douglass believed, they were, along with other popular entertainment features and concessions of the Midway, a major factor in the rising attendance figures which the world's fair enjoyed beginning in late June.

14
The Midway

Construction on the Midway had suffered some of the worst delays of any part of the fair, and by the time it was in full operation at the end of June, the fair's management had effectively given up—under financial pressure—all expectations of a "dignified and decorous" ethnological display under the control of Professor Putnam. There was, to be sure, a serious ethnological exhibit on the Midway, but very few of the two million people who crammed into the trained animal theater to see Hagenbeck's lions, tigers, and elephants ever went up to the second floor to see it.[1] The heavy messages, so inescapable in the main section of the exposition, gave way in the confusing hodge-podge of peoples, races, languages, entertainments, shops, restaurants, and architecture of the Midway to a more spontaneous kind of amusement. And for many

people it was undoubtedly a relief to pass from the Court of Honor to the "Streets of Cairo," with its sixty shops, its replica of a Moslem mosque, its camel and donkey rides, and its collection of Egyptians, Arabs, Sudanese, and Africans—all in native costume and all shouting come-ons in their native languages.[2]

In addition to the Cairo concession, which was operated by an Egyptian banker, the exotic entertainments included Persian, Japanese, and Indian (India) bazaars, a Moorish palace, a Chinese village and Sol Bloom's Algerian and Tunisian village, which included a Bedouin tent village, a Moorish cafe, and a "concert" hall for musical, juggling, and dancing performances. The North African dancing girls in the Algerian and Egyptian theaters drew the most attention during the summer for their speciality, the *danse du ventre.* As Bloom recalled: "When the public learned that the literal translation was 'belly dance' they delightedly concluded that it must be salacious and immoral. The crowds poured in. I had a gold mine."[3] Like many another woman who had to see what the men were so excited about, Mrs. D. C. Taylor marched into the Algerian theater, only to leave, as she said, singing "My Country 'tis of Thee" to herself.[4]

Not only were exciting Oriental, North African, and Middle Eastern concessions presented along the Midway, but several European cultural exhibits were also popular. There were German and Austrian villages with restaurants and shops staffed by their respective nationals in national dress, a Hungarian "Orpheum" or cafe providing music by Paul Olah's Gypsy Band, and a French cider press pavilion showing how French peasants made apple cider which was then served by country maids from Normandy. Perhaps the most extensive national display on the Midway was that of Ireland, under the charge of Lady Aberdeen, which included a model industrial village in which home industries such as lace and linen making were carried on. There was also an Irish museum, a model village store, a giant statue of Gladstone, a model of the ruins of Donegal Castle, and most importantly, a model of Blarney Castle (where, for a price, one could kiss a piece of Chicago sidewalk that passed for the Blarney Stone).

There was a giant mural panorama of the Swiss Alps (500 feet by 65 feet), models of the Blue Grotto of Capri, St. Peters in Rome, the Eiffel Tower, a Hawaiian volcano, and a Colorado gold mine, and an international beauty show. Libby Glass Company of Toledo, Ohio, and a separate group of Italian artisans demonstrated the arts of spinning and blowing glass. A preview of the motion picture was presented in the zoopraxiscope exhibit of animal locomotion. And the Pennsylvania Women's Auxiliary produced an inexpensive but comfortable model workingman's home. E. R. Johnson of Fall Brook, California, operated an ostrich farm of twenty-eight birds where visitors could enjoy the rare experience of eating an ostrich omelet, and Fleishmann's Yeast Company engaged

Jim Corbett to give demonstrations of how he had defeated the great John L. Sullivan.[5]

The more authentic ethnic displays included the Dohamony village, where one hundred native Africans demonstrated their domestic, religious, and marital customs; Sitting-Bull's Cabin, with a sign which read "War Dances Given Daily"; a Lapland village complete with reindeer; and a Dutch settlement which presented a number of typical South Sea island villages originally discovered by the Dutch. None of these, however, or any of the other attractions on the Midway, were as popular as the captive balloon ride, a facsimile of the one used at Paris that carried passengers 1,500 feet above the fairgrounds, and the great Ferris wheel, which became to the World's Columbian Exposition what the Eiffel Tower was to the Paris exposition of 1889.

Built by George Washington Gale Ferris, head of a large bridge-building concern in Pittsburgh, the 264-foot wheel dominated all the surrounding buildings, including the domes of the exhibition halls on the main grounds. It was the most popular attraction of the entire exposition. "No single enterprise on the Midway or the grounds proper [the Midway was apparently the grounds improper!] approached it either in patronage or in wonderment."[6] Actually, Ferris' wheel was two wheels, each 264 feet in diameter, between which thirty-six cars, each larger than a Pullman coach and capable of holding sixty persons, were suspended. When fully loaded, it could carry 2,160 people. The wheel rotated on an axle forty-five feel long and nearly a yard in diameter—the largest single piece of steel ever forged—and was supported by two great steel skeletal towers of such strength that the constructing engineers claimed it could easily withstand winds of one hundred miles an hour.[7] When put into operation, a two thousand horsepower engine moved the great wheel at the speed of one complete revolution every ten minutes. "What next?" asked Denton Snider. "Shall we not in time be able to invade the lunar territory."[8]

Perhaps the unrestrained carnival atmosphere of the Midway Plaisance provided a much needed escape from the harsh realities of daily living, or perhaps, it provided a patently un-selfconscious, eclectic, and noisy relief from the idealism of progress and unity so pervasive elsewhere on the fairgrounds. In any case, millions of Americans came and enjoyed them-selves at the Midway and, for many of them, it was the memory of their experiences there that they most cherished. Americans, and especially Chicagoans, it was said, had allowed themselves little time in their all-consuming desire to get ahead and to build up their country either for the develop-ment of a truly "cultivated" society or for simple enjoyment. The Midway, some observers thought, taught America to be joyously merry. "The first time that America turned out for an unrestrained good time was in Chicago; and that properly gives the city a strong claim to distinction as well as to grati-tude."[9]

The Midway, the decision of the management to "popu-larize" the fair, the newspaper and magazine reports, and bet-ter weather all contributed to the steady increase in attend-ance following the initial disappointment of May. June's figures were more than two and a half times those of the month before. July showed a considerably smaller increase, but attendance surged in August to over 3.5 million paid visitors, and the people continued to come. In September, the total reached over 4.5 million, and in the last month of the fair, 6,818,864 persons passed through the turnstiles, 30 per-cent more than came to Paris during its best month.[10] During the last three months of the exposition, it became more nearly "a World's Fair for the rich and the poor."[11] Most new immi-grants, migrants, blacks, and a large portion of the laboring classes were economically excluded from coming to Chicago to see the world's fair (the fifty-cent admission fee was itself re-strictive), but numerous associations, group excursions, and package plans developed by the railroads did enable a signifi-cant number of people of limited means to attend. Others, especially midwesterners, spent their life savings and even mortgaged their land to raise money for the trip.[12]

When the World's Columbian Exposition of 1893 finally closed on October 31, over 21.5 million paid admissions had been registered. Allowing for those who came more than once, the foreign visitors, and the several million free passes issued, it is probably a fair estimate that between 5 and 10 percent of the population of the United States actually visited the fair.[13] And considering the extensive coverage the fair received in all avenues of the popular media, it was a rare American who escaped at least some exposure to the celebration in Chicago in 1893. The fitting climax came on October 9, Chicago Day, when 716,881 people crowded into Jackson Park. "Each feature of the program except the fireworks was rendered al-most impossible by the masses of people who were everywhere about the grounds."[14] The following day, Ferdinand W. Peck and Anthony Seeberger carried a check for $1.5 million to the Illinois Trust and Savings Company which liquidated the last debts held against the Chicago Company.[15] Although a final financial assessment of the entire enterprise can only be esti-mated (see Appendix H), the Chicago Company did emerge with a small surplus to repay its private investors. The fact that it was able to do so, especially during a severe depression, and was able to collect all but 7 percent of the total subscribed stock, was a genuine triumph. Perhaps it was, as it was then thought to be, the greatest measure of the character of Chi-cago itself. Few cities have been able, before or since, to boast that they had their great world's fair and made it pay besides.

Part Four:
THE CULTURE

The great Fair was indeed a superb and appropriate symbol of our great nation, in its noble general design and in the inequalities of its execution; in its unexampled display of industrial energy and practical capacity; in the absence of the higher works of the creative imagination; in its incongruities, its mingling of noble realities and ignoble pretences, in its refinements cheek-by-jowl with vulgarities, in its order and its confusion—in its heterogeneousness and in its unity.

Charles Eliot Norton

15

Achievement and Influence

As with all the great world's fairs, the actual consequences of the World's Columbian Exposition of 1893 are difficult to assess accurately. So much was expected and so much attention was focused upon it, that it is not surprising that many extravagant claims have been made for the fair's impact on the national culture, for good and for ill.

Widespread admiration was expressed for American technology, factory management, inventiveness, organization, mass production, and especially for the extensive and novel uses of electricity. Foreign visitors were also impressed by the short hours and high pay of American workers and by the apparent importance attached to women in industry and the arts. Several European nations (France, Germany, and Great Britain especially) were represented by notable displays of their products and skills, but the contrast with the American exhibits overall was not as great as at the Philadelphia Centennial seventeen years earlier, and in the mechanical arts and sciences the United States was shown to have no superiors. The fair appeared in this sense a "triumphant celebration" of the age of the machine, and it did stimulate American entrance into the international commerce in goods on a more extensive scale than ever before.[1] "It is a well known fact," wrote Ferdinand Peck in 1899, "that more American firms have been able to form connections abroad and extend their foreign trade since 1893 than ever before, and to the Columbian Exposition might easily be traced the beginning of negotiations which have led to the closing of many recent large orders for American goods."[2] According to Joseph Rogers, the world's fair showed that "the American does things more quickly and more cheaply than any other nation on earth; and, as this is an unsentimental age, it is natural that he should get the trade from all over the world."[3] Agricultural and mining exhibits also stimulated interest at home and abroad, and led to greater economic investment and development of these industries. Oregon's exhibit, for instance, was so impressive that "inquiries from fruit dealers all over the United States multiplied tenfold," and the state's fruit industry expanded continuously thereafter.[4]

As in all previous fairs, new sales did not compensate every individual exhibitor for the expense of his display, and a few even came to financial ruin because of their overoptimism. A great many, however, found their investments rewarded. Indirectly, the world's fair stimulated new technological achievements, not only in electricity but in transportation as well. It also provided a popular boost to the careers of such show business personalities as Lillian Russell, who led her own company at the Columbia Theater downtown, and Florenz Ziegfeld, Jr., who had originally been commissioned by the fair to recruit military bands in Europe, but who began his first musical comedy revue instead.[5]

While the congresses of the sciences, social sciences, arts, religion and education demonstrated, as Merle Curti says, "great strides in American learning and scholarship," the great hopes for their widespread impact on the intellectual and cultural life both of the United States and of the world were largely unrealized.[6] The World Peace Congress especially, but also the association of various nations and states in the enterprise as a whole, gave rise to hopes that the exposition would be a positive agent for fostering international cooperation and brotherhood and even, eventually, an international confederacy.[7] The utopianism of all such visions, in 1893 at a world's fair, was made clear by the ominous presence of the American battleship and the largest military cannon ever cast, a display of the Krupp Iron Works of Essen, Germany.[8] "The objects which tend to increase the material happiness of human beings," remarked an Indian delegate, "are

not unaccompanied by others calculated to destroy human beings themselves and all their works in a twinkling. Steel armor plates and breech-loading guns of enormous sizes and powers stare at you with their ominous looks, and inform you that the present civilization has not been successful in abolishing the profession of freebooters, because instead of small associations we have large ones each of which consists of one nation or more. The innocent Siamese or the ignorant African, the red Indian or the passive Hindu, is driven to accept one of two alternatives, either to give up the fruits of his labor or to end his existence, whenever lawless Might finds it pleasant to civilize its victims, under the shelter of the law that: 'They have no rights who cannot successfully maintain them.' "[9]

Many Americans who visited the exposition or read the reports about it, however, saw what they wanted to see: the emergence of the United States as a world power, the equal of any of the great imperial powers of the Old World. "One might say that the Centennial represented Uncle Sam as a strong man rejoicing to run a race; that the Chicago Fair showed him rich in the possession of power and potential wealth."[10] Rather than stimulating a true cosmopolitanism, as Henry Fuller and many others hoped, the Columbian celebrations encouraged more generally a growing spirit of nationalism and were at least partially responsible for the adoption of such patriotic rituals as Columbus Day (instituted originally in the public schools by the National Association of School Superintendents as a special day for reading patriotic essays, singing songs, and similar activities) and the Pledge of Allegiance.[11] "In many respects," wrote Oswald Garrison Villard in 1939, that exhibition "marked the coming of age of the United States."[12]

If the fair increased the sense of national pride within the country at large, for Chicagoans it had even greater significance. It changed the city's image and became a landmark in its history. Nearly every history of Chicago written since 1893 has regarded the Columbian Exposition as either the beginning or the end of an era. "Since 1893 Chicago ought never to be mentioned as Porkopolis," asserted a British visitor, "without a simultaneous reference to the fact that it was also the creator of the White City, with its Court of Honor, perhaps the most flawless and fairy-like creation on a large scale, of man's invention. . . . It will to all time remain impossibly ridiculous to speak of a country or a city as wholly given over to the worship of Mammon which almost involuntarily gave birth to this ethereal emanation of pure uneconomic beauty."[13] In the years before the exposition, Chicago had been certain that it was the most American city in the land and that it was destined to be the nation's greatest commercial and industrial center. It was sensitive, however, to the charge that it could never be truly great, anymore than a nation or a civilization could be, until it also developed as a center of art and letters and acquired the refinements of a cultured society and a broader civic spirit. The Columbian Exposition, it was hoped, would channel and direct the exuberant energy and vigor of commerce and agriculture toward cultivation and education in order to correct this imbalance, and there were many who have argued since that this was the fair's most significant accomplishment.

The world's fair of 1893, according to Bessie Pierce, began a new epoch in the aesthetic growth not only of Chicago but of the Midwest and the entire nation.[14] "The importance of the Columbian Exposition," echoed Harry Thurston Peck, "lay in the fact that it revealed to millions of Americans whose lives were necessarily colourless and narrow, the splendid possibilities of art, and the compelling power of the beautiful."[15] And indeed, following the exposition, there appeared in ever increasing numbers, especially in the Midwest, "study groups" and "art clubs" (even Hull House formed one), literary circles and culture societies "enough to gladden the hearts of the most ardent artistic missionaries and the most devoted handmaidens of the muses."[16] More specifically, the impulse for establishing an American Academy for the training of art students in Rome and the Field Museum of Natural History in Chicago can be traced to the exposition.[17] The most extensive claims for the positive influence of the fair,

however, have not been restricted simply to the quickening of American esthetic sensibilities, but involved a recognition of the relationship between art and city planning.

The White City not only inspired many people to return to their own homes and towns and make them beautiful, but, according to Charles Moore, "the impulse to plan American cities for unity, amenity, and beauty was born of the Exposition."[18] From this point of view, it could be said that the Columbian Exposition had a decidedly reformist influence, and there is little question that it was at least an indirect factor in the development of the "City Beautiful" movement, and in particular Daniel Burnham's 1907 plan for Chicago.[19] Nevertheless, it is probably a distortion to conclude that the world's fair was "an early chapter . . . in the record of the decline of laissez-faire as the dominent American philosophy," or to assume that it actually encouraged an objective appraisal of the new urban and industrial problems of the nation.[20] For most people, at the time, the dream-like White City was simply too far removed from the actuality of real city life and real city problems for its lessons to seem directly transferable in any practical way. It is curious, however, that both the exposition's greatest admirers and its bitterest critics have accepted the doubtful premise that the fair had a direct and powerful influence upon city planning and American civic architecture over the next twenty years. Thus, two divergent images of the results of the world's fair have emerged: one, that it was a precursor of progressivism and led to serious attempts to create real, positive, beautiful and harmonious cities; and two, that it encouraged mechanically frigid duplication of outmoded and irrelevant modes of civic architecture and fostered the "rapid succession of Roman temples and baths, Florentine villas and French palaces and Gothic churches and universities, to say nothing of office buildings which retained ill-chosen souvenirs from all these crumbled civilizations."[21]

Critics have been sharply divided in their explanations of why the American architects, when given their greatest public opportunity, should have elected a reactionary and academic neoclassism and ignored the new urban forms of Chicago itself. Some have held Daniel Burnham responsible for "selling out" to the "academicians of the East" out of envy and a sense of cultural inferiority.[22] Others have suggested that with the death of both Henry Hobson Richardson in 1886 and John Root in 1891, the major creative forces in American architecture were gone and a vacuum was created which was then filled by conservative easterners.[23] The tendency to overrate the influence of the exposition has created the necessity to find a villain, none of which can be supported historically, and to obscure the fact that the world's fair of 1893 was of far greater significance as a reflector of the general culture than as an influence upon it. This tendency can be seen most clearly in the criticism of Louis Sullivan, the central figure in the architectural and cultural condemnation of the Columbian Exposition.

Sullivan, like Root, was the more artistically imaginative partner of his architectural firm—Adler and Sullivan—which, in company with Burnham and Root, Holabird and Roche, and several others, was a major force in the tall building innovations that characterized the Chicago School in the eighties and nineties.[24] Of the more than one hundred buildings erected by Adler and Sullivan before the firm dissolved in 1895, the Auditorium and the exposition's Transportation Building most clearly reflected Sullivan's sense of functional design, his elaborate yet vital ornamentation, and his experimental approach to polychromatic coloration. Sullivan wanted his architecture to express the indigenous spirit of American culture which he saw, as Larzer Ziff points out, as "strident acceleration."[25]

During the height of his personal and professional success, before Adler retired from the profession, Sullivan led a conspicuously fashionable life, with a fine residence in Chicago, a cottage in Mississippi (his place in nature), membership in the Chicago Club, and a large collection of books, rugs, paintings, jade, and tapestries.[26] Beginning in 1895, however, Sullivan's professional practice began to dwindle (chiefly because of a host of personal difficulties, including his well-

known arrogance and inability to get along with clients, and the severe depression-related contraction in the funds for new construction) until 1904, when he completed his last large commission. During the last twenty years of his life, when he was known primarily for a few small town bank buildings and his health and finances were deteriorating dramatically, he began writing long book-length exposés and became "less a critic and teacher and more a prophet and messiah."[27]

In 1922, Sullivan completed the *System of Architectural Ornament According with a Philosophy of Man's Power* and began his famous *Autobiography of An Idea*.[28] He finished the latter work in the last two years of his life, and in it he identified himself and his life with the career of the American democratic spirit. Since he then saw his own decline as having begun with the Columbian Exposition, he felt democracy itself betrayed by the failures of the dominant architecture of the fair:

> Thus Architecture died in the land of the free and the home of the brave,—in a land declaring its fervid democracy, its unique daring, enterprise and progress. Thus did the virus of a culture, snobbish and alien to the land, perform its work of disintegration; and thus ever works the pallid academic mind, denying the real, exalting the fictitious and the false, incapable of adjusting itself to the flow of living things, to the reality and the pathos of man's follies. . . . The damage wrought by the World's Fair will last for half a century from its date, if not longer. It has penetrated deep into the constitution of the American mind, effecting there lesions significant of dementia.[29]

The fair, Sullivan concluded, corrupted the American people, distorted their way of life, and destroyed their unique spirit. It handed over their trust in liberty to a feudal idea, which he personified in Daniel Burnham's passion for power. Burnham's career, not incidentally, had prospered while Sullivan's declined. "Within his system of thought," wrote Sherman Paul, "the Fair represented the Rhythm of Death, and when he spoke of a thought in decadence producing a form in decadence, the Fair was ever in his mind."[30] No critic, before or since, has matched the eloquent indictment of the *Autobiography,* but unfortunately, the followers and admirers of the "poet-seer of the Chicago School" have too often taken Sullivan's symbolic treatment of Burnham and the world's fair as literal description of their actual influence and relationship to him, American architecture, and American culture.

Actually, while Sullivan was directly involved in the artistic and architectural discussions that determined the final plan and design of the world's fair, there is no evidence whatever that he raised his voice in opposition before 1893.[31] According to that plan, only in the Court of Honor were the buildings controlled by the white neoclassic style, and in so far as Sullivan's Transportation Building was located on the lagoon he was free of stylistic restraints.[32] In his design for the building, Sullivan chose not to try to disguise the fact that it was a "great shed" meant to house transportation exhibits. The flat surfaces didn't look like marble and were enlivened by thirty shades of color and ornament.[33] Overall, the building itself has never been thought completely successful. The *Nation,* in August, 1893, called it a revelation of what the fair escaped by adopting the Renaissance style and prevailing whiteness elsewhere. "Up close the building is an entertaining salad of styles . . . but seen at a distance, all these details fail of effect, and the epithet 'shabby' applied to it by the London *Times* seems justified."[34] And Hugh Morrison, a more recent critic, has pointed out that the Transportation Building was by no means Sullivan's greatest work, nor did it—in terms of his career—indicate his passing greatness (his decline did not begin until several years later). Thus it "is not of such great import as the widespread familiarity with it and the popular notions of its place in Sullivan's career would suggest."[35] There was, however, a single isolated feature of the building— unrelated to the general scheme—which drew considerable national and international attention in 1893 and which one writer referred to as the "sphinx" of the fair because "it offers more problems and makes us ask more questions than we ask about anything else."[36]

For the central entrance to the building, Sullivan created a majestic composition of concentric arches, highly ornamented and gold-leafed throughout. Foreign visitors were much impressed with the boldness and originality of the design, which stood out in arrogant contrast to the familiar beaux-arts of the other buildings.[37] For most Americans, however, the golden gate to transportation had such a direct symbolic meaning that the artistic merits were of less concern.

Throughout the country's history, from its earliest beginnings, physical mobility—movement—had been associated with popular liberty and freedom and thus with the "golden" promise of the New World itself.[38] Transportation, the implements of mobility, meant more to the American people than simply the technology of minimizing distance. It was the means by which the American dream could be realized and it therefore became, and remains today, synonymous with that promise. In the nineteenth century, however, several major developments occurred that seemed to dramatically distort the meaning of these traditional cultural symbols. The first of these, before the Civil War, was the actual discovery of gold in California and the subsequent rush west, not for freedom, but for riches. (The material promise of wealth had always been present in the symbol of the West, but it had not heretofore seemed so blatant.) After the war, the nation's transportation systems (especially railroads and streetcars) expanded dramatically, but by the 1890s the results of that expansion seemed less to increase the freedom and prosperity of the many than to make millionaires out of a corrupt few, whose power appeared so great as to enslave the democracy itself.[39]

Sullivan's gilded gateway to the Transportation Building thus appeared to many Americans not as a symbol of American liberty, vitality and imagination, but as a symbol of the Gilded Age itself, their very antithesis. "The modern and realistic *rilievo* at the base of the Transportation Building," wrote H. C. Bunner in *Scribner's Monthly,* "does the completest justice to the Pullmancar end of our civilization."[40] It suggested the way the robber barons—Vanderbilt, Gould, Hill, Harriman, and J. P. Morgan—made their fortunes, and to one observer at least it even suggested how they spent them, in the "oriental opulence" of their private taste.[41] Critics looking back at the architecture of the fair from over the years have been puzzled by the white neoclassicism in the heart of the city where the modern problems of creating beautiful commercial buildings were first being solved, but for most Americans who saw it, the "sphinx of the fair" was Louis Sullivan's golden doorway.[42] While the White City probably had some influence on the popularity of classic forms in public and private architecture, it by no means introduced the trend nor was its effect as great as the followers of Sullivan have supposed.[43] There was no conspiracy by Daniel Burnham against

him, and the public was not tricked by a cabal of eastern reactionaries. It is more likely that the stylistic retreat in architecture, as unfortunate as it may have been, would have happened whether or not the dramatic display had occurred at Jackson Park.

As is true of the fair in general, the overall significance of the architecture does not lie in its influence upon the culture. Taken as a whole, the fair was not a major beacon to the future. In keeping with its nature as a Victorian institution, the Columbian Exposition is of greater importance as a reflector of the confusing variety and conflicting cultural patterns that characterized the period that Henry Steele Commager calls the "watershed of American history."[44]

16

A Confusion of Symbols

In response to the publicity surrounding the planning of the fair, James F. Muirhead was commissioned by the Baedecker publishing firm of Leipzig in the early nineties to tour the United States and write a handbook for foreign visitors. Although impressed by the dynamic qualities of American life, he was most forcefully affected by the apparent lack of coherence within the culture. "It may well be," he wrote, "that a long list of inconsistencies might be made out for any country, just as for any individual; but so far as my knowledge goes the United States stands out as preeminently the 'land of contrasts'—the land of stark, staring, and stimulating inconsistency."[1]

Muirhead's response to the country at large parallels the reaction of many disinterested observers who looked upon the World's Columbian Exposition as a reflector of American culture. All of the great world's fairs, of course, exhibited a degree of diversity and even inconsistency, but in none before or since 1893 was the "stark, staring" confusion of cultural signs so evident. Foreign visitors, who like Muirhead were separated from America by their native cultures, were in the best position to see it, and the record of their impressions is consequently the best source of this perspective. The London *Quarterly Review* summarized the basic foreign interpretation by stating that while the diversity of the fair showed that America had indeed emerged as a nation of "boundless wealth" and "inexhaustible vigour," the lack of any central theme left the really critical cultural questions unanswered: "How will they fare, to what will they finally attain, by what paths of suffering will they march to what new ideals?"[2]

Although such questions appeared most commonly in the foreign press and in the letters and reports of foreign visitors, several American writers were also sensitive to the conflicting messages embodied in the fair. Chief among the latter was Henry Adams, grandson of John Quincy Adams and great grandson of John Adams, who visited the world's fair on two occasions during the summer of 1893. Adams's initial estimate of the fair is unknown, but some fourteen years later, when he included a chapter on it in *The Education of Henry Adams,* he clearly saw it as a reflection of cultural confusion:

> The Exposition itself denied philosophy. One might find fault till the last gate closed, one could still explain nothing that needed explanation. As a scenic display Paris never approached it, but the inconceivable scenic display consisted in its being there at all—more surprising, as it was, than anything else on the continent, Niagara Falls, the Yellowstone Geysers, and the whole railway system thrown in, since these were all natural products in their place; while, since Noah's Ark, no such Babel of loose and ill-joined, such vague and ill-defined and unrelated thoughts and half-thoughts and experimental outcries as the Exposition, had ever ruffled the surface of the Lakes.[3]

Viewed objectively as a symbolic event, the fair does indeed suggest a disordered and confused culture. There is simply no consistent thread holding it together. The ideal and archaic Court of Honor, for instance, not only contrasted with the real-life Chicago eight miles away, but with the pandemonious Midway Plaissance, the eclectic state and foreign buildings, and the lagoon area within the fair itself. Even in the court, the finished and formal exterior of the major buildings was undercut by the raw engineering of the exposed interior skeletons and the multitude of exhibits they contained. While Paderewski performed Chopin for swooning audiences in the Court of Honor's Music Hall, Scott Joplin played ragtime for the pleasure-seeking throngs along the Midway; while

electricity illuminated an ideal vision of the new urban West, Carter Harrison declared Chicago a wide-open frontier town, and Buffalo Bill's Wild West Show did a booming business. Winning the world's fair for Chicago signalled the ascendancy of the West in national affairs, but eastern architects and artists were brought in to design it. The material exhibits of industry and science themselves were countered by the intellectual congresses and spiritual Parliament of Religions, the battleships and cannons by the World Peace Conference.

Similarly, the two predominant structures or artifacts to strike the entering visitor's eye suggest paradox as well. In the initial plans, most people were to have entered the fairgrounds from the great railway terminal by passing through the Administration Building into the Court of Honor. Richard Morris Hunt's golden dome, symbolic of unity, grandeur, and order, was to have provided the first and controlling impression of benign authority and solidity. As it happened, however, a dispute with the railroad companies over rates effectively cancelled the plan, and at least as many visitors actually entered the fair through the Midway where, instead of the golden dome, they confronted the enormous Ferris wheel—the epitome of mechanized money-making entertainment. The list of such conflicting cultural symbols presented by the Columbian Exposition is practically endless. A number of these have received attention in the earlier chapters, but for the present purpose one final illustration will, perhaps, be sufficient.

In view of the unprecedented official recognition given women at the exposition, it was often remarked that just as Columbus had once discovered America, the Columbian Exposition had now discovered woman. The existence of a Board of Lady Managers, the Woman's Department, the Congress of Representative Women, and the Woman's Building all lend support to the slogan. And yet, just what kind of woman it was that the fair discovered was unclear. Recognition in and of itself was not without its value, as Susan B. Anthony was quick to appreciate, but it is equally important to note that the fair provided no consistent image of woman's nature or cultural role. While much was said in the various congresses that questioned the charming, sentimental, dependent, and self-sacrificing Victorian stereotype of ideal womanhood, and much was claimed for woman's ability to compete fully and equally with man in the world outside the home, the traditional view of woman as somehow the ethical and moral superior of man was pervasive. The inherent confusion in these images was present not only in the speeches but throughout the exhibits and activities of the Woman's Department.

On the one hand, the fair displayed a remarkable collection of products and statistical studies designed to show the accomplishments of women in industry, manufacturing, science, art, literature, and the professions, and to break down the older view of woman's work and woman's place. Yet, on the other hand, a major effort was made to show the continuing predominance of women in the traditional areas of child rearing, education, the "divine art of healing," and cooking.[4] The Women's Building itself, the structure which President Palmer called "the American Woman's Declaration of Independence" and which gave a unique opportunity for talented women artists to demonstrate their achievements, was actually dominated by a heavy-handed treatment of "women's virtues." Candace Wheeler, who had charge of the interior decoration, described Sophia Hayden's neoclassic building as "the most peacefully human of all the buildings . . . like a man's ideal of woman—delicate, dignified, pure, and fair to look upon."[5] Two large allegorical murals were prominently displayed at either end of the main interior court. One, painted by Mary MacMonnies, was entitled "The Primitive Woman" and featured a group of women and children ministering to the male upon his return from the hunt; the other, by Mary Cassatt, presented "Modern Woman" playing music, dancing, and pursuing Fame (symbolized by a flock of ducks) heavenward.[6] One stereotype was juxtaposed against another.

The problem of reassessing the role and nature of woman in the nineties was further complicated by a fundamental confusion about sex itself. Discussions about the appropriate use of the nude in art, for example, had raged for nearly a decade, but at the world's fair, as Thomas Beer wryly noted, "the artists who essayed the nude announced by every concession of wind-blown drapery, floating vegetable matter, and opportune posture that they considered a naked body most obscene."[7] Daniel Chester French's sixty-foot statue of the Republic, an idealized version of the American woman—secular, chaste, and virginal—reigned above the dynamos in the Court of Honor, while in the theaters along the Midway young Algerian and Egyptian girls performed suggestive dances and the World's Congress of Beauties ("Forty Ladies from Forty Countries") paraded. Outside the fairgounds, of course, the world's oldest profession flourished.[8] Objections were raised and petitions were brought before both the mayor and the fair's managers concerning the "painted women" and the Midway dancers, but nothing was ever done. Similar confusion was reflected in such activities as the Woman's Dormitory Association, which was financed by private subscription for the purpose of providing inexpensive accommodations in Chicago for working women. While the idea was to encourage those who would otherwise be unable to come to the exposition and witness the progress of women toward full independence and equality, chaperones were provided to guarantee that their virtue and reputations were protected at all times.[9]

Adding to the paradoxical images of woman provided or generated by the fair itself, the association of several distinctive nineteenth-century women with the enterprise served to confuse the picture further. As notable American women which the world's fair brought to public attention, Susan B. Anthony, Jane Addams, and Bertha Honoré Palmer represented very different roles and values.

Susan B. Anthony, seventy-three-year-old president of the National American Woman Suffrage Association, was one of a dedicated handful of American women who had pioneered the cause of woman's rights since the early abolitionist days and had recognized the potential of world's fairs as instruments for spreading the message since the New York World's Fair of 1853. It was largely through her efforts that a Board of

Lady Managers was approved for the Columbian Exposition but, because of her political views, she was never offered an official position herself. Nevertheless, Anthony was a major public figure at the world's fair. During the four months she spent in Chicago in the summer of 1893, she addressed the various congresses on numerous occasions, attended many of the fair's functions, and was treated as a celebrity even by the Chicago press which had once delighted in ridiculing her.[10] Anthony's public acceptance, however, did not necessarily imply that her political and social views had become acceptable as well. By 1893 she had become a traditional figure, the grand dame of the American woman's movement, at a time when America was badly in need of traditional heroes (or heroines).[11]

Jane Addams, who was also prominent during the fair, represented a different type of American woman. Forty years younger than Susan B. Anthony, Addams was neither a crusading idealist nor a major political organizer. In 1889, following a series of acute personal crises, she purchased Hull House in the middle of Chicago's most decayed immigrant slums and began the social settlement activities which made her internationally admired as a model of the professional social service worker and a major figure in the Progressive Movement of the next century. In 1893, she was already widely known and respected for her charitable work and her empirical knowledge of the social conditions that existed at the core of the new American cities. Like Susan B. Anthony, Jane Addams was never offered a position within the world's fair organization but participated extensively in the congresses and other fair functions.

The most publicly prominent woman to be directly connected with the exposition was Bertha Honoré Palmer, the president of the Board of Lady Managers. The period between the 1800s and the beginning of World War I was the great age of the female social leader in America, of the dominent personality who "by a mixture of wealth, family, aggressiveness, social skill, originality, and a measure of publicity—was able to shape into a more or less compact group the casual, scattered materials cast up by successive tides of new riches and luxurious living."[12] Mrs. Potter Palmer, wife of Marshall Field's ex-partner, was the undisputed "queen" of Chicago society during these years, filling a role that was duplicated in varying degrees in New York, Boston, St. Louis, and San Francisco. From her castle on Lake Shore Drive, Bertha Palmer—the "Lady Astor of the Middle West"—set the social tone and dictated the cultural taste of Chicago's newly rich and powerful. In spite of the great competence with which she managed the Woman's Department and the startlingly modern views of woman's situation she expressed on several occasions, as a representative type she provided a third contrasting model of the new American woman.[13]

Taken as a whole, then, the World's Columbian Exposition offered a conflicting picture of the American woman, in its symbolic artifacts and exhibits and in its notably representative women. American culture, at least as far as women were concerned, seemed to be looking both forward and backward, but neither way wholly. Although the fair gave women more public attention than ever before and provided opportunities for them to participate more fully in such an important national enterprise, it did not thereby announce a revolution. The image of woman at the fair is as confusing and paradoxical as the image of American culture in general.

Many individuals at the time, and many since then, found little difficulty, of course, in selectively focusing upon this or that symbolic aspect of the fair to support a cultural theme or theory with which they were particularly concerned. Thus, the Columbian Exposition could provide dramatic evidence for criticizing American culture as materialistic, repressive, senile, escapist, imperialistic, unjust, naive, and imitative, among other things, or for celebrating it as idealistic, liberating, mature, realistic, humane, progressive, powerful, spirited, and original. By the very nature of its being a great world's fair in the Victorian era, the exposition was required to illustrate the actual diversity of American culture as a way of showing the American commitment to the nineteenth century values of change and expansion. The tensions and conflicts which such a presentation inevitably revealed were to be understood, however, as dynamic and progressive, rather than chaotic and confusing. In the final analysis, all such symbolic expressions should be comprehensible within the overall optimistic framework of the Victorian faith in the gradual evolution of civilization and the continuity of national identity. As we have seen, however, the changes which were rapidly transforming the country in the last quarter of the century and the growing sense of the depth of these changes created an undercurrent of doubt about the continuity of American life and a self-consciousness about the national character. Change, diversity, and even inconsistency do not in themselves present great cultural problems when they are understood as organic alternatives or choices—they may in fact be exhilarating. It is quite another matter when they appear as irreconcilably dialectic in nature—as a series of either/ors. For then the conflicts seem radical, penetrating the core of the culture and producing schism and insecurity.

One of the most famous expressions of this sense of cultural insecurity is Frederick Jackson Turner's classic paper "The Significance of the Frontier in American History," which he delivered before the same American Historical Association meeting that elected Henry Adams its president. The unique qualities of the national character, he argued, summarizing a myth that had been popular since the 1830s, were the peculiar product of the frontier experience. But now, he concluded, "four centuries from the discovery of America, at the end of a hundred years of life under the Constitution, the frontier has gone, and with its going has closed the first period of American history."[14] If American life and values—personal, material, social, and political—were wedded to an accident of geography, what would become of American democracy, freedom, equality, opportunity—of the culture itself, once that fortunate determining factor ceased to exist? Turner did not speculate on the future of a frontierless America, but the implications were unsettling enough. Although the full import of Turner's work was not appreciated immediately, the self-consciousness he expressed concerning the lack of an adequate means of cultural continuity was shared by many Americans in the late nineteenth century and was a second major theme of the World's Columbian Exposition.

To the foreign visitor, the disinterested traveller, or the cultural historian, the fair reflected the contrasts within America in the nineties. It also provided evidence of the general psychological insecurity resulting from the recognition of those tensions. And yet, as a great world's fair, the exposition had a further obligation—perhaps the overriding one at the time—to reaffirm the Victorian faith in control and order. The more the fair accurately mirrored the conflicts and self-doubt within the culture, the more important it was that it also provide an image of cultural unity and self-confidence. And it was the American who was most often captured by this latter vision, because he felt himself most in need of reassurance. Where the foreign observer saw a confusion of symbols at the fair, the American saw a convergence. And both were right.

17

The Vision of Unity

Prevented by their own self-consciousness from achieving a detached perspective, most Americans tended to dismiss the signs of change and conflict at the fair and to focus instead upon those aspects which suggested idealism and order. "Commercialism, industrialism, materialism *were* in the Fair," admitted a native Chicagoan thirty years later, "but these have all been lost in the remembrance of those ever-abiding things that came from the Spirit. . . ."[1] The organizers, designers, and publicizers of the fair were themselves sensitive to the cultural need for reassurance and had provided as much evidence for this interpretation as time, money, and imagination allowed. Increasingly, also, the story of the fair became a kind of triumphant epic of American civic spirit, teamwork, and self-sacrifice. Columbus was himself transformed into a man of great vision whose mission was to bring about the unification of all mankind. Similarly, the construction of the White City at the site of what had formerly been a swamp was seen as nothing less than the reenactment of the purpose of American civilization, to bring order out of chaos.[2] "The most important thought which the visitor is to realize for himself out of the Fair," wrote Denton Snider, "is this thought of unity."[3]

The world's congresses were, perhaps, the most remarkable of the activities of the exposition which stood for harmony in the face of conflict. The great popularity of the World's Parliament of Religions in particular, and the religious interest in the enterprise in general, provided a new basis for hope that the exposition itself would become the beginning of a unified spirit of tolerance, cooperation, and peace. If the world's religions could settle their differences, then religion might be able to reassert its traditional authority over the forces of chaos. As in most other areas, the permanent contribution of the parliament seems to have been very little. And the reason for this was that there was more fear than conviction behind the call. At best, Americans sought a unity at the world's fair to aid them in facing an uncertain and confusing future with confidence and optimism, one that would convince the older American stock, as Hugh Duncan put it, that they could meet the problems of the city, poverty, and labor in their own way without interference from outsiders or revolutionaries.[4] At worst, of course, such a pretense of harmony could permit Americans a dangerous escape from reality through fantasy, authoritarianism, or even a paternalistic Christianity wedded to imperialism and racism. "As Columbus discovered America," said one speaker on the last day of the parliament, "so must Americans find a true religion for the whole world, and show the people of all nations a new religion in which all hearts may find rest."[5]

The need to find an ordering principle within American life in the nineties also helps to better explain woman's role in the activities and organization of the enterprise. At the Congress of Representative Women, one of the delegates warned her audience that America was in grave danger of becoming divided into two separate parts—one rich and one poor. But women, she announced, have the capacity for healing the social, cultural, and economic fissures. Rather than insisting that modern forces had broken down and made inappropriate and unjust the older distinctions between male and female, it was argued that the times demanded an extension of the "power of womanliness" into a wider sphere of American life. For all the great organizational competence of the Board of Lady Managers and in spite of the numerous exhibits of woman's industry and art, the note of woman's moral superiority as a unifying principle, rather than woman's liberation, was most heavily struck at Chicago in 1893. "If men can't solve the labor crisis," said Mary Lease in the Labor Congress, for example, "let them stay home and the women will."[6] As

Thomas Beer later remarked, "it would be a long time yet before a woman would ask in print: 'Are women people?' "[7]

The popularized story of the fair, the intellectual and religious aspects, and the unique recognition given women were seized upon as indicators of a continuing commitment to control and order, but the most impressive and powerful lesson of unity was conveyed by the vision of the White City itself. Predominantly in the Court of Honor, science, architecture and art conspired to create a dreamlike scene under the spell of which the problems and complexities of modern life seemed to vanish. It was the overall planning, the unity of the whole and not the details, that produced the effect. "Whether we look upon this spectacle by day, under a blue sky that is clarified by the reflection of the limpid waters of Lake Michigan; or by night, when fretted with fires that outspangle the vault of heaven, with flying fountains bathed in floods of rainbow lights, and overlooking domes bejeweled with glittering crowns . . . we feel that the dream of hope has come true," wrote Candace Wheeler.[8] "Turn your eyes to whatever building you please, you see hosts of suns, moons, and satellites illuminating this model of an earthly heaven," added another visitor.[9] The visual impact was undiminished for those who came to the fair even late in the year. After hearing about it for six months, W. T. Stead was still overwhelmed when he viewed the scene on the evening before closing. "Nothing that I have ever seen," he wrote, "in Paris, in London, in St. Petersburg, or in Rome, could equal the effect produced by the illumination of the great white palaces that autumn night."[10]

Like so many others who came to Chicago looking for a hopeful sign or clue to the direction of American civilization, William Dean Howells shared with many of his countrymen a shaken but persistent faith in Christian progress modified by democracy and art as the solution to the problems of his time. He had, in fact, been hard at work since November, 1892, on a series of fictionalized "letters" for *Cosmopolitan Magazine* critiquing American society from that perspective. For Howells, the White City seemed the tangible embodiment of his vision of utopia, which he called "Altruria," and he subsequently included the fair in his December, 1893 "Letter of an Altrurian Traveller" as an illustration of the "possibilities already existing in the American civilization."[11] What made the White City so impressive to Howells was that it evinced cooperation instead of competition, idealism instead of materialism, beauty instead of ugliness, social responsibility instead of individual avariciousness, and art instead of business. "Yet it would be useless trying to persuade most Americans," the Altrurian concluded, "that the World's Fair City was not the effect, the fine flower, of the competition which underlies their economy, but was the first fruits of the principle of emulation, which animates our happy commonwealth [i.e., Altruria], and gives men as nowhere else on earth, a foretaste of heaven."[12]

There is little question, of course, that the vision was contrived or that its relationship to American social and material conditions was essentially dialectic. The great buildings were a facade, a magnificent stage prop, set in a landscape of fantasy in which the economic, political, racial, and sexual conflicts of the time had no place. The architectural style and the elaborate decoration was, for the most part, an insult to native American genius and in this sense the White City was indeed the "society's wax flower, preserved under glass and apart from reality."[13] Still, in another sense, the artificial vision of unity was a positive response to a real condition, that of the collective psychology of the nation. In the White City, Chicago and the country at large got what they felt they needed to counterbalance the materialism they feared, the confusion of traditional values and symbols, the lack of cultural and political leadership, and the dislocations they were experiencing. Louis Sullivan was as out of tune with this aspect of the American 1890s as Whitman would have been, because however well he may have sensed the enduring spirit of America's vigorous liberalism, he did not appreciate that the profound insecurity of the period demanded reassurance. Nor did Sullivan and his later followers, after the First World War had completely eliminated all possibility of maintaining

the older philosophy, adequately recognize that the Columbian Exposition was a great world's fair and as such a Victorian institution. Accordingly, in so far as architecture (and sculpture and mural painting) was presented at Jackson Park as art, its function was to serve as an ideal counterweight on the cultural scale to the confusing diversity of physical and material change. Architecture as an expression of the dominant cultural spirit and forces of the time was simply incomprehensible. Americans turned to art, as they did to woman, to control confusion, not reflect it, and this was the primary reason that the Chicago School's commercial design was never seriously considered nor the classic Renaissance style seriously challenged.

Montgomery Schuyler, a nineteenth-century critic of American architecture whose views have held up remarkably well, suggested three reasons why the use of the Renaissance style was so impressive: unity, magnitude, and illusion. The success of the Court of Honor, which was, as he said, "what everybody means when he speaks of the architecture of the Exposition," was first and foremost a success of unity.[14] The second success was one of magnitude, which was appropriate because "in this country mere bigness counts for more than anywhere else, and in Chicago, the citadel of the superlative degree, it counts for more, perhaps, than it counts elsewhere in this country."[15] The final success, and the most dangerous, he concluded, was one of illusion: "What the World's Fair buildings have first of all to tell us, and what they tell equally to a casual glimpse and to a prolonged survey is that they are examples not of work-a-day building, but of holiday building, that the purpose of their erection is festal and temporary, in a word that the display is a display and a triumph of occasional architecture."[16] As such, Schuyler had no quarrel with the architects or the architectural style that was chosen, but he was concerned that the neoclassic be recognized as having no direct relevance to the present or future direction of permanent architecture in America. "The White City is the most integral, the most extensive, the most illusive piece of scenic architecture that has ever been seen. That is praise enough for its builders, without demanding for them the further praise of having made a useful and important contribution to the development of the architecture of the present, to the preparation of the architecture of the future."[17]

As Schuyler was perceptive enough to recognize, the White City was indeed an illusion, and as an illusion it did not have to conform to the everyday practical realities of American life, as Sullivan might have wished. It was free, therefore, as few events ever are, to reflect the psychological conditions of the society—the fears inherent in a confusing period of swiftly accelerating change, and the almost desperate faith in the possibility of the human mind to understand and control the direction of those changes with as little reorientation of basic values as possible. The Victorian world had assumed that change could be controlled, not in order to eliminate it, but in order to hold it within the comprehensible boundaries of progress. But the Columbian Exposition, with its grand illusion of unity and harmony, demonstrated clearly how far the Victorian balance had been stretched.

Perhaps, more than anything, it was the illusion of promise that was most significant. "The Fair...was on the whole a great promise, even a great pledge. It, at least, forbids despair," wrote Charles Eliot Norton.[18] It was a promise to Henry George of what the people could still accomplish, to Harriet Monroe of what businessmen were capable of, and to Henry Fuller of what art could do. But it was the city, finally, that was the hero of the exposition; it was Chicago's brash faith and enthusiasm that made a promise of future unity, harmony, and beauty visual in the midst of incongruity. And it was Chicago that created the Midway with its ragtime and Ferris Wheel and festive diversity. All in all it was a vision of the positive city, a vision rarely seen in nineteenth century America. After the fair was over Americans could no longer deny the connection between civilization and the city. The world's fair accomplished this, at least. Still, the World's Columbian Exposition revealed that in the nineties, American civilization, under the pressure of its own psychological insecurity, sought control within a Victorian balance which set art over against life, and idealism against materialism in a clear dialectical pattern which offered no real solution, and which may have been false to much that was traditional in the culture. And it did so in order to affirm the predominant faith in progress. The world's fair did not originate the tension, nor the particular method of attempted solution, it simply revealed it more clearly than any other event of the period.

EPILOGUE

Still they are not lost, but have become internal—the soul's possession, which is immortal. . . . While they existed, they could perish, but having perished, they live.

Denton Snider

October 28, 1893, "American Cities Day" at the World's Columbian Exposition, was the next to last day of the fair. Little official effort was made to control the great crowd which stayed late into the night and seemed to regret the end of the White City. Mayor Harrison completed a busy day at Jackson Park that included a typically rousing speech before the visiting mayors, in which he said that "genius is but audacity, and the audacity of the 'wild and wooly West' and of Chicago has chosen a star, and has looked upward to it, and knows nothing that it cannot accomplish."[1] Booster to the end, the mayor went home tired but exhilarated, especially as he had just announced that he had asked a young woman to become his (third) wife. He felt young again and proud of Chicago. Shortly after arriving home he was called to the door where a man, unknown to Harrison but carrying a grievance and a revolver, shot him three times and fled. Chicago's world's fair mayor was dead within fifteen minutes.[2]

It had been the intention that the great fair would close, as it had opened, with an elaborate ceremony and a blaze of glory. Instead, there was a single brief speech and the flags were lowered to half-mast. "Tragedy marked its close, except in the Midway Plaisance, where brawling and lewd crowds, waving whiskey bottles and signs, rioted until the small hours. Loving, weeping processions . . . viewed the Mayor's bier at City Hall. And so he was buried, and at the same time the dream-city on the lake's edge ceased to be."[3]

The world's fair had meant, in practical terms, a short period of peace and goodwill for Chicago in which it was felt that reasoned discussion, tradition and idealism would have their chance to control an otherwise highly dangerous socio-economic situation, and indeed, the exposition had helped to hold off the worst effects of the economic panic that summer. Yet with the closing of the fair and the return of cold weather, unemployment skyrocketed and the streets of the city were filled once more with beggars, peddlers, tramps, and jobless men and women. "The most spectacular proof," wrote Julia Lathrop of Hull House, "of the poverty entailed upon Chicago by the general business depression of 1893, and locally by the inevitable human debris left by the World's Fair, could be daily seen during all the severer months of the winter of 1893 and 1894. It was a solid, pressing crowd of hundreds of shabby men and shawled or hooded women, coming from all parts of a great city . . . standing hour after hour with market-baskets high above their heads, held in check by policemen, polyglot, but having the common language of their persistency, their weariness, their chill and hunger."[4]

There was some discussion in the press about saving the fair's principal buildings as a permanent landmark of the city, but the cost of preserving them as functional buildings in which future exhibits might be shown was prohibitive and, in view of the immediate socio-economic concerns, there was little interest in preserving them simply for their architectural effect. The buildings eventually became the responsibility of the South Park Commission which was unable or unwilling either to have them dismantled or to take positive steps to maintain them. As a result, the White City became what it had never been during the months of the fair—a city of the poor, inhabited by vagrants and tramps throughout the winter of 1893/1894. Small fires caused damage and vandalism destroyed most of the decorative work and sculpture, but the larger classic structures survived intact until the evening of July 5, 1894, when, in the midst of the first serious clash between federal troops (led by ex-world's fair grand marshall General Miles) and striking railway workers, incendiaries set fire to the great buildings. Thousands of soldiers, strikers, and frightened citizens stood watching the tremendous pillars of flame that lit the sky above Chicago's South Side. In two hours "the one splendid beautiful thing that Chicago had ever created was reduced to a wilderness of ashes and gaunt and twisted girders."[5] As with Pullman's worker's utopia, the utopian dreams of Christian communities directed by liberal businessmen and Christian pastors went up in the smoke of that summer's night and the World's Columbian Exposition, which had been conceived out of that faith in a rebirth of order, ended in violence and flame.

In later years the three Columbian caravels were used by the Knights of Columbus to stage pageants of the discovery of America, La Rabida (the model convent which had held most of the relics of Columbus during the Fair) became a hospital for cardiac children, Atwood's Art Palace was refurbished and became Chicago's Museum of Science and   Industry   and the Midway (without the Ferris wheel, which was moved to Coney Island) became a popular dancing resort in the years before prohibition and eventually, with the replanning of Jackson Park, evolved into the tree-lined entrance to the University of Chicago of today.

Daniel Burnham, of course, went on to become one of the country's most famous early city planners and was elected president of the American Institute of Architects. Lyman Gage, a chief figure in the Chicago Company, was appointed secretary of the Treasury by William McKinley, and Sol Bloom was later elected to Congress, became an advisor to four Presidents on foreign affairs, and helped draft the Charter of the United Nations in 1945. Harriet Monroe ceased writing her own odes and began *Poetry Magazine,* in which she introduced the new twentieth-century directions of T. S. Eliot and Ezra Pound. By the end of 1895, Henry Codman and Charles Atwood, the fair's two young formalist designers, had both died prematurely (Atwood's death following mysterious personal difficulties that included drugs) and in 1907, perhaps most tellingly, when William Dean Howells once again picked up his story of the Altrurian Traveller in *Through the Eye of the Needle,* he merely mentioned that the Traveller had visited Chicago's great world's fair. There was no reference to the "glorious dream of universal brotherhood which Aristides (and Howells) enjoyed in 1893."[6]

Appendix A

The World's Fairs

City	Date	Area (acres)	Number of Exhibits	Receipts	Cost	Attendance
London	1851	26	13,939	$2,525,000	$1,775,000	6,039,195
New York	1853	13	4,854	$340.000	$640,000	1,250,000
Paris	1855	24½	20,839	£128,099	£1,000,000	5,162,330
London	1862	25	28,653	£459,631	£460,000	6,211,103
Paris	1867	41	43,217	£420,735	£800,000	6,805,969
Vienna	1873	40	25,760	£206,477	£2,200,000	6,740,000
Philadelphia	1876	236	30,000	$3,666,715	$8,980,000	8,004,274
Paris	1878	66	52,835	f23,700,000	f55,400,000	16,032,725
Sydney	1879	15	9,345	£210,372	£313,987	1,117,536
Melbourne	1880	20	12,792	£331,901	£330,330	1,330,279
London	1886	13	—	£249,861	£215,218	5,550,745
Paris	1889	72	61,722	f50,000,000	f44,000,000	32,350,297
Chicago	1893	686	65,000.	$28,787,532	$28,340,700	21,477,212
Paris	1900	336	80,000	£4,578,249	£4,660,000	39,000,000
Buffalo	1901	350	3,500	$5,534,643	$8,860,757	8,304,073
Glasgow	1901	—	—	£404,105	£350,600	11,559,649
St. Louis	1904	1,240	70,000	$12,185,500	$26,564,000	12,804,000
Liege	1905	173	16,119	f14,526,930	f14,451,813	7,000,000
London	1908	140	13,500	£798,771	£783,521	8,396,673
Brussels	1910	200	—	£692,933	£702,933	4,196,939
San Francisco	1915	635	80,000	$27,178,065	$24,690,770	13,127,103
Wembley	1924–1925	200	—	£2,814,935	£4,396,840	27,102,498
Philadelphia	1926	450	—	$5,000,000	$26,000,000	5,852,783
Paris	1931	500	12,000	f159,000,000	f225,000,000	33,500,000
Chicago	1933–1934	424	—	$43,589,154	$42,900,989	39,052,236
Brussels	1935	375	9,000	—	—	26,000,000
Paris	1937	250	11,000	f4,000,000	f17,000,000	34,000,000
New York	1939–1940	1,217	100,000	$48,287,767	$67,010,989	44,932,978
London	1951	—	—	£2,560,000	£11,500,000	18,000,000
Brussels	1958	500	17,000	—	$400,000,000	41,454,412
Seattle	1962	74	—	—	$100,000,000	9,639,969
New York	1965	646	—	$128,600,000	$150,000,000	51,607,548
Montreal	1967	1,000	—	—	$300,000,000	50,306,648
San Antonio	1968	93	—	—	—	6,400,000
Osaka	1970	815	—	—	$220,000,000	64,218,770

Source: Frederick P. Pittera, *Fairs of the World* (unpublished). Reprinted by permission of *The Encyclopedia Britannica, Inc.*, 1973 Edition.

Appendix B

**United States Appropriations
to Exhibitions and Fairs (to 1904)**

Foreign Fairs

City	Date	Appropriation
London	1862	$2,000.00
Paris	1867	$212,603.00
Vienna	1873	$200,000.00
Paris	1878	$190,000.00
Syndey & Melbourne	1879–1880	$20,000.00
Melbourne	1880	$8,000.00
Berlin	1882	$20,000.00
London	1886	$70,000.00
Melbourne	1888	$50,000.00
Brussels	1888	$35,000.00
Barcelona	1888	$28,380.96
Paris	1889	$250,004.66
Madrid	1892	$25,000.00
Bergen	1898	$20,000.00
Paris	1900	$1,427,500.00
Liege	1904	$5,000.00

Domestic Fairs

City	Date	Appropriation
Philadelphia	1876	$2,183,184.59
Louisville	1883	$10,000.00
New Orleans	1884	$1,650,000.00
Cincinnati	1888	$157,750.00
Chicago	1893	$5,840,329.64
Atlanta	1895	$200,000.00
Nashville	1897	$130,000.00
Omaha	1898	$240,000.00
Buffalo	1901	$1,015,000.00
Charleston	1902	$250,000.00
St. Louis	1904	$11,427,500.00
Portland	1905	$5,000.00

Source: Treasury Department Letter to the Senate, Dec. 29, 1904. Senate Document 65, 58th Congress, 3rd Session. Vol. 2–47.

Appendix C

The Act Creating the World's Columbian Expositions of 1893

An Act to provide for celebrating the four hundredth anniversary of America by Christopher Columbus by holding an International Exhibition of arts, industries, manufactures and the products of the soil, mine and sea, in the City of Chicago, in the State of Illinois.

WHEREAS, It is fit and appropriate that the four hundredth anniversary of the discovery of America be commemorated by an exhibition of the resources of the United States of America, their development, and of the progress of civilization in the New World; and

WHEREAS, Such an exhibition should be of a national and international character, so that not only the people of our Union and this continent, but those of all nations as well, can participate and should, therefore, have the sanction of the Congress of the United States; therefore,

Be it enacted by the Senate and House of Representatives of the United States of America in Congress assembled, That an exhibition of arts, industries, manufactures and products of the soil, mine and sea, shall be inaugurated in the year of eighteen hundred and ninety-two, in the City of Chicago, in the State of Illinois, as hereinafter provided.

Section 2. That a commission, consisting of two commissioners from each State and Territory of the United States and from the District of Columbia and eight commissioners-at-large, is hereby constituted to be designated as the World's Columbian Commission.

Section 3. That said Commissioners, two from each State and Territory, shall be appointed within thirty days from the passage of this act by the President of the United States, on the nomination of the Governors of the States and Territories, respectively, and by the President, eight Commissioners-at-large and two from the District of Columbia; and in the same manner within the same time there shall be appointed two alternative Commissioners from each State and Territory of the United States and the District of Columbia, and eight alternate Commissioners-at-large, who shall assume and perform the duties of such Commissioner or Commissioners as may be unable to attend the meetings of the said Commission; and in such nominations and appointments each of the two leading political parties shall be equally represented. Vacancies in the Commission nominated by the Governors of the several States and Territories, respectively, and also vacancies in the Commission-at-large and from the District of Columbia may be filled in the same manner and under the same conditions as provided herein for their original appointment.

Section 4. That the Secretary of State of the United States shall, immediately after the passage of this act, notify the Governors of the several States and Territories, respectively thereof, and request such nominations to be made. The Commissioners so appointed shall be called together by the Secretary of State of the United States in the City of Chicago, by notice to the Commissioners, as soon as convenient after the appointment of said Commissioners, and within thirty days thereafter. The said Commissioners, at said first meeting, shall organize by the selection of such officers and the appointment of such committees as they may deem expedient, and for this purpose the Commissioners present at said meeting shall constitute a quorum.

Section 5. That said Commission be empowered in its discretion to accept for the purposes of the World's Columbian Exposition such site as may be selected for such purpose at the expense of and tendered by the corporation organized under the laws of the State of Illinois, known as "The World's Exposition of eighteen hundred and ninety-two": *Provided,* That said site so tendered and the buildings proposed to be erected thereon shall be deemed by said Commission adequate to the purposes of said Exposition: *And provided,* That said Commission shall be satisfied that the said corporation has an actual *bona fide* and valid subscription to its capital stock which will secure the payment of at least five million dollars, of which not less than five hundred thousand dollars shall have been paid in, and that the further sum of five million dollars, making in all ten million dollars, will be provided by said corporation in ample time for its needful use during the prosecution of the work for the complete preparation of said Exposition.

Section 6. That the said Commission shall allot space for exhibitors, prepare a classification of exhibits, determine the plan and scope of the Exposition, and shall appoint all judges and examiners for the Exposition, award all premiums, if any, and generally have charge of all intercourse with the exhibitors and the representatives of foreign nations. And said Commission is authorized and required to appoint a Board of Lady Managers of such number and to perform such duties as may be prescribed by said Commission. Said Board may appoint one or more members of all committees authorized to award prizes which may be produced in whole or in part by female labor.

Section 7. That after the plans for said Exposition shall be prepared by said corporation and approved by said Commission, the rules and regulations of said corporation governing rates for entrance and admission fees, or otherwise affecting the rights, privileges, or interests of the exhibitors or of the public, shall be fixed or established by said corporation, subject, however, to such modification, if any, as may be imposed by a majority of said Commissioners.

Section 8. That the President is hereby empowered and directed to hold a naval review in New York Harbor, in April, eighteen hundred and ninety-three, and to extend to foreign nations an invitation to send ships-of-war to join the United States Navy in rendezvous at Hampton Roads, and proceed thence to the review.

Section 9. That said Commission shall provide for the dedication of the buildings of the World's Columbian Exposition in said City of Chicago on the twelfth day of October, eighteen hundred and ninety-two, with appropriate ceremonies, and said Exposition shall be open to visitors not later than the first day of May, eighteen hundred and ninety-three, and shall be closed at such time as the Commission may determine, but not later than the thirtieth day of October thereafter.

Section 10. That whenever the President of the United States shall be notified by the Commission that provision has been made for grounds and buildings for the uses herein provided for, and there has also been filed with him by the said corporation, known as "The World's Exposition of eighteen hundred and ninety-two," satisfactory proof that a sum not less than ten million dollars, to be used and expended for the purposes of the Exposition herein authorized, has in fact been raised or provided for by subscription or other legally binding means, he shall be authorized, through the Department of State, to make proclamation of the same, setting forth the time at which the Exposition will open and close, and the place at which it will be held; and he shall communicate to the diplomatic representatives of foreign nations copies of the same, together with such regulations as may be adopted by the Commission, for publication in their respective countries, and he shall, in behalf of the Government and people, invite foreign nations to take part in the said Exposition and appoint representatives thereto.

Section 11. That all articles which shall be imported from foreign countries for the sole purpose of exhibition at said Exposition, upon which there shall be a tariff or customs duty, shall be admitted free of payment of duty, custom fees, or charges, under such regulations as the Secretary of the Treasury shall prescribe; but it shall be lawful at any time during the exhibition to sell for delivery at the close of the Exposition any goods or property imported for and actually on exhibition in the Exposition buildings or on its grounds, subject to such regulations for the security of the revenue and for the collection of the import duties as the Secretary of the Treasury shall prescribe: *Provided,* That all such articles when sold or withdrawn for consumption in the United States will be subject to the duty, if any, imposed upon such articles by the revenue laws in force at the date of importation, and all penalties prescribed by law shall be applied and enforced against such articles, and against the persons who may be guilty of any illegal sale or withdrawal.

Section 12. That the sum of twenty thousand dollars, or as much thereof as may be necessary, be and the same is hereby appropriated out of any moneys in the Treasury not otherwise appropriated, for the remainder of the present fiscal year and for the fiscal year ending June thirtieth, eighteen hundred and ninety-one, to be expended under the direction of the Secretary of the Treasury for the purposes connected with the admission of foreign goods to said Exhibition.

Section 13. That it shall be the duty of the Commission to make report from time to time to the President of the United States of the progress of the work and, in a final report, present a full exhibit of the results of the Exposition.

Section 14. That the Commission hereby authorized shall exist no longer than until the first day of January, eighteen hundred and ninety-eight.

Section 15. That the United States shall not in any manner, nor under any circumstances, be liable for any of the acts, doings, proceedings or representations of the said corporation organized under the laws of the State of Illinois, its officers, agents, servants or employes, or any of them, or for the service, salaries, labor or wages of said officers, agents, servants or employés, or any of them, or for any subscriptions to the capital stock, or for any certificates of stock, bonds, mortgages or obligations of any kind issued by said corporation, or for any debts, liabilities or expenses of any kind whatever attending such corporation or accruing by reason of the same.

Section 16. That there shall be exhibited at the said Exposition, by the Government of the United States, from its Executive Departments, the Smithsonian Institution, the United States Fish Commission and the National Museum, such articles and materials as illustrate the function and administrative faculty of the Government in time of peace and its resources as a war power, tending to demonstrate the nature of our institutions and their adaptation to the wants of the people; and to secure a complete and harmonious arrangement of such a Government exhibit, a board shall be created to be charged with the selection, preparation, arrangement, safe-keeping and exhibition of such articles and materials as the heads of the several Departments and the directors of the Smithsonian Institution and National Museum may respectively decide shall be embraced in said Government exhibit. The President may also designate additional articles for exhibition. Such boards shall be composed of one person to be named by the head of each Executive Department, and one by the directors of the Smithsonian Institution and National Museum, and one by the Fish Commission, such selections to be approved by the President of the United States. The President shall name the chairman of said board, and the board itself shall select such other officers as it may deem necessary.

That the Secretary of the Treasury is hereby authorized and directed to place on exhibition, upon such grounds as shall be allotted for the purpose, one of the life-saving stations authorized to be constructed on the coast of the United States by existing law, and to cause the same to be fully equipped with all apparatus, furniture, and appliances now in use in all life-saving stations in the United States, said building and apparatus to be removed at the close of the exhibition and re-erected at the place now authorized by law.

Section 17. That the Secretary of the Treasury shall cause a suitable building or buildings to be erected on the site selected for the World's Columbian Exposition for the Government exhibits, as provided in this Act, and he is hereby authorized and directed to contract therefore, in the same manner and under the same regulations as for other public buildings of the United States; but the contracts for said building or buildings shall not exceed the sum of four hundred thousand dollars, and for the remainder of the fiscal year and for the fiscal year ending June thirtieth, eighteen hundred and ninety-two, there is hereby appropriated for said building or buildings, out of any money in the Treasury not otherwise appropriated, the sum of one hundred thousand dollars. The Secretary of the Treasury shall cause the said building or buildings to be constructed as far as possible of iron, steel and glass, or of such other material as may be taken out and sold to the best advantage; and he is authorized and required to dispose of such building or buildings, or the material composing the same, at the close of the Exposition, giving preference to the City of Chicago, or to the said World's Exposition, of eighteen hundred and ninety-two, to purchase the same at an appraised value to be ascertained in such manner as he may determine.

Section 18. That for the purpose of paying the expenses, transportation, care and custody of exhibits by the Government and the maintenance of the building or buildings hereinbefore provided for, and the safe return of articles belonging to the said Government exhibit, and for the expenses of the commission created by this Act, and other contingent expenses, to be approved by the Secretary of the Treasury, upon itemized accounts and vouchers, there is hereby appropriated for the remainder of this fiscal year and for the fiscal year ending June 30, 1891, out of any money in the Treasury not otherwise appropriated, the sum of $200,000 dollars, or so much thereof as may be necessary: *Provided,* That the United States shall not be liable, on account of the erection of buildings, expenses of the Commission or any of its officers or employés, or on account of any expenses incident to or growing out of said Exposition, for a sum exceeding in the aggregate $1,500,000.

Section 19. That the Commissioners and alternate Commissioners appointed under this Act shall not be entitled to any compensation for their services out of the Treasury of the United States, except their actual expenses for transportation and the sum of six dollars per day for subsistence for each day they are necessarily absent from their homes on the business of said Commission. The officers of said Commission shall receive such compensation as may be fixed by said Commission, subject to the approval of the Secretary of the Treasury, which shall be paid out of the sums appropriated by Congress in aid of such Exposition.

Section 20. That nothing in this Act shall be so construed as to create any liability of the United States, direct or indirect, for any debt or obligation incurred, nor for any claim for aid or pecuniary assistance from Congress or the Treasury of the United States in support or liquidation of any debts or obligations created by said Commission in excess of appropriations made by Congress therefor.

Section 21 That nothing in this Act shall be so constituted as to override or interfere with the laws of any State, and all contracts made in any State for the purposes of the Exhibition shall be subject to the laws thereof.

Section 22. That no member of said Commission, whether an officer or otherwise, shall be personally liable for any debt or obligation which may be created or incurred by the said Commission.

Appendix D

Preliminary and Final Classification System for Major Departments

Preliminary Classification

Department 1: Agriculture and Allied Industries
Department 2: Mines and Metallurgy
Department 3: Marine and Fisheries
Department 4: Manufacture and other Elaborative Industries
Department 5: Food and Its Accessories
Department 6: The House and Its Accessories. Costume and Personal Equipment
Department 7: The Pictorial, Plastic, and Decorative Arts
Department 8: Social Relations and Public Welfare
Department 9: Science, Religion, Education and Human Achievement
Department 10: Collective and Monographic Exhibits

Final Classification

Department A: Agriculture, Food and Its Accessories, Forestry and Forest Products, Agricultural Machinery and Appliances

Department B: Horticulture
Department C: Live Stock, Domestic and Wild Animals
Department D: Fish, Fisheries, Fish Products, and Apparatus of Fishing
Department E: Mines, Mining, and Metallurgy
Department F: Machinery
Department G: Transportation, Railways, Vessels, and Vehicles
Department H: Manufactures
Department J: Electricity and Electrical Appliances
Department K: Fine Arts, Painting, Sculpture, Architecture, Decoration
Department L: Liberal Arts, Education, Engineering, Public Works, Constructive Architecture, Music, and Drama
Department M: Ethnology, Archaeology, Progress of Labor and Invention, Isolated and Collective Exhibits, Woman's Work

Source: G. Browne Goode, *First Draft of a System of Classification for the World's Columbian Exposition* (Washington: Gedney and Roberts, 1890); *Classification of the World's Columbian Exposition Adopted by The World's Columbian Commission* (Chicago: Donohue and Heneberry, 1891).

Appendix E

Presidential Proclamation of December 24, 1890

WHEREAS, Satisfactory proof has been presented to me that provison has been made for adequate grounds and buildings for the uses of the World's Columbian Exposition, and that a sum not less than $10,000,000, to be used and expended for the purposes of said Exposition, has been provided in accordance with the conditions and requirements of Section 10 of an Act entitled "An Act to provide for celebrating the four hundredth anniversary of the discovery of America by Christopher Columbus by holding an International Exhibition of arts, industries, manufactures and the products of the soil, mine and sea, in the City of Chicago, in the State of Illinois," approved April 25, 1890.

Now, THEREFORE, I, Benjamin Harrison, President of the United States, by virtue of the authority vested in me by said Act, do hereby declare and proclaim that such International Exhibition will be opened on the first day of May, in the year of eighteen hundred and ninety-three, in the City of Chicago, in the State of Illinois, and will not be closed before the last Thursday in October of the same year.

And in the name of the Government and of the People of the United States, I do hereby invite all the nations of the earth to take part in the commemoration of an event that is preeminent in human history and of lasting interest to mankind by appointing representatives thereto, and sending such exhibits to the World's Columbian Exposition as will most fitly and fully illustrate their resources, their industries and their progress in civilization.

In TESTIMONY WHEREOF, I have hereunto set my hand and caused the seal of the United States to be affixed.

Done at the City of Washington, this twenty-fourth day of December, in the year of our Lord one thousand eight hundred and ninety, and in the independence of the United States the one hundred and fifteenth.

By the President: Benj. Harrison

James G. Blaine, Secretary of State

Appendix F

Memorandum of December 9 to the Committee on Grounds and Buildings

In our advisory capacity, we wish to recommend such action to you as will be productive of the best results, and will at the same time be in accord with the expressed sentiments of the architectural societies of America. The following suggestions relate only to the central group of buildings in Jackson Park, it being the intention from time to time to designate other architects for the various important structures that are to be erected in addition thereto:

That these buildings should be in their designs, relationships and arrangement, of the highest possible architectural merit, is of importance scarcely less great than the variety, richness and comprehensiveness of the various displays within them. Such success is not so much dependent upon the expenditure of money as upon the expenditure of thought, knowledge and enthusiasm by men known to be in every way endowed with these qualifications, and the results achieved by them will be the measure by which America, and especially Chicago, must expect to be judged by the world. Several methods of procedure suggest themselves:

First.   The selection of one man to whom the designing of the entire work should be entrusted.

Second.   Competition made free to the whole architectural profession.

Third.   Competition among a selected few.

Fourth.   Direct selection.

Far better than any of these methods seems to be the last. That is, to select a certain number of architects, choosing each man for such work as would be most nearly parallel with his best achievements. These architects, to meet in conference, become masters of all the elements of the problems to be solved, and agree upon some general scheme of procedure. The preliminary studies resulting from this to be compared and freely discussed in a subsequent conference and, with the assistance of such suggestions as your advisors may make, be brought into a harmonious whole.

The honor conferred upon those so selected would create in their minds a disposition to place the artistic quality of their work in advance of the mere question of emoluments; while the emulation begotten in a rivalry so dignified and friendly could not fail to be productive of a result which would stand before the world as the best fruit of American civilization.

> D. H. Burnham
> Chief of Construction
> John W. Root
> Consulting Architect
> F. L. Olmsted and Company
> Consulting Landscape Architects
> A. Gottlieb
> Consulting Engineer

Appendix G

Burnham's Letter of December 13, 1890, to the Eastern Architects

The enclosed recommendation was approved last night by the Board of Directors of the World's Columbian Exposition, and in the same resolution they empowered the Grounds and Buildings Committee to secure the services of five architects to design the main group of buildings at Jackson Park. The committee authorized me to confer with you with a view to your appointment.

It is intended to place the matter in your hands as to the artistic aspect only—first, of the group of buildings as a whole; second, of the separate buildings.

The committee are disposed to leave the method of designing to the five architects, and you may determine among yourselves whether to make a joint design of the whole work as one, or each to take separate parts, the result to be modified to meet such views as may be expressed in your conference from time to time.

This bureau will be expected to supply you with all data about materials, sizes, general dispositions and cost of buildings, and it is also to have charge of the constructional features, and finally of the execution of the same, but with the understanding that the artistic parts are to be carried out with your approval, and that you are from time to time to visit the work either in a body or separately, as may be determined. Our consulting architect, Mr. Root, would act as your interpreter when you should be absent, without imparting to the work any of his own feelings.

I realize the hesitancy you may feel in assuming responsibility for design when you do not fully control the execution of it. The Committee feels, however, that strictest economy of the two essentials—time and money—will be the best subserved by keeping the actual control of the work in the hands of one man and his bureau; and I can assure you that your intents and purposes of design, once agreed upon by the Committee, shall be carried out as you wish, and that they shall not be altered or meddled with, and when exigencies arise, making any important change necessary, you shall be consulted and have the matter the same as in original design.

D. H. Burnham
Chief of Construction

Appendix H

General Balance Sheets

I. Receipts and Expenses of the Chicago Exposition Company

Receipts

Capital Stock:	$5,607,075.28
City of Chicago:	5,000,000.00
Souvenir Coins:	1,929,120.00
Premium on Coins:	517,556.43
Gate Receipts:	10,601,175.41
Concession Receipts:	3,794,406.26
Interest:	68,090.50
General Receipts from Exhibitors:	807,450.44
Post-Exposition Receipts (Salvage, etc):	123,649.98
Total Receipts:	$28,448,524.30

Expenses

Operations:	$7,443,563.50
Preliminary Organization:	90,674.97
Construction:	18,562,528.04
Post-Exposition Expenses:	828,922.99
Estimated Net Liabilities:	114,626.22
Total Expenses:	$27,040,315.72
Balance:	1,408,208.58

II. Estimated Total Costs of the World's Columbian Exposition Disbursements from the

Chicago Company:	$27,040,315.72
U.S. Government Expenses:	2,668,875.00
Foreign Government Expenses:	6,571,520.00
State Appropriations:	6,020,830.00
Private Exhibitor's Expenses:	25,000,000.00
Grand Total:	$67,301,540.72

Sources: Auditor's reports of January 31, 1894 and June 30, 1895.

NOTES

Prologue

1. Ray Ginger, *Altgeld's America 1890–1905: The Lincoln Ideal Versus Changing Realities* (New York: Funk & Wagnals, 1958), p. 19.

2. *Chicago Times,* 2 May 1893, p. 1. *Chicago Record,* 2 May 1893, p. 1. Lloyd Lewis and Henry Justin Smith, *Chicago: The History of Its Reputation* (New York: Harcourt, Brace, 1929), p. 205.

3. *Chicago Times,* 2 May 1893, p. 1. *Chicago Record,* 1 May 1893, p. 1.

4. Lewis and Smith, p. 206.

5. *Chicago Record,* 2 May 1893, p. 1. *Chicago Herald,* 2 May 1893, p. 1. There were, fortunately, no deaths reported by the papers though there were numerous minor injuries.

6. *Dedicatory and Opening Ceremonies of the World's Columbian Exposition, Memorial Volume* by the Joint Committee on Ceremonies (Chicago: Stone, Kastler, and Painter, 1893), pp. 260–261. Hereafter referred to as *Dedicatory.*

7. *Chicago Daily Inter Ocean,* 2 May 1893, p. 1.

8. *Dedicatory,* p. 265.

9. The "Hallelujah Chorus" had to be cancelled due to a lack of space on the platform for the fifteen-hundred-member chorus.

10. Ginger, p. 18. Lewis and Smith, p. 207.

11. Lewis and Smith, p. 208. *Chicago Times,* 2 May 1893, p. 1.

Introduction

1. James B. Conant, in *Science and Common Sense* (New Haven: Yale University Press, 1951), p. 58, says that the impact of theoretical science upon applied engineering did not really begin to be felt until 1870. Taking the birth of modern science as somewhere around 1600, "it was two hundred years or more before the practical arts benefited much from science ... not until the electrical and dye-stuff industries were well started, about 1870, that science became of real significance to industry."

1   The Crystal Palace and the Origins of the Institution

1. Richard L. Schoenwald, "Introduction" to *Nineteenth Century Thought*, ed. Schoenwald (Englewood Cliffs: Prentice-Hall, 1965), p. 1.

2. Guy Stanton Ford, "International Exhibitions," in *Encyclopaedia of the Social Sciences* (New York: Macmillan, 1933) 6: 23.

3. Winston Churchill, *History of the English Speaking Peoples* (New York: Dodd, Mead & Co., 1958) 4: 67. See also George Lichtheim, *Marxism: An Historical and Critical Study* (New York: Praeger, 1961), p. 133.

4. Quoted in Churchill, p. 66.

5. G. R. Leighton, "World's Fairs: From Little Egypt to Robert Moses," *Harper's* 221 (July 1960): 28.

6. Ford, p. 23.

7. Quoted in Walburga Paget, "The Crystal Palace: A Reminiscence and a Suggestion," *Nineteenth Century* 71 (June 1912): 1178.

8. The initial fears about the Crystal Palace are noted by several writers but this particular illustration is found in Paget, p. 1178.

9. Ford, p. 23.

10. See Appendix A.

11. Churchill, p. 67.

12. Quoted in Paget, p. 1180.

13. There is almost general agreement on this point. See for example R. H. Mottram, "Town Life," in *Early Victorian England 1830–1865*, ed. G. M. Young (London: Oxford University Press, 1934), pp. 212–22.

14. Churchill, p. 68.

15. Paget, p. 1181.

2   The Growth and Character of the Institution

1. Leighton, p. 32.

2. Carleton J. H. Hayes in *A Generation of Materialism 1871–1900* (New York: Harper, 1941), p. 334, sees this aspect of the fairs as an index to the growing international character of material civilization. See also Ford, p. 26, and A. Karlen, "Capsule History of World's Fairs," *Holiday* 36 (July 1964): 69.

3. Lewis Mumford, *The Brown Decades* (New York: Dover, 1955), p. 231.

4. The standard approach to the fairs has been, as Ada Louise Huxtable has noted, to trace exhibition building as a "series of dramatic exercises in progressive technology, from the glass and metal of the Crystal Palace to the increasing spans engineered for various Machinery Halls." "You Can't Go Home to Those Fairs Again," *New York Times*, 23 Oct. 1973, sec. II, p. 27.

5. Ford, pp. 26–27.

6. Foreign representation was also occasionally affected by the symbolic theme of a particular fair. Germany and England, for example, officially ignored the Paris World's Fair of 1889 because it commemorated the French Revolution. See Ford, pp. 24–26.

7. See, for example, H. T. Wood (Secretary to the Royal Commission for the Chicago World's Fair of 1893), "Chicago and Its Exhibition," *Nineteenth Century* 31 (April 1892): 533–65, or Ferdinand W. Peck (Chief U.S. Commissioner to Paris in 1900), "The U.S. at the Paris Exposition of 1900," *North American Review* 168 (January 1899): 24–33. The parallels between this and Social Darwinism are clear enough. The world's fairs provided a platform for judging the fittest of nations. Failure to demonstrate that would be interpreted as losing out in the race for survival.

8. Helen Augur, "From the Crystal Palace to the World of Tomorrow," *Travel* 72 (April 1939): 7.

3   America and the Great World's Fairs

1. Merle Curti, "America at the World's Fairs: 1851–1893," *American Historical Review* 55 (July 1950): 833.

2. Curti, p. 833.

3. *Punch*, 20 (1851): 243, quoted in Marcus Cunliffe, "America at the Great Exhibition of 1851," *American Quarterly* 3 (1951): 199. This article gives an excellent overall account of U.S. participation and British reactions.

4. Curti, p. 840.

5. The *Westminster Review*, referring to the recent bloomer propaganda, admitted that Americans were introducing a more sensible kind of women's wear. See Curti, p. 838.

6. *Punch*, 21 (1851): 117, quoted in Cunliffe, p. 125.

7. Curti, p. 841.

8. *Brother Johnathon's Epistle to his Relations Both Sides of the Atlantic, but Chiefly to his Father, John Bull, Brother Johnathon Being a Leetle Riled by the Remarks Made by John Bull at his*

Small Wares Displayed at the Opening of the Grand Exhibition (Boston, 1852), pp. 4–6, quoted in Hugo A. Meier, "American Technology in the Nineteenth Century," in *The American Culture,* ed. Hennig Cohen (Boston: Houghton Mifflin, 1968), p. 203.

9. Curti, p. 843.

10. Curti, p. 844.

11. Curti, p. 846.

12. Curti, p. 834. The United States throughout this period depended upon European capital to develop its resources and the economic importance of the world's fairs to the continuing development of the country was not lost upon such men as Secretary of State Seward, who had submitted a report to President Johnson urging a substantial U.S. commitment to the Paris World's Fair of 1867. See Peck, pp. 25–30, and Meier, p. 203.

13. Quoted in Curti, p. 835.

14. George Frederick Kunz, "Management and Uses of Expositions," *North American Review* 175 (September 1902): 414.

15. Karlen, p. 68.

16. Augur, p. 10.

17. Howard Mumford Jones, *The Age of Energy* (New York: Viking, 1970), p. 139.

18. Curti, p. 834.

19. *Artistic Guide to Chicago and the World's Columbian Exposition* (Chicago: R. S. Peale Co., 1891), p. 371.

20. Joseph M. Rogers, "Lessons From the International Exhibitions," *Forum* 32 (November 1901): 502.

21. Jones, p. 142.

22. M. H. DeYoung, "The Columbian World's Fair," *Cosmopolitan* 12 (March 1892): 605.

23. At the Chicago World's Fair seventeen years later no such inferiority in the arts would be admitted.

24. Russell Lynes, *The Tastemakers* (New York: Harper, 1954), p. 115. See also John A. Kouwenhoven, *The Arts in Modern American Civilization* (New York: Norton, 1948), pp. 87–90.

25. Kunz, p. 417.

26. The unusual significance of the world's fair in America as a focal point of competition for the national capital is implied by the popular American expression for such events. Every American fair of the period had a formal title such as "The World's Columbian Exposition" or "The Pan-American World's Exposition," but they were popularly referred to as the Chicago World's Fair or the Buffalo World's Fair, indicating that a greater importance was attached to their national urban meaning than to their international reason for being.

27. The raw newness of American cities and the enormous expanse of the country made hopes for stimulating extensive international tourism less important in America than they were in Europe. Thus, city rivalry in American world's fairs had less to do with predictions of indirect economic gain than elsewhere. See Ford, p. 24.

28. Edo McCullough, *World's Fair Midways* (New York: Exposition Press, 1966), pp. 29–71.

29. The Sawyer Tower, originally planned for one hundred feet, was the forerunner of the Eiffel Tower constructed for the Paris World's Fair of 1889. See McCullough, p. 33.

30. McCullough, p. 34.

31. Rogers, p. 506.

4   Energy and Uncertainty

1. Dee Brown, *The Year of the Century: 1876* (New York: Scribner's, 1966), p. 137.

2. Kouwenhoven, pp. 25–26.

3. Brown, p. 130.

4. Neil Harris, ed., *The Land of Contrasts 1889–1901* (New York: George Braziller, 1970), p. 7. Typewriter had a double meaning. It could mean either the machine itself, or its female operator.

5. Brown, p. 168. The entry of seven new western states into the Union between 1876 and 1896, and the corresponding rise in importance of the Midwest in determining the direction of American life, is indicative of a development that might have been noted at the centennial if it had been recognized as such. The West was to be henceforth a place to live in, not just to speculate upon and exploit. Officially, however, the rise of the West was ignored.

6. Brown, p. 43.

7. Whitman actually did revise an old poem, called it "Song of the Exposition," and offered it to the press. See Brown, p. 44.

8. Brown, p. 44.

9. Brown, p. 51.

10. Brown, pp. 117–120.

11. Edward C. Kirkland, *Dream and Thought in the Business Community 1860–1900* (1956; reprint ed., Chicago: Quadrangle Paperbacks, 1965) p. 3.

12. Kirkland, p. 4.

13. Kirkland, p. 6.

14. Thomas Beer, *Hanna, Crane, and the Mauve Decade* (New York: Knopf, 1941), p. 53.

15. See Kirkland, pp. 8–10.

16. 1873 and 1893; the other two are 1837 and 1929.

17. Kirkland, p. 7.

18. Real property, or tangible assets, are today still often referred to as securities.

19. Kirkland, p. 10.

20. Kirkland, pp. 16–18.

21. Kirkland, p. 147.

22. Robert H. Wiebe, *The Search for Order, 1877–1920* (New York: Hill and Wang, 1967), p. 12.

23. Arthur M. Schlesinger, *The Rise of the City: 1878–1898* (New York: Macmillan, 1933), pp. 67–76.

24. Schlesinger, p. 79.

25. See Morton and Lucia White, *The Intellectual Versus the City* (New York: Mentor, 1962) especially the last three chapters.

26. Schlesinger, p. 79.

27. Schlesinger, p. 76.

28. Schlesinger, pp. 61–64.

5   The Representative City

1. The first railroad line from Chicago was completed in 1848 and the first connection between the city and the eastern seaboard was accomplished in 1853. See Helen R. Jeter, *Trends of Population in the Region of Chicago* (Chicago: University of Chicago Press, 1927), p. 17.

2. Wood, p. 555.

3. Bessie Louise Pierce, *A History of Chicago 1871–1893* (New York: Knopf, 1957) 3: 10.

4. The city's first major captain of industry, Silas McCormick, was a Virginian, while its two meatpacking giants, Swift and Armour, were natives of Massachusetts.

5. Most people who acknowledge Chicago's remarkable growth in the period have assumed, probably incorrectly, that city life in these early years completely neglected the higher aspects of culture. Though most of the records of social and cultural interests and activities have been subsequently lost, there are indications—notably Harriet Martineau's descriptions of Chicago in 1836—of the existence of a refined and educated class of early Chicagoans. See Archibald Byrne, "Walter L. Newberry's Chicago," *Newberry Library Bulletin* 3 (August 1955): 262–263, which is exerpted in Carl Condit, *The Chicago School of Architecture* (Chicago: University of Chicago Press, 1964), p. 18.

,6. The story goes that the fire started in the barn behind the O'Leary cottage, when Mrs. O'Leary's cantankerous cow kicked over the kerosene lamp into the straw during a milking. The irony of the story is that the fire which destroyed Chicago left the O'Leary cottage unharmed.

7. Condit, p. 19.

8. Harold M. Mayer and Richard C. Wade, *Chicago: Growth of a Metropolis* (Chicago: University of Chicago Press, 1969), p. 117.

9. Hawthorne had written in his Preface to *The Marble Faun* (1859) that "Romance and poetry, ivy, lichens, and wallflowers need ruin to make them grow." After 1871, Chicago had the prerequisites.

10. Mayer and Wade, p. 117.

11. Mayer and Wade, p. 117.

12. The emotional value of the 1871 disaster to the city can be felt even today. Witness the adoption of the "Chicago Fire" as the nickname of Chicago's short-lived World Football League franchise.

13. "Development of Arts and Letters," in Ernest L. Bogart and Charles M. Thompson, eds., *The Industrial State 1870–1893, The Centennial History of Illinois* (Springfield: Illinois Centennial Commission, 1920) 4: 188.

14. W. T. Stead, *Chicago Today: The Labour War in America* (1894; reprint ed., New York: Arno Press, 1969), p. 87.

15. Lewis and Smith, p. 141.

16. Fuller, p. 198. 1880 was the peak year for agriculture in Cook County, thereafter the acreage devoted to farming declined. See Jeter, p. 9, for statistical data on the agricultural development of the Chicago region.

17. Schlesinger, p. 87.

18. Pierce, p. 20.

19. Jeter, pp. 18–19.

20. Mayer and Wade, p. 176.

21. Mayer and Wade, pp. 152–3, Jeter, p. 24, Pierce, p. 20. Between 1870 and 1890 the percentage of Afro-Americans in Chicago remained nearly constant at roughly one per hundred, or 1 percent.

22. Mayer and Wade, pp. 152–154.

23. Pierce, p. 20. In 1884, Potter Palmer built his $250,000 castle on what would later be Lake Shore Drive. Mayer and Wade, p. 144.

24. Mayer and Wade, pp. 124–128.

25. Mayer and Wade, p. 188.

26. Mayer and Wade, p. 118.

27. Thomas Robert Dewar, *A Ramble Round the Globe* (London: Chatto & Windus, 1894), p. 66.

28. Alan Pinkerton had been drawn initially to Chicago in these years to take up the fight as a city official against the rampant crime, and having failed, formed his famous, or infamous, private detective organization. An abolitionist, active in the underground railroad (he had put up John Brown and his sons on their way to Harper's Ferry), who guarded Abraham Lincoln against threats on his life, by the 1880s he was providing hired armies for industrialists to combat the rise of American unionism. See Ernest Poole, *Giants Gone: Men Who Made Chicago* (New York: McGraw-Hill, 1943), pp. 60–3.

29. Sol Bloom, *The Autobiography of Sol Bloom* (New York: Putnams' Sons, 1948), p. 124.

30. Quoted in Bessie Louis Pierce, ed., *As Others See Chicago: Impressions of Visitors 1673–1933* (Chicago: University of Chicago Press, 1933), p. 385.

31. Quoted in Pierce, *As Others See Chicago*, p. 305.

32. Ernest L. Bogart and John Mabry, eds., *The Modern Commonwealth, The Centennial History of Illinois* (Springfield: Illinois Centennial Commission, 1920) 5: 91. Lewis and Smith, p. 233.

33. Noble Canby, "Some Characteristics of Chicago," *Chautauquan* 15 (August 1892): 610, quoted in Pierce, *As Others See Chicago*, p. 369.

34. "Municipal History and Present Organization of the City of Chicago," *Bulletin of the University of Wisconsin* (Madison: University of Wisconsin, 1898), Economics, Political Science, and History Series, 2, No. 2, p. 158.

35. Stead, p. 100.

36. Bloom, p. 125.

37. Ginger, p. 23.

38. Quoted in Pierce, *As Others See Chicago,* p. 276.

39. Quoted in Pierce, *As Others See Chicago,* p. 352.

40. Pierce, *A History of Chicago,* p. 56.

41. "Map Notes and Comments," *Hull House Maps and Papers: A Presentation of Nationalities and Wages in a Congested District of Chicago Together with Comments and Essays on Problems Growing out of the Social Conditions* (1895; reprint ed., New York: Arno Press, 1970), p. 5.

42. As Ray Ginger has noted, child labor had existed for many years but the isolation and permanence of the tenement districts made the situation in the late nineteenth century more tragic and inhuman. "Child workers in 1850 in the Massachusetts cotton mills became foremen before they were twenty-one; child workers of 1890 in the sweatshops of Chicago became tubercular or rachitic before they were thirty." Ginger, p. 34.

43. Ginger, p. 38.

44. Ginger, p. 55.

45. Ginger, p. 49.

46. The trial of the Chicago anarchists was the turning point for Emma Goldman, according to Van Wyck Brooks in *The Confident Years* (New York: Dutton, 1952), p. 167. Two years earlier, she thought America "glorious." For the class antagonism revealed in the attacks on Altgeld see Joseph Dorfman, *Thorstein Veblen & His America* (New York: Viking, 1935), p. 94.

47. Brooks, p. 168.

48. Quoted in Pierce, *As Others See Chicago,* p. 288.

49. See Pierce, *A History,* p. 24.

50. Bernard Duffey, *The Chicago Renaissance in American Letters: A Critical History* (Michigan State Press, 1954), p. 32.

51. Quoted in Duffey, p. 27.

52. "Art and Labor," in *Hull-House Maps and Papers,* p. 178.

53. Stead, p. 91.

54. "Regional Studies in America: The Chicago Model," in *American Studies,* a supplement to *American Quarterly* 8 (October 1974): 29.

6 Genesis and Growth of the Idea

1. See Felix Gilbert's *Toward the Farewell Address* (Princeton: Princeton University, 1961) for the early roots of American

attitudes toward the Western hemisphere and Henry Nash Smith's *Virgin Land* (New York: Vintage, 1950) for a discussion of the development of the Western hero.

2. "The last Columbian Century Anniversary," *Harper's Weekly* 33 (17 August 1889) : 665.

3. Among those who claimed the original suggestion was Hinton Rowan Helper, who is said to have proposed in 1879 "a matchlessly grand World's Columbian Exposition" for St. Louis in 1892. See William Walton, *Art and Architecture of the World's Columbian Exposition* (Philadelphia: George Barrie, 1893), 1: ix.

4. William E. Cameron, ed., *The World's Fair, Being a Pictorial History of the Columbian Exposition, . . . with a Description of Chicago . . . with an Introduction by Thomas W. Palmer, Including a chapter on the Woman's Department by Frances E. Willard* (Chicago J. R. Jones, 1893), p. 126. Cited hereafter as *Pictorial History.*

5. Zaremba, who was much impressed by the Pan American exhibits at the centennial, claimed to have begun writing letters to promote the idea of a greater world's fair in honor of Columbus as early as 1876. See Ben C. Truman, ed., *History of the World's Fair* (Chicago: Monarch Book Co., 1893), p. 21, and *Dedicatory,* pp. 51–54.

6. *Chicago Times,* 16 February 1882, p. 3, col. 1.

7. Truman, p. 21, and *Dedicatory,* p. 51.

8. It was largely due to Anderson's suggestion that a naval review in New York harbor, as a way to get the national government to support the project, became a part of the original bill for the Columbian celebration. See Hubert H. Bancroft, *The Book of the Fair* (1894; reprint ed., New York: Bounty, n.d.), p. 37.

9. Various proposals mentioned at the time ranged from the erection of a Columbian memorial in Washington to the combining of a Columbian celebration with one honoring the centennial of the adoption of the Constitution over a period of three years (1889–1892). See *Dedicatory* p. 54, and Maurice F. Neufeld, "The Contribution of the World's Columbian Exposition of 1893 to the Idea of a Planned Society in the United States" (Ph.D. diss., University of Wisconsin, 1935), p. 30.

10. Charles Moore, *Daniel H. Burnham: Architect, Planner of Cities* (Boston: Houghton Mifflin, 1921), 1:31.

11. The editorials which did appear on the subject mentioned the value of such a fair for the development of the Mississippi Valley and the West, and one (*Inter Ocean,* 16 May 1883) said it would serve to "introduce the North and South anew in a city free from prejudice and animosities." See Francis L. Lederer, "The Genesis of the World's Columbian Exposition" (M.A. thesis, University of Chicago, 1967).

12. Bloom, p. 111, and *Dedicatory,* p. 54.

13. Quoted in Fuller, p. 210. See also Lederer, pp. 3–4, and Pierce, *History of Chicago,* p. 501. The Interstate Industrial Exposition had been established in 1873, and gave annual exhibitions of industrial products in its own building in Chicago. Increasingly, more space was also given to artistic works. (The exhibit of 1885 included more than 400 paintings, mostly by Americans). See Fuller, p. 200.

14. Lederer, p. 7.

15. Quoted in Lederer, p. 8.

16. Quoted in Lederer, p. 8.

17. *Dedicatory,* p. 54.

18. *Pictorial History,* p. 126.

19. Lederer, p. 14.

20. *Pictorial History,* p. 126.

21. *Pictorial History,* p. 127, and Lederer, p. 14.

22. *Pictorial History,* p. 126.

23. As early as September, 1887, American magazines like the *Building Budget* began publishing prospective views of the major fair buildings as they were being constructed on the Champs de Mars. Donald Hoffman, *The Architecture of John Wellborn Root* (Baltimore: Johns Hopkins, 1973), p. 222.

24. "Suggestions for the Next World's Fair," *Century Magazine* 17 (April 1890) : 845.

25. This incident is quoted in Theodore Stanton, "The International Exhibition of 1900," *Century Magazine* 51 (December 1895) : 314.

26. Quoted in Amos W. Wright, "World's Fair Progress," *Harper's Weekly* 33 (31 August 1889) : 707.

27. The New York Finance Committee which met on August 20 included Cornelius Vanderbilt, William Rockefeller, Jay Gould, and August Belmont, among others. It was proposed that a company be formed with an authorization to issue $15,000,000 in stock. Potential gate receipts were estimated at $7,500,000 and it was proposed that the building erected for the fair be turned over afterwards to the city. Charles A. Dana, who was elected Chairman of the Buildings

and Site Committee, wrote a check for $10,000 to cover the initial expenses and a committee was dispatched to visit and report on the Paris Exposition. See Wright, p. 707.

28. Amos W. Wright, "World's Fairs of 1889 and 1892," *Harper's Weekly* 33 (10 August 1889) : 652.

29. Wright, "The World's Fairs of 1889 and 1892," p. 652. "Everything conspires," he concluded, "to make the World's Fair of 1892 at New York what it purports to be—a thoroughly representative occasion."

30. "The World's Fair of 1892," *Harper's Weekly* 33 (3 August 1889) : 614.

31. *Pictorial History,* p. 130.

32. Quoted from Lederer, p. 16.

33. Pierce, *History of Chicago,* p. 502.

34. "The Meanest City in America," *Chicago Tribune,* 22 July 1889, quoted in Lederer, p. 17.

35. Quoted in Lederer, p. 20.

36. "The Farmer at the World's Fair," *Chicago Tribune,* 26 September 1889, quoted in Lederer, p. 34.

37. *Chicago Tribune,* 23 July 1889, quoted in Lederer, p. 35.

38. Quoted in Lederer, p. 34.

39. *Chicago Tribune,* 26 September 1889, quoted in Lederer, p. 34. Rudyard Kipling, who was touring America during this period, remarked that there was "some sort of dispute between New York and Chicago as to which town shall give an exhibition of products, and through the medium of their most dignified journals the two cities are ya-hooing and hi-yi-ing at each other like opposition newsboys." This is quoted in Robert Shackleton, *The Book of Chicago* (Philadelphia: Pennsylvania Publishing Co., 1920), p. 230. H. C. Brown in his *In Golden Nineties,* (Hastings-on-Hudson: Valentine Manual, Inc., 1928), which focuses mostly upon New York during the decade, called the contest between New York and Chicago "acrimonious" (p. 356). H. C. Bunner in his article "The Making of the White City," *Scribner's Monthly* 12 (October 1892) : 403, described the newspaper debate as an "extraordinary exhibition of indecorum," one which brought credit to neither city and was carried on "with the brutal acrimony of an English parliamentary campaign and the sputtering hysteria of an interpelation in the French Chamber of Deputies."

40. Quoted in Lederer, p. 26.

41. "Raising the Sectional Issue to get the Fair," *Chicago Tribune,* 28 September 1889.

42. "Why St. Louis is out of the Race," *Chicago Tribune,* 1 October 1889, quoted in Lederer, p. 28.

43. *Pictorial History,* p. 127.

44. Willis J. Abbot, "The Makers of the Fair," *Outlook* 48 (18 November 1893) : 884.

45. *Chicago Tribune,* 2 August 1889, quoted in Lederer, p. 42. By August 6, standing committees had been established on finance, transportation, preliminary expenses, congressional action, and local and national promotion. These included over 150 men, most of whom Lederer found listed in *The Elite Directory, Who Was Who in America,* or *The Dictionary of American Biography.* The bulk of this early organizational work seems to have been done by Thomas B. Bryan, Jefferey, Davis, and Gage. See Lederer, pp. 43–44, *Pictorial History,* p. 127, and Neufeld, p. 31.

46. *Dedicatory,* p. 55, Neufeld, p. 33, *Pictorial History,* pp. 128–129.

47. Neufeld, p. 34.

48. A representative sample of the original pamphlets and circulars is held by the Chicago Historical Association. One of the more humorous examples is a flyer, originally addressed to the citizens of New York by a native son in Chicago, that was returned by some New Yorkers with the remark that Chicago hasn't the room for an exhibition and that "New York is the place. We are the people. We have the boodle."

49. *Pictorial History,* p. 130, and Neufeld, p. 37.

50. *Pictorial History,* pp. 130–131.

51. Francis apparently felt that there was a conspiracy between the Senate and the Chicago people to "rub St. Louis' face in the mud." He would wait fourteen years to have his compensation as the chief organizer and promoter of the St. Louis World's Fair of 1904. See G. R. Leighton, "The Year St. Louis Enchanted the World," *Harper's Magazine* 221 (August 1960) : 38.

52. Rossiter Johnson, ed., *A History of the Columbian Exposition* (New York: Appletons, 1897–1898), 1: 11.

53. Johnson, p. 12 and Neufeld, p. 35.

54. Johnson, p. 12 and Neufeld, p. 36.

55. *Pictorial History,* p. 131.

56. Neufeld, p. 36.

57. "The World's Fair of 1892: Chicago favored by the House of Representatives," *Scientific American* 62 (March 1890) : 146–7.

58. *Pictorial History*, p. 132. Another reason for the fair being given to Chicago over New York was a political one. New York was controlled by the infamous—and Democratic—Tammany Hall organization which could be expected to use the fair (real estate contracts, building and construction, concessions, etc.) as a means to increase its financial and political strength. The experience of John A. Roebling's Brooklyn Bridge was too recent to be easily forgotten. A Republican Congress would not have been in any mood to allow such fat pickings to fall into Tammany's hands. See Brown, *In Golden Nineties,* p. 356.

59. Quoted in Harry Thurston Peck, *Twenty Years of the Republic 1885–1905* (New York: Dodd, Mead, & Co., 1906), p. 350. There may have even been some relief felt in New York when Chicago was given the fair because of some fear that a fair near Central Park would ruin it. A large unoccupied area just north of the park had been tentatively chosen as the site, and a real estate boom had ensued. With the selection of Chicago, a number of the speculators, rather than Central Park, were brought to ruin. See Brown, p. 356 and Bunner, p. 402. Charles Dana Gibson's drawings also support this. See F. D. Downey, *Portrait of An Era As Drawn by C. D. Gibson* (New York: Scribners, 1936).

60. H. T. Wood in "Chicago and Its Exhibition," *Nineteenth Century* 31 (April 1892) : 559, said that New York was "at first incredulous, then exasperated" by Chicago's success. "She does not love her pushing, energetic sister." It was the *pride* of New York that was injured. New York is the *de facto capital* of the United States and "the rise of a second capital cannot be pleasing."

61. Neufeld, pp. 28–38.

62. Neufeld, p. 38 and *Dedicatory,* p 55.

63. *Dedicatory,* p. 55. See Appendix C.

7   Organization

1. "The World's Fair of 1892: Chicago favored by the House of Representatives," p. 146.

2. F. A. Walker "America's Fourth Centenary," *Forum* 8 (February 1890) : 618.

3. Walker, pp. 612–618.

4. Walker, p. 615.

5. Walker, p. 612.

6. Walker, p. 616.

7. P. T. Barnum, "What the Fair Should Be," *North American Review* 150 (March 1890) : 400. As for novel features, Barnum suggested obtaining the loan of the mummy of Ramses II from Egypt.

8. George Berger, "Suggestions for the Next World's Fair," *Century* 17 (April 1890) : 845.

9. Berger, p. 845.

10. Berger, p. 847.

11. Berger, p. 848.

12. "The Columbian Exposition and American Civilization," *Atlantic Monthly* 71 (May 1893) : 581.

13. Quoted in Brooks, p. 170.

14. See, for example, H. C. Bunner, p. 402, and especially Julian Ralph, "Our Exposition at Chicago," *Harper's Monthly* 71 (May 1893) : 581.

15. It is ironic that Congress, out of fear that the Chicago Company would run the fair like a business venture (it was, after all, a corporation which sold stock and whose stockholders could naturally be expected to realize a profit from their investment) chose to enlarge the company's capital subscription rather than assume financial responsibility itself. See Appendix C.

16. Yet, the mechanism which was established by the act creating the exposition ultimately proved to be more of an obstacle to efficient planning and decision making.

17. The president of the Centennial Commission, General Joseph R. Hawley, had advised against the future use of joint government/local corporation management in his report on the Philadelphia World's Fair. See Neufeld, p. 40.

18. Quoted in *Pictorial History*, p. 145.

19. The committees which were established included an Executive, Rules and ByLaws, Tariffs and Transportation, Foreign Affairs, Fine Arts, Science, History, Literature and Education, Agriculture, Livestock, Horticulture, Finance, Auditing, Ceremonies, Classification, Manufactures, Commerce, Mines and Mining, Fisheries, Electricity, Forestry, Machinery, Printing, Grounds and Buildings, Federal Legislation, Awards and World's Congresses.

20. "Organization of the World's Fair," *Harper's Weekly* 34 (26 July 1890) : 578; *Dedicatory,* p. 56.

21. At the meeting on April 4, nearly four hundred thousand shares of stock were voted in electing the Board of Directors. The

names of the first directory can be found in *Pictorial History,* p. 132. At the April 30 meeting, the executive officers were elected: Lyman T. Gage, the vice-president of the First National Bank of Chicago, was elected president of the corporation; Thomas B. Bryan, a lawyer-banker and former president of the Chicago Sanitary Fair of 1865, and Potter Palmer, a real estate investor and former partner of Marshall Field, were named first and second vice-presidents, respectively; Anthony F. Seeberger was elected treasurer; Benjamin Butterworth was elected secretary; and William K. Ackerman was elected auditor. Chairmen of the initial standing committees were also elected, the first of these being Ferdinand W. Peck and DeWitt C. Creiger, of Finance and Bylaws and Grounds and Buildings, respectively.

22. Neufeld, p. 49.

23. See David H. Crook, "Louis Sullivan, The World's Columbian Exposition, and American Life," (Ph.D. diss., Harvard University, 1963), p. 303.

24. *Harper's Weekly* 34 (26 July 1890): 578. Potter Palmer, for instance, the second vice-president and a retired millionaire, received no salary.

25. Hereafter called the Chicago Company.

26. *Harper's Weekly* 34 (4 October 1890): 779; *Artistic Guide,* p. 214; *Pictorial History,* p. 153; *Harper's Weekly* 34 (26 July 1890): 578.

27. The city of Chicago's voluntary decision to increase its indebtedness to support the fair is a good example of the civic interest of the city in the project after the reformation of the Exposition Company.

28. See Appendix A. The major American world's fairs, putting more emphasis on space, almost always exceeded those of other nations of the same period.

29. Mayer and Wade, p. 102.

30. Newfeld, p. 90; *Harper's Weekly* 34 (26 July 1890): 578.

31. *Harper's Weekly* 34 (26 July 1890): 578.

32. The state stipulated that filled land could be used by the exposition for one year and then become the property of the city of Chicago to be used as a public park. All buildings must be dismantled. *Pictorial History,* p. 153. The city council's ordinance pledged the city up to $2 million for piling and filling and also required that the ground afterward become a city park. It also ordered the fair directors to make no unilateral bargain with Illinois Central for use of the lake front occupied by its tracks. "Chicago World's Fair," *Scientific American* 63 (2 August 1890): 70–1.

33. *Pictorial History,* p. 153. "It was the only time in the history of that company that its proverbial policy of greed resulted in benefit to the City of Chicago." *Pictorial History,* p. 153.

34. Hoffman, p. 224.

35. Hoffman, p. 224; Moore, p. 32.

36. Moore, p. 32.

37. This committee was one of the first established by the Chicago Company, having been established before Congress gave the fair to Chicago, and was one of the most important and hardest working of the committees in the early planning stage of the fair. Johnson says that the committee sat almost daily from the spring of 1890 until August of 1892 (Johnson, *A History of the World's Columbian Exposition,* 1: 48) and its members included many of the more influential figures in Chicago and the Exposition Company: DeWitt Cregier, Lyman Gage, George Davis, Joseph Medill, Charles Schwab, Potter Palmer, Edward Jefferey, Robert A. Waller, and others served at various times on the committee (see Neufeld, p. 95).

38. *Pictorial History,* p. 153.

39. Moore, p. 33.

40. Bancroft, p. 53.

41. Hoffman, p. 225; Crook, p. 245.

42. *Harper's Weekly* 34 (4 October 1890): 779.

43. Neufeld, p. 47.

44. Neufeld, p. 52.

45. Lewis and Smith, pp. 203–204.

46. *Harper's Weekly* 34 (4 October 1890): 779.

47. Neufeld, p. 56.

48. A minority report was also submitted by President Gage recommending General D. H. Hastings of Pennsylvania for consideration, but Davis was elected by a slight majority of the commissioners. Born in Massachusetts, Davis had served as a colonel in the Union Army and after the war became active in Republican politics and was elected three times to Congress. At the time of his appointment as director-general, he was acting as treasurer of Cook County. *Harper's Weekly* 34 (4 October 1890): 779; *Pictorial History,* p. 149.

49. *Pictorial History,* p. 149; G. Brown Goode, *First Draft of a System of Classification for the World's Columbian Exposition*

(Washington: Press of Gedney and Roberts, 1890) ; *Harper's Weekly* 34 (22 November 1890) : 915.

50. *Harper's Weekly* 34 (4 October 1890) : 779; Neufeld, p. 56; Hoffman, p. 225.

51. "World's Columbian Exposition," *Harper's Weekly* 34 (22 November 1890) : 914.

52. Neufeld, a recent student of the administrative policy of the fair, for example, holds that the evolution of a general administrative procedure is "a study of how these two groups learned to cooperate in the work before them." Neufeld, p. 23.

53. "World's Columbian Exposition," *Harper's Weekly* 34 (22 November 1890) : 914.

54. Ibid.

55. Neufeld, p. 58.

56. *Pictorial History,* p. 150; Neufeld, p. 58–9.

57. Neufeld, p. 60.

58. Neufeld, p. 61.

8   The Site, the Plan, and the Design

1. Harriet Monroe, *John Wellborn Root* (Boston and New York: Houghton Mifflin, 1896), p. 223.

2. Neufeld, p. 96; Moore, p. 34.

3. Hoffman suggests that this was done at Burnham's request at least in part "to sanction his newly acquired pre-eminence." Hoffman, p. 230.

4. Moore, p. 34. See also Carl Condit's discussion of Burnham and Root in his *Chicago School of Architecture.*

5. "The one faculty," wrote Montgomery Schuyler, "that was absolutely indispensable to the success of a practitioner of architecture in Chicago." William Jordy and Ralph Coe, ed., *American Architecture and Other Writings* (Cambridge: Harvard University Press, 1961), 2: 405.

6. See Hoffman, p. 247; Schuyler, p. 407.

7. Hoffman, p. 223.

8. Eugene Pike was a former client of Burnham and Root and John B. Sherman had given the firm their first large commission in 1874 and subsequently became Burnham's father-in-law in 1897. See Hoffman, p. 223.

9. Root had himself favored major use of the Lake Front because the fair would then leave an improved area in the heart of the city and possibly a few permanent buildings. Monroe, p. 218.

10. *Harper's Weekly* 34 (6 December 1890) : 951; Monroe, p. 230.

11. Several of the commissioners who drove out to the "swampy wilderness" considered it absurd and demanded that the South Park Board retract their restrictions on the use of Washington Park or else the commission would compel Congress to remove the fair from Chicago. Monroe, p. 230.

12. Monroe, p. 232.

13. Hoffman, p. 226. Jackson Park was approved as the principal site, although the Lake Front was still to have some features (Art Gallery, Annex, Music Hall). "Management of the World's Fair," *Harper's Weekly* 34 (6 December 1890) : 951. Actually, it was not until February of 1891 that plans for permanent world's fair buildings on the Lake Front were finally abandoned. *Artistic Guide,* p. 341.

14. See Appendix E; *Pictorial History,* p. 156.

15. The plan that was submitted by Burnham was the famous "brown paper plat done in pencil" by Root. It was executed in a fairly rough, large scale and the specifications were quite sketchy, but the general features of the scheme were clear. Moore, p. 36.

16. Moore, pp. 35–36; Hoffman, p. 226.

17. Hoffman, p. 225.

18. Crook, p. 253. Edward T. Jeffery, the chairman of the Grounds and Buildings Committee, had been sent to Paris to report on the exposition and had been greatly impressed.

19. Hoffman, p. 226.

20. Monroe, p. 218.

21. Hoffman, pp. 225–226; Monroe, pp. 224–225.

22. Moore, p. 35; Crook, p. 248; Monroe, p. 225.

23. Hoffman (quoting Burnham), p. 226; Moore, p. 35. Monroe says that Olmsted recommended that the most imposing building be located at the head of the court, but in any case, the model was once again the Parisian one. Monroe, p. 225. Chicago wanted to surpass Paris in the clear span of its largest building (Manufactures) and in the overall space in the main halls. This was proposed by Edward T. Jeffery who had succeeded Joseph Mendill on the Grounds and Building Committee. Hoffman, p. 223.

24. Hoffman says that Burnham, at least, never seemed bothered by the "disparity between architectural pomp and mysteri-

ous sylvan scenery" (Hoffman, p. 226), and that Olmsted, who had originally agreed to allow smaller buildings on the island, later fought to keep it entirely free from construction "as a foil to the artificial grandeur and sumptuousness of the other parts" (Hoffman, p. 227).

25. His revised plan for Jackson Park of 1895 eliminated any trace of the Court of Honor and the only formal landscaping specified was near the Fine Arts Building, the one fair building designed to outlast the fair. Hoffman, p. 227.

26. These were: Agriculture (500' X 800'), Horticulture (250' X 998'), Fisheries (165' X 335'), Mines (350' X 700'), Machinery (492' X 846'), Transportation (256' X 960'), Manufactures and Liberal Arts (787' X 1687'), Electricity (345' X 690'), Fine Arts (320' X 500'), Administration (262' X 262').

27. Adler and Sullivan had just completed the famous Chicago Auditorium and Beman had built the town of Pullman several years before. Hoffman, p. 227.

28. Root never had expected to design many of the actual fair buildings and he had predicted, even before Chicago was selected, the architects who would be invited. Hoffman, p. 230.

29. Monroe, p. 235.

30. Olmsted had altered Burnham's original somewhat and Root had rewritten it. Hoffman, p. 230. See Appendix F.

31. The list included Richard M. Hunt, McKim, Mead and White, and George Post of New York, Peabody and Stearns of Boston, and Van Brunt and Howe of Kansas City.

32. There was no question that the architects listed were national leaders in their profession, but the opposition emphasized that Chicago money was paying for the fair, and the Chicago architects were equally as competent as the easterners and much more progressive. See Monroe, p. 236. Both Burnham and Root, according to Monroe, wanted to give the great fair a national character by inviting the country's leading architects to take part (p. 235). In addition, inviting guest architects from outside of Chicago seemed an excellent way to overcome some of the disappointment of the other cities who had wanted the fair. Hoffman, p. 230.

33. Moore, p. 40; Hoffman, p. 231. See Appendix G.

34. McKim had been a leading advocate of the classical style for several years and it was probably he who made the initial suggestion. Mead reported later that he could recall no opposition being made to the use of the classical motif, but then at this time there wasn't much interest in participation at all. Moore, p. 41; Charles Moore, *The Life and Times of Charles Follen McKim* (1929; reprint ed., New York: Da Capo, 1970), p. 111.

35. Moore, *McKim,* p. 113. Nonetheless, Root went East at the first of the year and after a short meeting with the eastern architects came away depressed over their attitude toward the enterprise. They apparently shared the public feeling that Chicago would produce nothing better than a cattle-show, that westerners would never give art a chance, and that beautiful effects couldn't be accomplished with such large buildings in the monotonous surroundings of Chicago in so short a time. Monroe, p. 249.

36.. Quoted in Hoffman, p. 233.

37. The five were Burling and Whitehouse, Jenny and Mundie, Henry Ives Cobb, S. S. Beman, and Adler and Sullivan.

38. Monroe, p. 240; Hoffman, p. 234; Moore, *McKim,* p. 113.

39. Hoffman, p. 234.

40. Root was out of town but returned later in the day. It was his fortieth birthday. *Pictorial History,* p. 116.

41. It was a cold winter day, gloomy and overcast, and the grounds looked particularly forbidding. Robert Peabody, Burnham recalled later, shouted to him from a pier, "Do you mean to say that you really propose opening a fair here by '93?" "Yes," Burnham replied, "we intend to." "It can't be done," said Peabody. "That point," responded Burnham, "is settled." Quoted in Moore, *Burnham,* p. 43.

42. Quoted in Moore, *Burnham,* p. 43. Later Burnham remarked to Charles Moore that "it was the same old appeal that the Chicago men were brought up on," quoted in Hoffman, p. 235.

43. Hoffman, 253; Moore, *Burnham,* p. 46.

44. With the death of his partner of twenty years, and the chief designer of their private firm, Burnham seemed to take his job as chief of construction of the fair even more seriously than before. He literally threw himself into the work of the fair, assuming more and more responsibility for its outcome and an increasing amount of authority for decision making.

The work was divided as follows: Hunt—the Administration Building (the dominant structure of the Court of Honor and the entrance point to the fair); Peabody and Stearns—Machinery Hall; George Post—the giant Manufactures and Liberal Arts Building; Van Brunt and Howe—Electricity; S. S. Beman—Mines and Mining; Adler and Sullivan—Transportation; Cobb—Fisheries; Burling and Whitehouse—Venetian Village; Jenney—Horticulture; McKim, Mead and White—Agriculture.

Burnham had originally thought that Adler and Sullivan should be assigned the Music Hall, a lesser building then to be on the Lake Front, because of their success with acoustics in Chicago's Auditorium, but when they objected, he first offered them the Art Building (also expected to be on the Lake Front) and finally assigned them the Transportation Building. Crook, p. 268. Burnham also knew the feeling of the Committee on Grounds and Buildings that Chicago's architects should be better represented in the Court of Honor (S. S. Beman's Mines Building was the only one tentatively assigned) and they desired the Agricultural Building to be given to a Chicago firm. (Hoffman quotes a January 6 letter of Burnham's to that effect, p. 234.) Burnham, however, assigned the Agriculture building to McKim.

45. Neufeld, p. 110.

46. Moore says that Burnham had foreseen the need of an advisor on sculptural decoration and had written Saint-Gaudens asking his advice in selecting the sculptors. Moore, *Burnham*, p. 46.

47. *Pictorial History*, p. 167. He had had a long and extremely successful relationship with McKim, Mead and especially Stanford White, and had just completed work on the three sculpted panels for the entrance to McKim's Boston Public Library.

48. Moore, *Burnham*, p. 46. Almost every revision of Root's initial plan of November, 1890, was toward greater axiality and formality. Hoffman gives a concise and convincing illustrated analysis of the evolution of Root's plan in his *Architecture of John Root*, pp. 227–229.

49. Daniel H. Burnham and Francis D. Millet, *The Book of the Builders* (Chicago: Columbia Memorial Pub., 1894), p. 29.

50. Quoted in Moore, *McKim*, pp. 118–119; and Moore, *Burnham*, p. 47.

51. Quoted in Hoffman, p. 221.

52. By the end of February, the Board of Directors of the Chicago Company had decided in order to keep costs down, that all remaining fair buildings projected for the Lake Front (the Fine Arts Building and the Music Hall) should be relocated at Jackson Park. In order to make this accommodation, it was decided that the Venetian Village, originally planned for the end of the pier of the Grand Court, would be replaced by Saint-Gauden's idea of columns, Music Hall, peristyle and casino. Whitehouse of Burling and Whitehouse

—who had been appointed to do the Venetian Village—became ill and was forced to refuse Burnham's offer of designing the Fine Arts Building, while Adler and Sullivan had earlier rejected the Music Hall in favor of the Transportation Building. This was the situation which led up to Charles Atwood's appointment as designer of two of the fair's most prominent structures—the Art Building and the monumental peristyle group. Atwood subsequently was given responsibility for numerous smaller buildings (Terminal Station, Forestry, Dairy, et al.) and for "finishing" details like the obelisk and grand colonnade entrance to the livestock pavilion, the latter "a very odd portal," as Hoffman says, p. 229.

53. Even Hoffman, who is generally unimpressed with Atwood's designs, concedes this much, p. 221.

54. Hoffman, p. 227; H. C. Bunner, in *Scribner's Monthly*, said that it was Codman's work that made the water an effective feature of the setting, heightening the impressiveness of the architecture. He was the author of the "water show in the heart of the landshow." (p. 413)

55. Quoted in Moore, *Burnham*, p. 50. Granger, in his biography of McKim says that McKim persuaded the others to adopt the uniform color. See Alfred Hoyt Granger, *Charles Follen McKim* (Boston: Houghton Mifflin, 1913), p. 57.

56. Quoted in Moore, *Burnham*, p. 50.

57. Burnham remembered Millet for his organization of the "white-wash gang," the painters who used the novel method of spray painting invented by a New Yorker (which later came into general use of painting freight cars and automobiles) and for his ability to keep the artists from fighting among one another. Moore, *Burnham*, pp. 50–56.

58. *Pictorial History*, p. 168.

59. *Pictorial History*, p. 169.

60. Daniel Burnham, "The Building of the Exposition," *A Week at the Fair* (Chicago: Rand, McNally, 1893), p. 31.

61. For example, see Frank Millet, "The Designers of the Fair," *Harper's Monthly* 85 (November 1892): 872–873; and H. C. Bunner, "The Making of the White City," *Scribner's Monthly* 12 (October 1892): 417.

62. Burnham, *The Book of the Builders*, p. 6; Burnham, "The Building of the Exposition," p. 31.

63. Hoffman, p. 235.

64. H. C. Bunner, "The Making of the White City," *Scribner's*

Monthly 12 (October 1892) : 417. As Rossiter Johnson later wrote, "The life of the Director of Works [the title later given to Burnham] and his staff was like that of soldiers on the field." Johnson, *A History,* 1: 159.

65. Moore, *Burnham,* p. 53. Burnham was reported to have been overheard, at one point, muttering, "By heaven, I've undertaken to build this fair, and I'm going to do it." *Pictorial History,* p. 239.

66. Willis J. Abbot, "The Makers of the Fair," *Outlook* 48 (18 November 1893) : 884.

67. Perhaps he thought that the harmony of those masters would be communicated to the workers. Edgar Lee Masters, *A Tale of Chicago* (New York: Putnam's Sons, 1933) , p. 250.

68. Lewis and Smith, *Chicago,* p. 204.

69. Lewis and Smith, *Chicago,* p. 188; Ginger, *Altgeld's America,* p. 17.

70. Moore, *Burnham,* p. 51.

71. Millet, "The Designers of the Fair," p. 872.

72. Millet, "The Designers of the Fair," p. 878.

73. A combination of plaster and jute fibre, this plaster-of-Paris was adaptable to almost all forms of handling. It was easily and cheaply prepared, could be made coarse or fine, and when mixed with cement, became water-resistant. When wet, "staff" could be molded or cast into shape and when dry it became tough and stiff like wood and, like wood, could be bored, sawed, nailed, and colored.

74. Millet, "The Designers of the Fair," p. 878.

75. Other contributing sculptors were Olim Warner, Paul Barlett, Edwin Kennys, Louis Saint-Gaudens (Augustus' brother) , Carl Bitter, Larken G. Mead, Phemister Proctor, Bela Pratt, Rohl-Smith, Bush-Brown, Rideout, Boyle, Mora, Waagen, Baur, Blankenship, and Partridge. The artists also included Julian Alden Neir, Walter Shirlaw, James Carol Beckwith, Edwin Howland Blashfield, Robert Reid, Edward Emerson Simmons, Charles Stanley Reinhart, David Maitland Armstrong, George Willoughby Maynard, William Leftwich Dodge, McEwen, Earle, and Weir. Moore, *Burnham,* p. 55; *A Week at the Fair,* p. 135; *Pictorial History,* pp. 171–173.

76. Daniel Chester French is most famous today for his seated statue of Lincoln in the Lincoln Memorial in Washington, D.C. (1922) .

77. French's Republic was colossal indeed, sixty-five feet tall (making an even one hundred feet with the pedestal) and weighing thirty-five tons, its little finger was two feet, three inches long and its nose was thirty inches. His treatment of the Republic was formal, almost archaic, and cold. Draped in heavy ropes to suggest a lawyer's gown, a breast-plate and sword partly revealed, and holding in her outstretched hands a globe surmounted by an eagle and a staff with the liberty cap, the figure's rigid appearance was relieved only partially by a more natural treatment of the facial features. The graceless weight of the statue earned it the name "Big Mary" during the fair. Shackleton, *The Book of Chicago,* p. 253.

MacMonnies' fountain, on the other hand, executed primarily in the sculptor's studio on the Boulevard Montparnasse in Paris, and said to have been inspired, however unlikely, by a sketch made by Columbus, expressed at least some sense of movement and youth. The idea of the work was to present Columbia, genius of liberty, riding upon the Ship of State (or boat of progress) , holding a torch in her right hand and being propelled by the oars of science and art while Father Time manned the helm. On either side of this principal allegorical group were two of the largest electric fountains ever built. Each of the basins was sixty feet in diameter and included over one hundred fifty jets capable of throwing their two inch wide streams of water over one hundred feet into the air. The fountain was fully lighted by electricity, built by the Edison Company, and the pumps and electrical controls were housed in the Machinery Building. The cost of operating the lights and pumps was estimated at nearly $1,000 a night. *A Week at the Fair,* pp. 78–79.

9   Finance and Promotion

1. In November 1890, Georges Berger had suggested that an adequate estimate of the cost of producing a world's fair in the United States might run as high as $17 million for the major buildings, landscaping, operating expenses, and administration. It was a large figure, he admitted, but "the Americans are a rich people; they can afford to pay soundly for the glory which awaits them." Berger, p. 850.

2. The Report of the President is quoted in *Artistic Guide to Chicago,* pp. 217–218; and it agrees substantially with the figures estimated by the Budget Committee on February 20, 1891, which are quoted in Neufeld, pp. 83–84.

3. The plans for the Manufacturers and Liberal Arts Building, for example, had been accepted in the spring of 1891 and the Chicago Company had let contracts when the National Commission

changed its mind, increased the space for exhibitors, and doubled the original cost of the building. Even then, when the building was finally erected and was the largest enclosed structure in the world, the National Commission had promised more space than it held and several annexes had to be built and paid for by the Chicago Company. *Artistic Guide to Chicago*, p. 285.

4. Neufeld, p. 76.

5. "Report of the Chairman of the Committee on Grounds and Buildings," to the Board of Directors, 2 September 1891, quoted in *Pictorial History*, p. 181.

6. President Harrison's message to Congress is excerpted in *Pictorial History*, pp. 182–183.

7. Julian Ralph in *Harper's Monthly* wrote that many congressmen held a strong suspicion that a petition for aid was an attempt by the city to fleece the national public. In "Our Exposition at Chicago," *Harper's Monthly* 84 (January 1892) : 214.

8. Throughout the debate the Senate had been more sympathetic to the fair than the House.

9. Neufeld, p. 79. The text of the appropriating act can be found in *Pictorial History*, pp. 184–185.

10. Paris in 1889 had averaged fifty thousand paid visitors per Sunday. Almost since the proposal of holding a Columbian celebration was first made public, Congress had been besieged with hundreds of petitions from orthodox religious groups and journals to require the fair to remain closed on Sunday. Part of it had to do with religious concerns, but a part of it also had to do with Chicago's reputation as held especially in the East. See *Harper's Weekly* editorial, "The World's Fair," 34 (4 October 1890) : 779; and Kunz, "Management and Uses of Expositions," p. 417.

11. Neufeld, p. 80. *Pictorial History*, p. 186.

12. Taking note of this, *The Journal of the Franklin Institute* in May of 1892 said that Congress should feel it incumbent "both in point of actual obligation and that the national honor may be maintained before the world, to provide the means for meeting the excess of expenditures which the action of its representative [the National Commission] rendered necessary." From an editorial "The World's Fair," *Journal of the Franklin Institute*, 133 (May 1892) : 363.

13. Ralph had by this time become *Harper's* chief correspondent on the developments of the fair. See Ralph, "Our Exposition at Chicago," *Harper's Monthly*, 84 (January 1892) : 209.

14. R. E. A. Dorr, "How We Told the World of the White City's Wonders," in *A Week at the Fair*, p. 33.

15. There was some difficulty in sending Charles Graham's large, beautifully colored pictures through the foreign mails as they were larger than the International Postal Union allowed, but John Wanamaker (developer of the department store in 1877 and postmaster general) was able to arrange a special agreement with foreign postal officials permitting the pictures to pass into their postal systems. See Dorr, p. 34.

16. *Pictorial History*, p. 158.

17. Dorr, p. 35.

18. Sol Bloom, about whom more will be said, related an amusing incident in this connection. He had a flair for advertising and was often called in to explain one thing or another to reporters. On one occasion when the Manufactures Building was just underway, reporters were given long lists of statistics about its tremendous size: "I could feel they weren't in the least interested in the number of acres or tons of steel, so I said, 'Look at it this way—it's going to be big enough to hold the entire standing army of Russia!' I had no idea then, any more than I have at this moment, of the size of the Russian army. But the papers liked it and the phrase caught on." Bloom, p. 120.

19. Dorr, p. 35.

20. France, England, Germany, Spain, Japan, China, Mexico, Peru, Honduras, Salvador, Costa Rica, Columbia, Cuba, Venezuela, Turkey, Denmark, and the Dominican Republic. *Artistic Guide*, p. 219.

21. See F. D. Thomas, "The Sultan and the Chicago Exhibition," *Magazine of American History* 26 (October 1891) : 291, for Turkey's reaction; Stanton, "International Exhibition of 1900," p. 317, for France and Germany; and *Artistic Guide to Chicago*, p. 277, for Japan.

22. See Ralph, *Harper's Monthly* 84 (January 1892) : 211.

23. In some states, especially in the South, there were statutes prohibiting the spending of public funds on buildings outside the state. In those cases, private means, which took longer to accumulate, had to be relied upon. Of the nine states which finally failed to erect a structure at Jackson Park, six were from the South.

24. A. B. Farquhar, ed., *Pennsylvania at the World's Columbian Exposition* (Harrisburg: Meyers, n.d.), p. 29.

25. Johnson, *A History*, 4: 2.

26. Neufeld, pp. 176–178.

27. Neufeld, pp. 178–179.

28. Neufeld, pp. 179–180.

29. Neufeld gives the best detailed account of the organizational and administrative development of the World's Congress Auxiliary.

30. Quoted in *Artistic Guide*, p. 287.

31. A. M. Kimball and W. Wellner, "Fairways to Freedom: World's Fairs and Centennials as Battle Grounds in American Women's Struggles for Equal Rights," *Independent Woman* 17 (November 1938) : 360.

32. Kimball and Wellner, p. 361.

33. Ida Husted Harper, *The Life and Work of Susan B. Anthony* (Indianapolis and Kansas City: Bowen and Merril Co., 1898), 2: 743; Rheta Childe Dorr, *Susan B. Anthony: The Woman who Changed the Mind of a Nation* (New York: American Studies Press, 1928), p. 304.

34. Harper, p. 744.

35. "Management of the Fair," *Harper's Weekly* 34 (6 December 1890) : 915.

36. "An executive body composed wholly of women, acting with government authority, was a sight to fix the gaze," wrote Francis Willard, President of the National Women's Christian Temperance Union. *Pictorial History*, p. 448.

37. Moore, *Burnham*, p. 47.

38. Bernard Jacoby, for example, submitted a plan for a structure called the "Hanging Gardens of Babylonia." His idea was to construct two large steel and glass buildings arranged on a system of cables between sixteen four-hundred-foot steel columns. One building would be suspended three hundred fifty feet in the air while the other was on the ground. Each building would contain a restaurant, an orchestra, and an elaborate roof garden and could accommodate two thousand people per trip. For some "unexplained reason," the Hanging Garden was never built. *Artistic Guide,* p. 377.

39. In the first draft of his classification plan recommended to the commission, Goode wrote that the goal of the exposition "is to expound as far as may be the steps of progress of civilization and its arts in successive centuries, and in all lands up to the present time—to be, in fact, an *Illustrated Encyclopedia of Civilization*. It is to be so generous in its scope that in its pictorial and literary remains will be preserved the best record of human culture in the last decade of the Nineteenth Century." G. Brown Goode, *First Draft of a System of Classification for the World's Columbian Exposition*, p. xi.

40. Julian Ralph reported in January of 1892 that the department had an officer in Africa "who is in correspondence with Tippu-Tib for fifteen pygmies." Ralph, *Harper's Monthly* 84 (January 1892) : 209.

41. *Dedicatory*, p. 41.

42. Bloom had been to Paris in 1889, was impressed by the Algerian Village there, and had contacted a troupe of Algerians for an American tour. When he learned of the proposed Chicago exposition, he applied for permission to exhibit his troupe and was waiting for the fair officials to decide what to do about the Midway when Michael De Young of the management approached him with the offer of supervising amusements. Bloom, pp. 106–117.

43. Bloom, p. 119.

44. As related in his *Autobiography*, Bloom's experience with the Algerians provides an interesting and revealing story. He had wired the Algerian troupe of dancers, sword swallowers, glass eaters, etc., to come in April of 1893, but they arrived in New York a year before they were expected. (They had the month right but the year wrong.) Meeting them at the ship, Bloom saw the Algerians straggling off apparently without a leader and so began shouting in French and English to get their attention. A huge, angry black man walked up to him. "I suggest that you be more civil, otherwise I may lose my temper and throw you into the water," he said with a heavy English accent. "Who are you?" Bloom asked. "For simplicity, you may call me Archie," came the condescending response. "That is the name they used in London where I lived for ten years as body guard to my master. At present I am responsible for conveying my associates to a place called Chicago. I understand it is somewhere in the hinterland." Bloom hired him on the spot and with his help got the Algerians to Chicago and then put them to work in constructing the Midway. By mid-summer of 1892 they had part of the Algerian Village completed and Bloom began regular performances. By dedication day in October, he recalled, he was "out of the red." Bloom, pp. 121–123.

10 Dedication Day

1. Distinguished visitors would need the time to get to Chicago and the twenty-first was the real anniversary of Columbus' landing

according to the Gregorian calendar. See Bruwaert, in Pierce, *As Others See Chicago*, p. 337. New York had the honor of beginning the Columbian celebration with a naval parade down Fifth Avenue on October 12. Brown, *In Golden Nineties*, p. 357.

2. *Artistic Guide*, p. 323.

3. "Higher Aspects of the Columbian Exposition," *Dial* 13 (1 November 1892) : 263.

4. A full list of those attending can be found in *Pictorial History*, pp. 190–194, which also contains the complete dedication program.

5. The opening chorus of the hymn set the tone of the proceedings: "All hail and welcome nations of the earth, Columbia's greeting comes from every State! Proclaim to all mankind the world's new birth, of freedom, age on age shall consecrate. The universal brotherhood of peace, shall be Columbia's inspiring song." *Pictorial History*, p. 194.

6. *Pictorial History*, pp. 197–198.

7. Thomas Palmer's Address in *Pictorial History*, p. 201.

8. *Pictorial History*, pp. 207–210.

9. Quoted in Lewis and Smith, p. 200.

10. Hundreds of people had sent odes for consideration; one even offered a vision that would take six weeks to deliver! *A Week at the Fair*, p. 134.

11. *Pictorial History*, p. 217.

12. *Pictorial History*, p. 200.

13. *Pictorial History*, pp. 225–226.

14. *Pictorial History*, p. 203.

11 Final Preparations

1. Bancroft says that in the last days before opening, the number of workers at the park reached upwards of forty thousand men. Bancroft, p. 91.

2. *Pictorial History*, p. 234. During this last feverish period, a strike was called by the Carpenter's Union which, had it not been averted, would have made the May 1 deadline impossible.

3. Neufeld, p. 81; *Pictorial History*, p.234.

4. Quoted in *Pictorial History*, p. 233.

5. Great Britain, France, Germany, Russia, Holland, Italy, Spain, Argentina, and Brazil were all represented in the thirty-five-ship fleet that also included a replica of Columbus' original squad-

ron. The three tiny caravels—built in Palos, Spain—provided an interesting contrast to the huge steel-plated cruisers of the modern navies.

6. As a further example of the general congressional attitude toward the Columbian Exposition, Henry Villard recalled that as chairman of the reception committee of the New York Chamber of Commerce for the foreign dignitaries invited by the United States, he found that while Congress had extended the invitations, no money had been appropriated for receiving or entertaining the nation's guests. Fearing national humiliation, but unable to get any help from the government, Villard raised the money privately to pay for the parade, a banquet at the Waldorf, and a formal ball at Madison Square Garden. See Henry Villard, *The Memoirs of Henry Villard* (Boston: Houghton Mifflin, 1904), 2: 365–367.

7. *Chicago Daily Inter Ocean*, 1 May 1893, p. 1; *Chicago Herald*, 1 May 1893, p. 1. Largely because of the influence of Charles McKim, Burnham had been the subject of a testimonial dinner in New York in March at which several hundred guests (Charles Eliot Norton, William Dean Howells, E. L. Godkin, and Charles Dudley Warner among them) saluted the work of the artists and architects of the fair and presented Burnham with a gallon-sized, engraved loving cup. After Burnham had spoken, Richard Watson Gilder—editor of *The Century*—read his poem, "To the White City."

> Say not 'Greece is no more'!
> Through the clear morn
> On light winds bourne
> Her white-winged soul sinks on the New World's breast.
> Ah, happy West—
> Greece flowers anew, and all her temples soar!

Quoted in Clara M. Kirk, *W. D. Howells: Traveller From Alturia 1889–1894* (New Brunswick: Rutgers University Press, 1962), p. 101.

8. Moore, *Burnham*, p. 69.

9. Lewis and Smith, p. 188.

10. Claudius O. Johnson, *Carter Harrison I* (Chicago: University of Chicago Press, 1928), p. 30.

11. Lewis and Smith, p. 188. Tom O'Brien, King of the Bunko Men, is reported to have pocketed more than a half a million for a few months work during the fair. See Ginger, p. 23.

12. Wendt and Kogan, p. 47.

13. The spiritual/moral guardians also descended upon the city in response to rumors of such concentrated temptation. The Moody

and Sankey Home was opened near the fairgrounds where "Mr. Moody, aided by other eminent divines, will hold constant services, and strive to win the erring of their ways, and spur on the virtuous to further works of righteousness." See *A Week At The Fair*, p. 246.

14. Duffey, p. 4; C. Johnson, pp. 28–29.

15. Lewis and Smith, p. 178.

16. He had, in addition, been a strong supporter of the Philadelphia centennial in 1876 while he served as a congressman. See C. Johnson, p. 66.

17. He owned property in the notorious First Ward and was friendly with the "sporting" element of the city. A Marion, Indiana, man was overheard to remark that "if Old Carter Harrison's elected Mayor, I'm goin' to Chicago to the Fair, but I'm goin' to wear nothing but tights and carry a knife between my teeth and a pistol in each hand." See Lewis and Smith, p. 178.

18. At one point, Harrison bought the *Times* in order to have a public voice with which to defend himself. See Masters, *A Tale of Chicago*, pp. 252–253.

19. Sol Bloom, the manager of the Midway, for instance, got his start in Chicago politics working for Harrison's election because he "thought he would be the best possible man to have in City Hall during the Fair." See Bloom, p. 131.

20. There is the story that when the mayor met Princess Eulalie of Spain upon her arrival in Chicago, he rode up, as was his custom, on his big white stallion, wearing a silk top hat instead of his usual felt one. The band was to have played "Hail to the Chief," but when they saw the mayor they struck up a popular song "Where Did You Get That Hat?" The crowd and Harrison enjoyed the joke. See C. Johnson, p. 159. And yet, Bloom could ask, "How could he be an excellent mayor in every activity that met the eye and at the same time head such a notorious administration?" Bloom, p. 132.

21. James Dedge, *The Columbian Exposition of 1893: What to See and How to Get There* (London: The Polytechnic Institute, 1893), p. 23.

22. Dredge, p. 22.

23. Thomas had labored for years to establish a permanent American symphonic orchestra in Boston, but when the Boston Symphony was finally organized in 1881, the conductorship was given to a German musician imported for the purpose. Ten years later, his career at its lowest point, he was approached by Charles Norman Fay, a Chicago businessman, with the proposal that he come to Chicago and form an orchestra. Money was no problem. Thomas's reply was immediate: "I would go to hell if they would give me a permanent orchestra." Irving L. Sablosky, *American Music* (Chicago: University of Chicago Press, 1969), pp. 92–93.

24. Fuller, "Development of Arts and Letters," p. 216.

25. There was more than a little irony in the relationship between the fair and the university because, as Thorstein Veblen was quick to notice, the university was built along the Midway and not next to the Court of Honor. The Divinity School and the classrooms of John Dewey and Jacques Loeb took shape within a few hundred yards of the Ferris Wheel, the Streets of Cairo, and the Ostrich Farm. See Dorfman, p. 98. and Sherman Paul, *Louis Sullivan: An Architect in American Thought* (Englewood Cliffs: Prentice-Hall, 1962), p. 98.

An anonymous limerick in the Thirtieth Anniversary Exhibit collection of the Chicago Historical Society gives a somewhat down to earth impression of university life during the year of the fair:

> Oh, there were more Profs than students,
>   but then we didn't care;
> They spent their days in research work,
>   their evenings at the Fair.
> And life upon the Campus
>   was one continual swing,
> We watched the Ferris Wheel go round,
>   and didn't do a thing.

26. Quoted in Caro Lloyd, *Henry Demarest Lloyd, 1847–1903*. (New York: Putnam's Sons, 1912), 1: 161.

27. The exposition was to receive from the railroads a payment of five cents per passenger brought from Chicago and ten cents for each brought from outside the city limits. Unfortunately, the railroads didn't use the terminal and it ended, as Neufeld says, "a beautiful, well-planned failure." Neufeld, p. 145.

28. *The Daily Columbian*, the fair's official bulletin, was actually an eight page composite. The first five pages consisted of the front pages of Chicago's leading newspapers—*The Herald, Inter Ocean, Record, Times* and *Tribune*—and the last three pages contained such information as the locations of special exhibits, bureaus or departments, lists of important dates, foreign council addresses, hospitals, telephone and telegraph offices, rail and steam-

ship tables, and short descriptive articles or human interest stories. Moses Handy was general editor and the paper was issued from Machinery Hall.

29. The French commisssioner reported that a peanut company had paid the fair 500,000 francs for the exclusive rights to sell "a sort of pistachio that is quite popular in Chicago," and another had paid 800,000 to sell popcorn. "To keep children quiet, people often buy them a little bag, not of candy, but of toasted corn," he remarked. "It is detestable but it suffices to occupy the youngsters." See Pierce, *As Others See Chicago,* p. 334.

30. The Guards, numbering sometimes fifteen hundred, were supervised by U.S. Army officers detailed by the War Department and by Chicago Police and were instructed to be examples of courtesy and helpfulness.

31. Neufeld states that their effectiveness accounted for the recovery of 95 percent of all property stolen during the fair. See Neufeld, p. 161.

32. The Waukesha Hygeia Mineral Springs Company also had a concession for mineral water supposedly imported from Wisconsin.

33. Neufeld, p. 165.

34. On July 11, the Cold Storage Building, which served as the fair's ice house, caught fire and was completely destroyed despite the heroic efforts of the firemen, fifteen of whom died while scores of others were injured, in the clear sight of one hundred thousand helpless and horrified onlookers. *Memorial Volume,* p. 36, and *Pictorial History,* p. 803.

35. Neufeld, p. 155. *A Week at the Fair,* p. 182.

36. Neufeld, pp. 150–152.

37. Henry G. Prout, *A Life of George Westinghouse* (New York: American Society of Mechanical Engineers, 1921), p. 140.

38. *The Chicago Herald,* 4 May 1893, reported that the guards wanted $75 a month instead of the $60 they were being paid and that U.S. Army officers, who held ranking positions, were in sympathy with their petitions which Burnham had thus far ignored.

39. Lewis and Smith, p. 208; Bogart and Mathews, pp. 394–397.

40. To stimulate gate receipts, Millet and William E. Curtis even staged fake fights on the Midway, while phoney letters of outrage appeared in the Chicago papers. According to Charles Moore, "people flocked to see the barbaric encounters." Moore, *Burnham,* p. 64.

41. There were probably twenty thousand amateur bands in the United States by 1900 and band music was felt to be indispensable to the festivities of American towns and cities. See Sablosky, p. 103.

42. Sablosky, p. 105; *Pictorial History,* p. 723.

43. *Artistic Guide,* p. 300.

44. Although a less ambitious series of classical concerts had been a failure at the Philadelphia World's Fair, leaving the Theodore Thomas Orchestra nearly in bankruptcy, he viewed the Columbian Exposition as an opportunity to finally realize his dream to make "lofty" music popular in America. See Sablosky, p. 104.

45. Bloom, p. 139.

46. Chicago *Daily Inter Ocean,* 4 May 1893, p. 1. The caption to the story reads "Fine Feminine Frenzy."

47. Bloom, p. 140; Moore, *Burnham,* p. 58.

48. Lewis and Smith, p. 210. When asked, once again, to suggest a musical plan for the St. Louis World's Fair in 1904, his advice was, "Have plenty of band music, out of doors." Sablosky, p. 103.

49. *Memorial Volume,* p. 34.

50. The conclusions of the court can be found in *Pictorial History,* pp. 764–767.

51. *Memorial Volume,* p. 35. Perhaps, as Lewis and Smith suggest, the reason that Sunday opening was not popular was that the people were not thrilled by a curtailed world's fair (p. 209), and yet the main entertainment section of the fair, the Midway, was allowed to operate at "full blast." It would seem more likely that the failure of Sunday opening to prove popular was that opening an exhibition on the Sabbath had been inconceivable in the United States, and to do so was in effect to violate the order and form of such undertakings. As Senator Hawley had said in a speech before the U.S. Senate the year before: "Up to this time there had never been a State exhibition, a State fair, a country fair, or a city fair or a circus, or a show of any description, opened on Sunday. There has never been a secular convention, social, political, scientific, literary, or commercial that has not adjourned over Sunday." Quoted in Kunz, "Management and Uses," p. 417.

52. *Memorial Volume,* p. 35.

53. *Pictorial History,* p. 767. For the attitudes of one of the directors involved, see Charles H. Dennis, *Victor Lawson: His Time and His Work* (New York: Greenwood Press, 1935), pp. 160–161.

54. Lewis and Smith, p. 209.

12 The World's Congress

1. The unusual blending of the sacred and the secular has been one of the most remarkable characteristics of American culture. The need to insist upon it so vigorously at the time of the fair is thus a good indication of the general concern about losing this dimension of the national identity.

2. John H. Barrows, "The Religious Possibilities of the World's Fair," *Our Day* 10 (August 1892) : 560.

3. Barrows, p. 563.

4. Barrows, p. 569.

5. Barrows, p. 571.

6. Joseph Cook, *Our Day* 12 (December 1893) : 499–509.

7. Cook, p. 507.

8. Walton, p. v. Columbus, as the man who discovered the West, was seen more and more as an agent of God, instead of an adventurer, and the fair generated increasing interest in his life and character. (Over forty new editions of works on Columbus were published in the United States according to the *American Catalog.*) The July, 1893, issue of the London *Quarterly Review,* for example, in a review of an essay based on four new British works on Columbus, said that even if one could not "be sure where America will turn, or how she will turn out, nevertheless if the most momentous of all events in the history of mankind was the conquest of the Greek and Roman world by Christianity, the other which marks a fresh chapter in that History and gives un-exampled scope to the Christian message, was the five weeks' voyage of Columbus." No third event seems likely to rival "the wild dedication and the vision of progress" which has long been "extant in human instinct." See "Discovery of America," *The Quarterly Review* 177 (July 1893) : 41.

9. The nineties produced a flood of bestsellers written from this new perspective, the most famous of which, *In His Steps,* was written by a Topeka minister, Charles Sheldon, who in 1889 devised a kind of serial-fiction sermon in order to interest young college people in Christian ethics. It is not surprising that Sheldon used Chicago as his setting for the great transformation. See Luther Mott, *Golden Multitudes: The Story of Best-Sellers in the United States* (New York: Macmillan, 1947), pp. 193–195.

10. James B. McClure, ed., *World's Fair Sermons by Eminent Divines at Home and Abroad* (Chicago: Rhodes and McClure, 1893), p. 59.

11. Henry C. Kinny, *Why the Columbian Exposition Should be Opened on Sunday: A Religio-Social Study* (Chicago: Rand, McNally, 1892), p. 9.

12. "Higher Aspects of the Columbian Exposition," *Dial* 13 (1 November 1892) : 264.

13. Quoted in *A Week at the Fair,* p. 78.

14. See for example Candace Wheeler, "A Dream City," *Harper's Monthly* 86 (May 1893) : 86; or W. H. Gibson, "Foreground and Vista at the Fair," *Scribner's Monthly* 14 (July 1893) : 29.

15. Mrs. D. C. Taylor, *Halcyon Days in the Dream City,* (Kankakee, Illinois: 1894), p. 7.

16. . Henry James, ed., *The Letters of William James* (Boston: Atlantic, 1920), 1: 348. From a letter of September 22, 1893.

17. Henry van Brunt, "The Columbian Exposition and American Civilization," *Atlantic Monthly* 71 (May 1893) : 581.

18. Quoted in Pierce, *A History of Chicago,* p. 510.

19. Neufeld, p. 336.

20. Barrows, p. 564.

21. George Dana Boardman, *The Parliament of Religions: An Address Before the Philadelphia Conference of Baptist Ministers* (Philadelphia: National Baptist Printing Agency, 1893), p. 5.

22. Boardman, p. 16.

23. *Pictorial History,* p. 686.

24. The building was originally expected to be designed by John Root and was a joint project of the exposition and the Chicago Art Institute. The Institute contributed $400,000 and the Chicago Exposition Company provided $200,000 for the erection of a building that would be suitable for the congresses during the period of the fair and would afterwards become a new permanent home for the institute's expanding collection. The Art Institute was another example of Chicago's selfconscious desire to outgrow its reputed vulgarity. "It has long been the fashion in eastern circles to ridicule Chicago," said a writer in *The Artistic Guide to Chicago* in a paragraph describing the project, "as a home of the sordid money-getter, the souless real-estate speculator, and the unenlightened and unregenerate packer of pork. This may have been true of the Chicago of a decade ago, but the city today counts among its residents some of the most liberal patrons of art in the world—men who love art for art's sake, and do not hesitate to pay liberally for any production having merit, no matter who the artist may be." *Artistic Guide to Chicago,* p. 228. Root's early drawings show rich

coloration and a certain degree of Richardsonian vitality, but following his death, the design was given to Shepley, Rutan, and
Coolidge of Boston and they provided an "Italian Renaissance
building, the details classic" which was obviously influenced by
Charles McKim. See Hoffman, p. 236.

25. *Quoted in Artistic Guide,* p. 287.

26. Johnson, *A History,* vol. 4, p. 7.

27. Quoted in Johnson, *A History,* vol. 4, p. 8. *The Dial* hu-
morously warned the auxiliary to guard against the "fanatics" who
would be waiting for just such an opportunity as the congresses.
Examples of things to beware of were Christian Scientists in the
Medical Congress, theosophy in the Religious Congress, spelling
reformers in the Philology Congress, and an over abundance of Iowa
and Kansas poets in the Congress of Authors. It was probably useless
to keep fanatics out of the Temperance Congress—"which has its
raison d'etre in fanaticism"—or the Sunday Rest Congress, however.
"World's Congress Auxiliary," *Dial* 13 (16 December 1892) : p. 377.

28. Maurice Neufeld has done the most work on this aspect of
the fair, though his emphasis is upon the evidence of the recognition
of social problems and the need for collective planning to find
solutions.

29. Quoted in Neufeld, p. 238. See also U.S. Bureau of Education, *Education at the World's Columbian Exposition* (Washington:
Government Printing Office, 1896), p. 424.

30. Neufeld, p. 138.

31. Neufeld, p. 333.

32. U.S. Bureau of Education, pp. 425–435.

33. See Larzer Ziff, *The American 1890's: Life and Times of a
Lost Generation* (New York: Viking, 1966), pp. 101–108, and
Hugh D. Duncan, *The Rise of Chicago as a Literary Center 1885–
1920* (Totowa, N.J.: Bedminster Press, 1964), pp. 77–78.

34. Hoffman, p. 244.

35. Neufeld, p. 274.

36. Neufeld, p. 271.

37. See Neufeld, pp. 223–224.

38. Quoted in Wayne Andrews, *The Battle for Chicago* (New
York: Harcourt, Brace, 1946), p. 152.

39. See Pierce, *A History of Chicago,* p. 509; Ginger, *Altgeld's
America,* p. 21; and Neufeld, pp. 209–303. Samuel Gompers, president of the AFL, spoke at several sessions and assured his audience
that the labor movement intended to stay free from all "isms" and

violence and work for the simple objectives of shorter hours (the
eight-hour day) and higher pay. Booker T. Washington, while
pointing out the evils of the crop-lien system, said that the real solution for ignorant labor was education and intelligence. Other important speakers at the congress included Professors John R. Commons and Richard T. Ely, Mr. and Mrs. Henry Demarest Lloyd,
Florence Kelly of Hull House (who described the sweat-shop system
and the child labor situation in Chicago), and General James B.
Weaver, the Populist Party's first presidential candidate (in 1892),
who argued that only when the farmer's economic problems were
solved could city workers expect jobs. The most radical ideas concerning the labor situation which might have been heard during the
fair, but which were largely ignored, came from an ex-member of the
Indiana Legislature, Eugene V. Debs, who had the same month of
August helped found the first lodge of the American Railway
Union, an industrial rather than a craft union. He spoke on the
need to consolidate labor more completely than ever before. Debs'
speech, condemning all paternalistic ideas of "what we can do for
labor," was a prediction of the violent confrontation which began
the following year at Pullman. See Ginger, pp. 154–155.

40. Joint Committees of both men and women were never appointed, but a Woman's Branch of the World's Congress Auxiliary
was organized under the direction of Mrs. Potter Palmer (president
of the Board of Lady Managers) and Mrs. Charles Henrotin with
the option of meeting and acting separately or in conference with
the primary all-male committee.

41. Nearly half of all the organizations represented were from
the United States and although they were individually devoted to
different purposes, their major interests were in the areas of religion,
charities, moral reform, and education. See Neufeld, pp. 308–310.

42. Harper, *Susan B. Anthony,* p. 746; Neufeld, p. 309.

43. The record of the proceedings of the Women's Department
is the most complete of any of the congresses held during the exposition due to the fact that it was privately collected and printed. May
Wright Sewell's *World's Congress of Representative Women* (Chicago: Rand, McNally, 1894) in two volumes is the best edition
of the addresses and papers, while Mary K. O. Eagle's *The Congress
of Women Held in the Women's Building, World's Columbian Exposition* (Philadelphia: International Publishing Company, 1895)
gives a supplemental account of the more informal meetings conducted in the Women's Building.

44. See Pierce, *As Others See Chicago*, p. 337.

13   The Exhibits

1. Rogers, "Lessons from International Expositions," p. 507. A similar experience is in store for any general student who attempts to read through the catalogues of exhibits (for example, Bancroft's *Book of the Fair*) to get an overall idea of what was shown at Chicago.

2. Pinchot's exhibit was the "first exhibit of practical forestry ever made in the United States." Gifford Pinchot, *Breaking New Ground* (New York: Harcourt, Brace, 1947), p. 57.

3. By far the best summary of the development of various industrial machinery at the time was published in 1892 by Benjamin Butterworth, U.S. Commissioner of Patents and a director of the Columbian Exposition. The book—*The Growth of Industrial Art* (1892; reprint ed., New York: Knopf, 1972)—has been recently republished.

4. Quoted in Pierce, *As Others See Chicago*, p. 346.

5. Beer, p. 31. Even J. P. Morgan thought the French exhibits looked as if they had been picked by a committee of chambermaids.

6. Quoted in Pierce, *As Others See Chicago*, p. 504.

7. Quoted in Hoffman, p. 220.

8. Quoted in Pierce, *As Others See Chicago*, p. 332.

9. *A Week at the Fair*, p. 214.

10. *A Week at the Fair*, p. 146.

11. According to Frank W. Grogan, the designer, the "idea of having a battleship (emblematic of power) for the Navy Department exhibit originated with Commodore R. W. Meade, U.S.N." *A Week at the Fair*, p. 152.

12. *A Week at the Fair*, p. 111.

13. Richard H. Pratt, *Battlefield and Classroom: Four Decades with the American Indian*, ed. Robert M. Utley (New Haven: Yale, 1964), p. 303.

14. Carlisle students participated in both the New York parade and that in Chicago in the fall before the fair opened under the banner "Into Civilization and Citizenship," and Pratt brought five hundred of his students to the fair during the summer where they gave several public performances of their marching and musical skills. See Pratt, pp. 277–303.

15. New York was the only state to appoint a black woman to the board and even that was done against threats of resignation by several of the other managers.

16. See Louis R. Harlan, *Booker T. Washington* (New York: Oxford, 1972), p. 207.

17. *The Daily Columbian*, 9 May 1893, p. 1.

18. "The Reason Why," *The Reason Why the Colored American is Not in the World's Columbian Exposition*, ed. Ida B. Wells (Chicago: Ida B. Wells, 1893), p. 80.

19. "Introduction" to *The Reason Why*, p. 4. Douglass was himself appointed an official commissioner to the fair—by the Republic of Haiti—through whose "courtesy the Colored American received from a foreign power the place denied to him at home." Barnett, p. 81.

20. Douglass, p. 9.

14   The Midway

1. *Memorial Volume*, p. 43.

2. The racket from the Midway "barkers" became so loud that at one point an order was issued to cease all vocal advertising. The result was, for a time, a sea of waving placards, but "by degrees the lecturers recovered their voices, and before the close the Midway had outhowled all previous records." *Memorial Volume*, p. 41.

3. Bloom, p. 135.

4. Taylor, p. 6. The reputation of the dancers on the Midway has probably exceeded the actual facts. The belly dance was indeed introduced there, but the "Hootchy-Kootchy"—a vulgarized version that subsequently became the stock of amusement parks across the country was not. Neither, as many reports would have it, was the famous Coney Island nude dancer "Little Egypt" at the fair. As Bloom states, and as director of the Midway he was in the best position to know, "At no time during the Chicago Fair did this character appear on the Midway." See Bloom, pp. 135–136.

5. Actually, the omelets were made from chicken eggs and at one point a crisis arose when a strike disrupted deliveries from Chicago poultry men. Bloom canvassed the grocers and restaurants on the South Side for anything with a shell on it, and "for a few days the ostrich-egg omelets were more subtly flavored than usual: in addition to hen's eggs, they contained duck, goose, and turkey eggs." "For all I know," Bloom wrote, "they might have had a few ostrich eggs in them." Bloom, p. 137.

6. *Memorial Volume,* p. 191. Some people, according to Bloom, spent all day on it. Bloom, p. 138.

7. *Pictorial History,* p. 669.

8. Denton J. Snider, *World's Fair Studies* (Chicago: Sigma Pub. Co., 1895), p. 25.

9. Shackleton, *The Book of Chicago,* p. 227.

10. *Memorial Volume,* p. 38.

11. Charles H. Herman, *Recollections of Life and Doings in Chicago: 1886–1918* (Chicago: Normandie House, 1945), p. 109.

12. Lewis and Smith, p. 211. The tales of such sacrifices are legendary. Hamlin Garland, for instance, urged his aging parents on their Dakota farm to "sell the cook stove if necessary and come. You must see this fair!" (See Ginger, p. 21.) And Teresa Dean overheard a man say: "I tell everybody in my town that they must come to the Fair. And if they can't get the money to come any other way, they better knock a man down gently, and take his money, and then after they return from the Exposition, go to work and pay back in installments the man they've robbed." Teresa H. Dean, *White City Chips* (Chicago: Warren Publishing Company, 1895), p. 293. Perhaps the most unusual determination was shown by a Texas woman, Mrs. Lucille Rodney, who walked from Galveston on railroad ties—a distance of thirteen hundred miles—to get to Chicago. *Chicago Record,* 31 July 1893, p. 1.

13. The population of the United States as of July 31, 1893, according to the census figures, was 66,970,000. See Crook, p. 331.

14. *Memorial Volume,* p. 37.

15. *Memorial Volume,* p. 38.

15   Achievement and Influence

1. See, for example, Gilman Ostrander, *American Civilization in the First Machine Age* (New York: Harper, 1970), p. 3.

2. "U.S. at the Paris Exposition in 1900," p. 27.

3. "Lessons from International Expositions," p. 508.

4. See Fred A. Shannon, *The Farmer's Last Frontier* (New York: Farrar and Rinehart, 1945), p. 266.

5. See Herman, *Life and Doings,* pp. 112–113; and McCullough, *World's Fair Midways,* pp. 43–48.

6. "America at the World's Fairs," p. 855.

7. Several writers have claimed that the world's fairs, and especially the Columbian Exposition, were in fact instrumental in en-couraging the antiwar leagues and international arbitration groups which emerged in the next twenty years. See W. O. Partridge, "The Educational Value of World's Fairs," *Forum* 33 (March 1902): p. 126.

8. The eighty-seven-foot gun, almost twice the size of America's largest, had a range of sixteen miles and fired a projectile weighing 2,300 pounds. German engineers speculated that if it were fired the concussion would shatter every building in Jackson Park. *A Week at the Fair,* p. 111.

9. Quoted in Pierce, *As Others See Chicago,* p. 341.

10. Rogers, p. 510.

11. Bancroft, *The Book of the Fair,* p. 98.

12. Oswald G. Villard, *Fighting Years* (New York: Harcourt, Brace, 1939), p. 92.

13. Quoted in Pierce, *As Others See Chicago,* p. 351.

14. *A History of Chicago,* pp. 511–512.

15. *Twenty Years of the Republic, 1885–1905,* p. 352.

16. Lynes, *The Tastemakers,* p. 148. Still, it could not be said that the exposition began this trend. The ground had been well prepared in the previous decade.

17. See Moore, *Burnham,* p. vii, and John William Tebbel, *The Marshall Fields* (New York: Dutton, 1947), p. 81. The Field Museum (now the Museum of Science and Industry) began with a nucleus of exhibits left over from the fair and was housed in the Art Palace.

18. Moore, *Burnham,* p. vii.

19. The Chicago Civic Federation was formed in the fall of 1893 with the stated purpose of furthering municipal reforms and projects. The federation was a "driving force" behind the creation of the Chicago Plan. See Crook, p. 378.

20. Neufeld, p. 71. Both Neufeld and Crook have argued for this interpretation.

21. Mumford, *The Brown Decades,* p. 141.

22. See, for example, Wayne Andrews, *The Battle For Chicago,* p. 149.

23. See Louis Mumford, "Two Chicago Fairs," *New Republic* 65 (21 January 1931): 271.

24. The Chicago Auditorium, financed like the world's fair by stock subscription, was the firm's greatest public triumph and to many its completion in 1889 marked the emergence of a mature Chicago.

25. Ziff, p. 22.

26. See Sherman Paul, *Louis Sullivan: An Architect in American Thought.*

27. Crook, p. 124.

28. See Crook, p. 2.

29. Louis H. Sullivan, *The Autobiography of an Idea* (1924; reprint ed., New York: Dover, 1956), p. 325.

30. Paul, p. 51.

31. See Hoffman, *The Architecture of John W. Root,* p. 253.

32. It was Sullivan's suggestion, adopted by the architects at their first meeting in Chicago, that the transportation exhibits be separated from those in the Machinery Building. See Crook, p. 277.

33. In the use of color and unusual ornamental detail, Sullivan was joined by Henry Cobb, whose Fisheries Building was also on the lagoon.

34. "The Columbian Exposition," *The Nation* 57 (24 August 1893): 133.

35. Hugh Morrison, *Louis Sullivan, Prophet of Modern Architecture* (New York: Norton, 1935), p. 137. The building did not even function well.

36. *World's Fair Studies,* p. 154.

37. The *Union Controle des Arts Decoratifs* awarded Sullivan three medals for the doorway, not the building, the next year. See Morrison, p. 136.

38. The inscription at the base of the Statue of Liberty reads:

> Give me your tired, your poor
> Your huddled masses yearning to be free,
> The wretched refuse of your teeming shore,
> Send these, the homeless, tempest-tossed to me:
> I lift my lamp beside the golden door.

39. The Populists' hostility toward the "Goldbugs" and the gold standard was never simply an expression of their views on financial policy.

40. "The Making of the White City," *Scribner's Monthly* 12 (October 1892): 416.

41. See Snider, p. 154. Chicago had its own infamous example, Charles Yerkes, who had made a fortune by cornering streetcar construction.

42. Interestingly enough, it was Burnham who first suggested to Sullivan that he make "one grand entrance toward the east and make this much richer than either of the others you had proposed." From a letter of 11 February 1891 quoted in Crook, p. 298.

43. A conservative classic formalism could be observed emerging in numerous other aspects of the culture as diverse as drama and the law.

44. Henry Steele Commager, *The American Mind* (New Haven: Yale University Press, 1950), p. 41.

16   A Confusion of Symbols

1. James F. Muirhead, *The Land of Contrasts: A Briton's View of His American Kin* (London, 1898), p. 7.

2. "The Discovery of America," *Quarterly Review* 177 (October 1893): 40.

3. Henry Adams, *The Education of Henry Adams* (1918; reprint ed., Boston: Houghton Mifflin, 1961), p. 340. At least for the purposes of his critical stance in the book, Adams had assumed the perspective of the outsider in search of answers about the direction of America.

4. A model children's home was built by the Women's Department next to the Woman's Building from funds raised by a bazaar held at Mrs. Palmer's mansion in December, 1892. A model hospital and kitchen was also operated by the Women's Department and many state exhibits emphasized woman's traditional dominance in the domestic arts. California women, for instance, prepared a giant "Jelly Palace," twenty-five feet high, made from filled jelly jars and lighted by electricity. There was, in addition, a cook book of favorite autographed recipes published by the Board of Lady Managers.

5. Quoted in David Burg, *Chicago's White City of 1893* (Lexington: University of Kentucky Press, 1976), p. 144.

6. Burg, p. 164.

7. *Mauve Decade,* p. 32.

8. According to Beer, one of New Orleans' leading procuresses brought "her entire stock, suitably costumed, on a holiday to broaden their minds." *Mauve Decade,* p. 29.

9. See Bancroft, p. 73.

10. Harper, p. 752.

11. Anthony was not one of those who wished to see the fair closed on Sundays and when questioned about it by a clergyman she added that in her opinion a young man would learn more from

Buffalo Bill's Wild West Show than from listening to an intolerant sermon. Cody, hearing of Anthony's remarks, not only sent her box seat tickets for a performance but rode over and saluted her during the opening. Anthony stood and returned the bow and "for a moment these two typical Americans faced each other to the wild applause of thousands." Dorr, p. 306. It would be hard to imagine a more incongruous pair of heroes.

12. Wecter, p. 344.

13. There were, of course, considerable differences among the female leaders and societies of the various cities—Chicago was not New York and Mrs. Palmer was not merely an imitation of the eastern imitation of European aristocracy.

14. *American Historical Association Annual Report for 1893* (Washington: 1894), p. 227.

17   The Vision of Unity

1. Elizabeth Faulkner to The Chicago Historical Society, n.d. [1923], in the Columbian Exposition Collection of the Chicago Historical Society.

2. This theme, the creation of the garden from the wilderness, is one of the most traditional interpretations of the meaning of the American experience, going back at least as far as the Puritan settlement.

3. *World's Fair Studies,* p. 66. Snider even believed that the circular Ferris Wheel was the embodiment of a single unifying idea.

4. *The Rise of Chicago as a Literary Center,* p. 80.

5. Quoted in Newfeld, p. 335. That "true religion" was Protestantism according to Henry King Carrol whose address, "The Present Religious Condition of America," was based on the 1890 census of churches. "It is the little bodies," he said, "... that give religion in the United States such a divided aspect. If most of them were blotted out we should lose little that is very valuable; but much that is queer in belief and practice." The two major reasons for the undesirable pluralism were race and "imported beliefs." Quoted in Robert T. Handy, *Religion in the American Experience: The Pluralistic Style* (Columbia: University of South Carolina Press, 1972), p. 192.

6. Quoted in Neufeld, p. 229. At the opening ceremonies of the Woman's Building, Mrs. Palmer expressed the conflict in the women's goals: "If we can really find, after careful search, any women mounted upon pedestals, we should willingly ask them to step down in order that they may meet and uplift their sisters." Quoted in Mary Eagle, p. 27.

7. *Mauve Decade,* p. 34.

8. Quoted in Burg, p. 136.

9. Vedant, in Pierce, ed., *As Others See Chicago,* p. 348.

10. Stead, in Pierce, *As Others See Chicago,* p. 357.

11. Kirk, p. 97.

12. William Dean Howells, *Letters of an Altrurian Traveller,* Clara M. Kirk and Rudolf Kirk, eds., (1893; reprint ed., Gainesville, Florida: Scholars' Facsimiles and Reprints, 1961), p. 21.

13. Ziff, p. 85.

14. "Last Words About the World's Fair," *Architectural Record* 3 (January-March 1894) : 283.

15. Schuyler, p. 283.

16. Schuyler, p. 286.

17. Schuyler, p. 287. What he feared as much as the classicism was the extensive use of the photograph in reporting the fair. That technical innovation, at least as it was used for the fair, made the buildings look "real" and did not convey the "illusion" of the world's fair context, which was the only context which made them both possible and appropriate.

18. Quoted in Kirk, p. 104.

Epilogue

1. Quoted in Lewis and Smith, p. 214.

2. The assassin, Patrick Eugene John Prendergast, was possessed with the notion that the mayor had conspired against his appointment as a corporation council for the city. He was later defended by Clarence Darrow who used the case to introduce the novel plea of insanity. See Ginger, p. 216, and Lewis and Smith, p. 214.

3. Lewis and Smith, p. 214.

4. "The Cook County Charities," in *Hull House Maps,* p. 158.

5. W. T. Stead, *Chicago To-Day: The Labour War in America,* p. 249.

6. Kirk, p. 112.

BIBLIOGRAPHY

Abbot, W. J. "Makers of the Fair." *Outlook* 48 (18 November 1893):
884–85.

Adams, Henry. *The Education of Henry Adams*. 1918. Reprint.
Boston: Houghton Mifflin, 1961.

Afalo, F. G. "The Promise of International Exhibitions." *Fortune*
73 (May 1900): 830–39.

American Institute of Architects, Chicago Chapter. *A Challenge to
Civic Pride: A Plea for the Preservation and Rehabilitation of
the Fine Arts Building of the World's Columbian Exposition*.
Chicago: American Institute of Architects, 1923.

Andrews, Wayne. *The Battle for Chicago*. New York: Harcourt,
Brace, and Co., 1946.

Artistic Guide to Chicago and the World's Columbian Exposition.
Columbian Art Company. Chicago: R. S. Peale, 1891.

As Others See Chicago: Impressions of Visitors, 1673–1933. Edited by
Bessie Louise Pierce. Chicago: University of Chicago Press,
1933.

Augur, Helen. "From the Crystal Palace to the World of Tomorrow." *Travel* 72 (April 1939): 6–13.

Baker, W. T. *Answer of the President of the World's Columbian
Exposition to Questions Propounded by the Honorable A. M.
Dockery*. Chicago: Rand, McNally, 1892.

Bancroft, Hubert Howe. *The Book of the Fair*. 1894. Reprint. New
York: Bounty Books, n.d.

Barnum, P. T. "What the Fair Should Be." *North American Review*
150 (March 1890): 400–401.

Barrows, John H. "Religious Possibilities of the World's Fair." *Our
Day* 10 (August 1892): 560.

Beer, Thomas. *Hanna, Crane, and the Mauve Decade*. New York:
Knopf, 1941.

Berger, George. "Suggestions for the Next World's Fair." *Century* 17 (April 1890) : 845–50.

Bloom, Sol. *The Autobiography of Sol Bloom.* New York: G. P. Putnam's Sons, 1948.

Boardman, George Dana. *The Parliament of Religions: An Address Before the Philadelphia Conference of Baptist Ministers.* Philadelphia: National Baptist Printing Co., 1893.

Brooks, Van Wyck. *The Confident Years.* New York: Dutton, 1952.

Brown, Dee. *The Year of the Century: 1876.* New York: Scribners, 1966.

Brown, H. C. *In Golden Nineties.* Hastings-on-Hudson: Valentine's Manual, Inc., 1928.

Buel, J. W. *The Magic City, A Massive Portfolio of Original Photographic Views of the Great World's Fair.* Philadelphia: Historical Publishing Co., 1894.

Bunner, H. C. "Making of the White City." *Scribner's Monthly* 12 (October 1892) : 398–418.

Burg, David F. *Chicago's White City of 1893.* Lexington: University of Kentucky Press, 1976.

Burnham, Daniel H., and Millet, Francis D. *The World's Columbian Exposition; the Book of the Builders.* Chicago: Columbian Memorial Publications, 1894.

Butterworth, Benjamin. *The Growth of Industrial Art.* 1892. Reprint. New York: Knopf, 1972.

The Century: 1847–1946. Edited by Rodman Gilder. New York: Century Association, 1947.

"Chicago." *The Quarterly Review* 177 (October 1893) : 297–328.

"Chicago's World's Fair." *Scientific American* 63 (2 August 1890) : 70–71.

Churchill, Winston. *History of the English Speaking Peoples.* 4 vols. New York: Dodd, Mead, 1958.

Classification of the World's Columbian Exposition Adopted by the World's Columbian Commission. Chicago: Donohue and Henneberry, 1891.

"The Columbian Exposition." *The Nation* 57 (24 August 1893) : 132–33.

Conant, James B. *Science and Common Sense.* New Haven: Yale University Press, 1951.

Condit, Carl. *The Chicago School of Architecture: A History of Commercial and Public Building in Chicago Area 1875–1925.* Chicago: University of Chicago Press, 1964.

Congress of Women Held in the Woman's Building, World's Columbian Exposition. Edited by Mary K. O. Eagle. Philadelphia: International Publications, 1895.

Cook, Joseph. "Promises and Perils of the World's Columbian Exposition." *Our Day* 12 (December 1893) : 499–509.

Crook, David H. "Louis Sullivan, the World's Columbian Exposition, and American Life." Ph.D. dissertation, Harvard University, 1963.

Cunliff, Marcus. "America and the Great Exhibition of 1851." *American Quarterly* 3 (Summer 1951) : 115–27.

Curti, Merle. "America at the World Fairs, 1851–1893." *American Historical Review* 55 (July 1950) : 833–56.

Cutler, Harry Gardner. *The World's Fair: Its Meaning and Scope.* Chicago: Star Publishing Co., 1892.

Dean, Teresa H. *White City Chips.* Chicago: Warren Publishing Co., 1895.

Dennis, Charles H. *Victor Lawson: His Time and His Work.* New York: Greenwood Press, 1935.

De Young, Michael H. "The Columbian World's Fair." *Cosmopolitan* 12 (March 1892) : 599–605.

Depew, Chauncey M. "International Fair, Chicago 1890." *Magazine of American History* 24 (July 1890) : 66–68.

Dewar, Thomas R. *A Ramble Round the Globe.* London: Chatto and Windus, 1894.

"The Discovery of America." *The Quarterly Review* (London) 177 (July 1893) : 1–41.

Dorfman, Joseph. *Thorstein Veblen and His America.* New York: Viking, 1935.

Dorr, Rheta C. *Susan B. Anthony: The Woman Who Changed the Mind of a Nation.* New York: AMS Press, 1928.

Downey, F. Davis. *Portrait of an Era as Drawn by C. D. Gibson.* New York: Scribners, 1936.

Draft of a System of Classification Prepared for the Committee on Classification. Chicago: Rand, McNally, 1890.

Dredge, James. *The Columbian Exposition of 1893: What to See and How to Get There.* London: The Polytechnic Institute, 1892.

Drew, William A. *Glimpses and Gatherings, During a Voyage and Visit to London and the Great Exhibition in the Summer of 1851.* Augusta, Me.: n.p., 1852.

Duffey, Bernard. *The Chicago Renaissance in American Letters: A*

Critical History. East Lansing: Michigan State College Press, 1954.

Duncan, Hugh Dalziel. *The Rise of Chicago As a Literary Center 1885–1920*. Totowa, N. J.: Bedminster Press, 1964.

Early Victorian England 1830–1865. Edited by G. M. Young. 2 vols. London: Oxford University Press, 1934.

Fine Arts at the World's Columbian Exposition; Being a Collection of Artotypes of the Most Famous Paintings and Statuary Exhibited at the World's Fair. Chicago: Rand, McNally, 1894.

Ford, Guy Stanton. "International Exhibitions." *Encyclopedia of the Social Sciences*. New York: Macmillan, 1933. 6: 23–27.

Fuller, Henry B. "Development of Arts and Letters." *The Industrial State 1870–1893* Edited by Ernest L. Bogart and Charles M. Thompson. *The Centennial History of Illinois*. Springfield: Illinois Centennial Commission, 1920. 4:188–216.

Gandhi, V. R. *The Jain Philosophy*. Edited by B. F. Karbhari. Bombay: Tripathi and Co., 1911.

Gibson, W. H. "Foreground and Vista at the Fair." *Scribner's* 14 (July 1893) : 29.

Gilbert, Felix. *Toward the Farewell Address*. Princeton: Princeton University Press, 1961.

Ginger, Ray. *Altgeld's America 1890–1905: The Lincoln Ideal Versus Changing Realities*. New York: Funk and Wagnalls, 1958.

Goode, G. Brown. *First Draft of a System of Classification for the World's Columbian Exposition*. Washington: Gedney and Roberts, 1890.

Granger, Alfred Hoyt. *Charles Follen McKim*. Boston: Houghton Mifflin, 1913.

The Great Exhibition, London 1851; The Art-Journal Illustrated Catalogue of the Industry of All Nations. London: George Virtue, 1851.

Handy, Robert T. *Religion in the American Experience: The Pluralistic Style*. Columbia: University of South Carolina Press, 1972.

Harlan, Louis P. *Booker T. Washington: The Making of a Black Leader 1856–1901*. New York: Oxford University Press, 1972.

Hawthorne, Julian. *Humors of the Fair*. Chicago: E. A. Weeks, 1893.

Harper, Ida H. *The Life and Work of Susan B. Anthony*. 2 vols. Indianapolis: Bowen and Merrill, 1898.

Hayes, Charleton J. H. *A Generation of Materialism 1871–1900*. New York: Harper, 1941.

Hermann, Charles H. *Recollections of Life and Doings in Chicago 1886–1917*. Chicago: Normandie House, 1945.

"Higher Aspects of the Columbian Exposition." *Dial* 13 (1 November 1892) : 263–65.

A History of the World's Columbian Exposition. Edited by Rossiter Johnson. 4 vols. New York: Appleton, 1898.

History of the World's Fair. Edited by Ben C. Truman. Philadelphia: Monarch Book Co., 1893.

Hoffman, Donald. *The Architecture of John Wellborn Root*. Baltimore: Johns Hopkins University Press, 1973.

Howells, William Dean. *Letters of an Altrurian Traveller*. Edited by Clara M. and Rudolf Kirk. 1893. Reprint. Gainesville, Florida: Scholars' Facsimiles and Reprints, 1961.

Hull-House Residents. *Hull-House Maps and Papers: A Presentation of Nationalities and Wages in a Congested District of Chicago Together with Comments and Essays on Problems Growing Out of the Social Conditions*. 1895. Reprint. New York: Arno Press, 1970.

Huxtable, Ida Louise. "You Can't Go Home to Those Fairs Again." *The New York Times,* 28 October 1973, section II, p. 27, col. 1.

James, William. *The Letters of William James*. Edited by Henry James. 2 vols. Boston: Atlantic Press, 1920.

Jamieson, Duncan R. "Women's Rights at the World's Fair, 1893." *Illinois Quarterly* 37 (December 1974) : 5–20.

Jeter, Helen Rankin. *Trends of Population in the Region of Chicago*. Chicago: University of Chicago Press, 1927.

Johnson, Claudius O. *Carter Henry Harrison I*. Chicago: University of Chicago Press, 1928.

Joint Committee on Ceremonies. *Dedicatory and Opening Ceremonies of the World's Columbian Exposition, Memorial Volume*. Chicago: Stone, Kastler and Painter, 1893.

Jones, Howard M. *The Age of Energy*. New York: Viking, 1970.

Josephson, Matthew. *The Robber Barons*. New York: Harcourt, Brace, and World, 1934.

Karlen, A. "Capsule History of World's Fairs." *Holiday* 36 (July 1964) : 68–69.

Keeler, Clinton. "The White City and the Black City: The Dream of Civilization." *American Quarterly* 2 (Summer 1950) : 112–17.

Kimball, A. M. and Wellner, W. "Fair Ways to Freedom: World's Fairs and Centennials as Battle Grounds in American Women's

Struggle for Equal Rights." *Independent Woman* 17 (November 1938) : 343–61.

Kinney, Henry C. *Why the Columbian Exposition Should Be Open on Sunday: A Religio-Social Study.* Chicago: Rand McNally, 1892.

Kirk, Clara M. *W. D. Howells: Traveller from Altruria 1889–1894.* New Brunswick, New Jersey: Rutgers University Press, 1962.

Kirkland, Edward C. *Dream and Thought in the Business Community 1816-1900.* 1956. Reprint. Chicago: Quadrangle, 1964.

Kirkland, J. "Cost and Resources of the World's Fair." *Chautauquan* 16 (December 1892) : 268.

Kirkland, Joseph. *The Story of Chicago.* 2 vols. Chicago: Dibble Publishing Co., 1894.

Knutson, Robert. "The White City—The World's Columbian Exposition of 1893." Ph.D. dissertation, Columbia University, 1956.

Kouwenhoven, John A. *The Arts in Modern American Civilization.* New York: Norton, 1948.

Kunz, George F. "Management and Uses of Expositions." *North American Review* 175 (September 1902) : 409–22.

The Land of Contrasts 1880–1901. Edited by Neil Harris. New York: George Braziller, 1970.

"Last Columbian Century Anniversary." *Harper's Weekly* 33 (17 August 1889) : 655.

Lederer, Francis L. "The Genesis of the World's Columbian Exposition." M.A. thesis, University of Chicago, 1967.

Leighton, G. R. "World's Fairs: From Little Egypt to Robert Moses." *Harper's Monthly* 221 (July 1960) : 27–37.

Leighton, G. R. "The Year St. Louis Enchanted the World." *Harper's Monthly* 221 (August 1960) : 38–47.

"Lessons of Exhibitions." *Review of Reviews* 21 (June 1900) : 731–32.

Lewis, Lloyd and Smith, Henry J. *Chicago: The History of Its Reputation.* New York: Harcourt, Brace, 1929.

Lichtheim, George. *Marxism: An Historical and Critical Study.* New York: Praeger, 1961.

"Literary Tributes to the World's Fair." *Dial* 15 (1 October 1893) : 176–78.

Lloyd, Caro. *Henry Demarest Lloyd, 1847–1903: A Biography.* 2 vols. New York: G. P. Putnam's Sons, 1912.

Lynes, Russell. *The Tastemakers.* New York: Harper, 1954.

"The Making of the White City." *Scribner's Monthly* 12 (October 1892) : 416.

"Management of the Fair." *Harper's Weekly* 34 (6 December 1890) : 949–53.

Martin, Jay. *Harvests of Change.* Englewood Cliffs, N. J.: Prentice-Hall, 1967.

Masters, Edgar Lee. *The Tale of Chicago.* New York: G. P. Putnam's Sons, 1933.

Maxwell, Gerald. "Great International Exhibitions." *Westminister Review* 170 (December 1908) : 673–83.

Mayer, Harold M., and Wade, Richard C. *Chicago: The Growth of a Metropolis.* Chicago: University of Chicago Press, 1969.

McCullough, Edo. *World's Fair Midways: An Affectionate Account of American Amusement Areas.* New York: Exposition Press, 1966.

Meier, Hugo A. "American Technology and the Nineteenth Century World." *The American Culture.* Edited by Hennig Cohen. Boston: Houghton Mifflin, 1968.

Midway Types: The Chicago Times Portfolio of Midway Types. Chicago: American Engraving Company, 1893.

Millet, Francis D. "Designers of the Fair." *Harper's Monthly* 85 (November 1892) : 872–83.

The Modern Commonwealth, 1893–1918. Edited by Ernest L. Bogart and John M. Mathews. *The Centennial History of Illinois,* vol. 5. Springfield: Illinois Centenniel Commission, 1920.

Monroe, Harriet. *John Wellborn Root.* 1896. Reprint. Park Forest, Ill.: Prairie School Press, 1966.

Moore, Charles. *Daniel H. Burnham; Architect, Planner of Cities.* 2 vols. Boston: Houghton Mifflin, 1921.

Moore, Charles. *The Life and Times of Charles F. McKim.* Boston: Houghton Mifflin, 1929.

Morrison, Hugh. *Louis Sullivan, Prophet of Modern Architecture.* New York: Norton, 1935.

Mott, Frank Luther. *Golden Multitudes: The Story of Best Sellers in the United States.* New York: Macmillan, 1947.

Muirhead, James F. *The Land of Contrasts: A Briton's View of His American Kin.* London, 1898.

Mumford, Lewis. *The Brown Decades: A Study of the Arts of America 1865–1895* New York: Dover, 1955.

Mumford, Lewis. "Two Chicago Fairs." *New Republic* 65 (21 January 1931) : 272.

Neeley's History of the Parliament of Religions and Religious Congresses at the World's Columbian Exposition. Edited by Walter R. Houghton. Chicago: F. T. Neely, 1893.

Neufeld, Maurice F. "The Contribution of the World's Columbian Exposition of 1893 to the Idea of a Planned Society in the United States." Ph.D. dissertation, University of Wisconsin, 1935.

Neufeld, Maurice F. "The White City: The Beginnings of a Planned Civilization in America." *Journal of the Illinois State Historical Society* 27 (April 1934) : 71–93.

Neville, Amelia. "World's Fairs of the Past." *Overland Monthly* 58 (August 1911) : 152–54.

Nineteenth-Century Thought: The Discovery of Change. Edited by Richard L. Schoenwald. Englewood Cliffs, N. J.: Prentice-Hall, 1965.

Official Directory of the World's Fair. Edited by Moses P. Handy. Chicago: W. B. Conkey, 1893.

"Organization of the World's Fair." *Harper's Weekly* 34 (26 July 1890) : 577–78.

Ostrander, Gilman. *American Civilization in the Frst Machine Age 1890–1940.* New York: Harpers, 1970.

Pagent, Walburga. "Crystal Palace: A Reminiscence and a Suggestion." *Nineteenth Century* 71 (June 1912) : 1176–84.

"Panorama of World's Fairs." *Literary Digest* 120 (5 October 1935) : 21.

Partridge, William O. "Educational Value of World's Fairs." *Forum* 33 (March 1902) : 121–26.

Paul, Sherman. *Louis Sullivan: An Architect in American Thought.* Englewood Cliffs, N. J.: Prentice-Hall, 1962.

Peck, Ferdinand W. "The United States at the Paris Exposition of 1900." *North American Review* 158 (January 1899) : 24–33.

Peck, Harry T. *Twenty Years of the Republic, 1885–1905.* New York: Dodd, Mead, 1906.

Pennsylvania and the World's Columbian Exposition. Edited by A. Farquhar. Harrisburg: E. K. Meyers, n.d.

Pierce, Bessie L. *A History of Chicago 1871–1893.* New York: Knopf, 1957.

Pinchot, Gifford. *Breaking New Ground.* New York: Harcourt, Brace, 1947.

Pittera, Frederick P., et al. "International Exhibitions and Fairs." *Encyclopaedia Britannica,* 1973.

Poole, Ernest. *Giants Gone: Men Who Made Chicago.* New York: McGraw-Hill, 1943.

Pound, Ezra. *Patria Mia.* Chicago: R. F. Seymour, 1950.

Pratt, Richard H. *Battlefield and Classroom: Four Decades with the American Indian, 1867–1904.* Edited by Robert M. Utley. New Haven: Yale University Press, 1964.

Prior, Frederick J. *Columbian Exposition Dedication Ceremonies Memorial.* Chicago: Metropolitan Art Engraving Co., 1893.

Prout, Henry G. *A Life of George Westinghouse.* New York: American Society of Mechanical Engineers, 1921.

Ralph, Julian. "Our Exposition at Chicago." *Harper's Monthly* 84 (January 1892) : 205–6.

The Reason Why the Colored American Is Not in the World's Columbian Exposition: The Afro-American's Contribution to Columbian Literature. Edited by Ida B. Wells. Chicago: Ida B. Wells, 1893.

Report of the President to the Board of Directors of the World's Columbian Exposition. Chicago: Rand, McNally, 1898.

Revised Catalogue of the Department of Fine Arts. Edited by The Department of Fine Arts. Chicago: W. B. Conkey, 1893.

Rogers, Joseph. "Lessons from the International Exhibitions." *Forum* 32 (November 1901) : 502–504.

Roper, Laura W. *A Biography of Frederick Law Olmsted.* Baltimore: Johns Hopkins University Press, 1973.

Sablosky, Irving L. *American Music.* Chicago: University of Chicago Press, 1969.

Schlereth, Thomas J. "Regional Studies in America: The Chicago Model." *American Studies* supp. to *American Quarterly* 8 (October 1974) : 29.

Schlesinger, Arthur M. *The Rise of the City 1878–1898. A History of American Life,* vol. 10. New York: Macmillan, 1933.

Schuyler, Montgomery. *American Architecture and Other Writings.* Edited by William H. Jordy and Ralph Coe. 2 vols. Cambridge: Harvard University Press, 1961.

Schuyler, Montgomery. "Last Words about the World's Fair." *Architectural Record* 3 (January-March 1894) : 271–301.

Sewell, May Wright. *World's Congress of Representative Women.* 2 vols. Chicago: Rand, McNally, 1894.

Shackleton, Robert. *The Book of Chicago*. Philadelphia: Penn. Publishing Co., 1920.

Shannon, Fred A. *The Farmer's Last Frontier*. New York: Farrar and Rinehart, 1945.

Shepp, Daniel B. *World's Fair Photographed*. Chicago: Globe Bible Co., 1893.

Smith, Henry N. *Virgin Land: The American West as Symbol and Myth*. New York: Vintage, 1950.

Snider, Denton J. *World's Fair Studies*. Chicago: Sigma Publishing Co., 1895.

Sparling, Samuel E. "Municipal History and Present Organization of the City of Chicago." *Bulletin of the University of Wisconsin*. no. 23, Economics, Political Science and History series, vol. 2 (1898), 75–188.

Stanton, Theodore. "The International Exhibition of 1900." *Century Magazine* 51 (December 1895): 314.

Stead, William T. *Chicago Today: The Labour War in America*. 1894. Reprint. New York: Arno Press, 1969.

Sullivan, Louis H. *The Autobiography of an Idea*. 1924. Reprint. New York: Dover, 1956.

Taylor, Mrs. D. C. *Halcyon Days in the Dream City*. Kankakee, Ill.: n.p., 1894.

Tebbel, John W. *The Marshall Fields*. New York: Dutton, 1947.

Thompson, F. D. "The Sultan and the Chicago Exhibition." *Magazine of American History* 26 (October 1891): 289–95.

Tozer, Lowell, "A Century of Progress, 1833–1933: Technology's Triumph Over Man." *The American Culture*. Edited by Hennig Cohen. Boston: Houghton Mifflin, 1968.

Treseder, Mable L. *A Visitor's Trip to Chicago*. Edited by Sheldon T. Gardner. 1893. Reprint. Chicago: n.p., 1943.

Turner, Frederick Jackson. "The Significance of the Frontier in American History." *American Historical Association Annual Report for 1893*. Washington: 1894.

U. S. Bureau of Education. *Education at the World's Columbian Exposition, Including Reports and Comments by American and Foreign Educators and Delegates*. Washington: U. S. Government Printing Office, 1896.

U. S. Bureau of Labor. *The Slums of Baltimore, Chicago, New York, and Philadelphia*. Washington: U. S. Government Printing Office, 1894.

Van Brunt, Henry. "The Columbian Exposition and American Civilization." *Atlantic Monthly* 71 (May 1893): 577–88.

Vijyanandsuri. *The Chicago-Prashnottar: Questions and Answers on Jainism for the Parliament of Religions*. AGRA: Damodar Printing Works, 1918.

Villard, Henry. *The Memoirs of Henry Villard*. 2 vols. Boston: Houghton Mifflin, 1904.

Villard, Oswald G. *Fighting Years*. New York: Harcourt, Brace, 1939.

Walford, Cornelius. *Fairs, Past and Present: A Chapter in the History of Commerce*. 1883. Reprint. New York: A. M. Kelley, 1968.

Walker, Francis A. "America's Fourth Centenary." *Forum* 8 (February 1890): 612–21.

Walton, William. *The World's Columbian Exposition*. 3 vols. Philadelphia: G. Barrie, 1893.

A Week At the Fair. Chicago: Rand, McNally, 1893.

Wendt, Lloyd and Kogan, Herman. *Bosses in Lusty Chicago: The Story of Bathhouse John and Hinky Dink*. 1943. Reprint. Bloomington: Indiana University Press, 1967.

Wheeler, Candace. "A Dream City." *Harper's Monthly* 86 (May 1893): 86.

White, Morton, and White, Lucia. *The Intellectual Versus the City*. New York: Mentor, 1962.

Wiebe, Robert H. *The Search for Order 1877–1920*. New York: Hill and Wang, 1967.

Wood, Henry Truman. "Chicago and Its Exhibition." *Nineteenth Century* 31 (April 1892): 553–65.

"World's Columbian Exposition." *Harper's Weekly* 34 (22 November 1890): 912–16.

"World's Congress Auxiliary." *Dial* 13 (16 December 1892): 377–79.

World's Congress of Religions—Addresses and Papers Delivered Before the Parliament. Edited by J. W. Hanson. Chicago: W. B. Conkey, 1894.

World's Congress of Representative Women, May 15–22, 1893. Edited by May W. Sewall. Chicago: Rand McNally, 1894.

"The World's Fair." *Harper's Weekly* 34 (4 October 1890): 779.

"The World's Fair." *The Journal of the Franklin Institute* 133 (May 1892): 363.

World's Fair, Being a Pictorial History of the Columbian Exposi-

tion, . . . with a Description of Chicago . . . with an Introduction by Thomas W. Palmer, Including a Chapter on the Woman's Department by Frances E. Willard. Edited by William E. Cameron. Chicago: J. R. Jones, 1893.

"World's Fair Officers." *Harper's Weekly* 35 (1 August 1891) : 588.

"The World's Fair of 1892." *Harper's Weekly* 43 (3 August 1889) : 614.

"World's Fair of 1892—Chicago Favored by the House of Representatives." *Scientific American* 62 (8 March 1890) : 146.

World's Fair Sermons by Eminent Divines at Home and Abroad. Edited by James Baird McClure. Chicago: Rhodes and McClure, 1893.

World's Parliament of Religions. Edited by John Henry Barrows. 2 vols. Chicago: W. B. Conkey, 1893.

Wright, Amos W. "World's Fairs of 1889 and 1892." *Harper's Weekly* 33 (10 August 1889) : 652.

Wright, Amos W. "World's Fair Progress." *Harper's Weekly* 33 (31 August 1889) : 707.

Ziff, Larzer. *The American 1890s: The Life and Times of a Lost Generation.* New York: Viking, 1966.

INDEX